Secrets of the Remote Workforce

BY EMPLOYEES.
FOR EMPLOYEES.

Teresa Douglas
Holly Gordon
Mike Webber

© 2018 Teresa Douglas, Holly Gordon, and Mike Webber

Published by 750 Publishing, a division of Kaplan, Inc.
750 Third Avenue
New York, NY 10017

10 9 8 7 6 5 4 3 2 1

ISBN: 978-1-5062-4856-1

Acknowledgments

There were many people who helped move this book from an idea into reality, and we would like to thank them for their support. Jim Shevlin started this project in the first place, and then let us run with it. Lola Disparte contributed hours of her time toward the writing and editing of this book. Paula Fleming took time off from her holidays to copy edit our writing so we would have a clean copy to submit for publication.

Caitlin Duke joined the team at the 11th hour and helped us write, organize, and edit the vignettes and pro tips in a very short amount of time. We wouldn't have made our deadline without her.

We would also like to thank all of the Kaplan colleagues, past and present, who contributed vignettes, pro tips, or personal experiences to our book. Thank you Corinne Simon, Ibrahim Husain, Christine Terrell, Dru Ciotti, Bobby Amirebrahimi, Brian Sabel, Evan Gaughan, Rei Champion, Walker Williams, Julie Minnich, Melanie McKay, Jenn Freeman, Yeo Ju Choi, Kristin Robinson, Sascha Strelka, Chrissy Damasco, Elle Mastenbrook, Dustin Semo, Patrick Reagan, Kate Mitsakis, Melody Young and Katie Stanfield. Sharing your personal experiences helped us to create a book that is truly by employees, for employees.

A big thank you to the team at 750 Publishing for their flexibility and willingness to nurture this book and help it see the light of day.

TABLE OF CONTENTS

Before You Begin

In midsummer 2010, I received a strange call from my manager. I was instructed to make myself available at 4:00 p.m. and to be in a place where I could talk freely without my fellow employees hearing. It was both mysterious and unsettling, but most of all it was intriguing.

When I dialed into the rather large conference call, I realized the presenter was the much-admired CEO of our division. His first words were galvanizing: "If you are not able to keep a secret, please leave this call immediately." And so it began.

The next hour was spent detailing an audacious plan to completely shift the current business model for Kaplan Test Prep, the world's leader in the field.

On November 3, 2010 (just a few months from that midsummer call), Kaplan would essentially flip a switch and change from a brick-and-mortar organization, with 170 physical locations throughout the United States, Canada, and Europe, to a predominantly virtual company where almost 90 percent of all employees would work from home. While on the surface Kaplan would continue to service students as it always had, the organizational structure behind that service would transform completely.

—Jim Shevlin

That provides the background for this book. On a single day in 2010, a 70-year-old, industry-leading company completely embraced the remote workforce and implemented an entirely new organizational structure. Written after the fact, this book is about the lessons learned from that extreme transformation—by employees, for employees.

This book is about being a remote worker, from the perspective of remote workers. By detailing the many lessons we learned transitioning from traditional offices to remote ones, we hope to help others understand how to enter, enjoy, and thrive in the wonderful world of working from home (or a library, or a coffee shop, or an exotic island). We have tried to write honestly and directly about the physical aspect of this type of work. We have tried to portray the mental challenges of this job. But most importantly, we have tried to provide words to convey the extraordinarily novel emotional and psychological considerations of working within this structure.

The main thrust of this book is not about how to manage a remote workforce—at least, not directly. As their titles clearly indicate, many of the books available today about working remotely are focused, with varying levels of success, on this management challenge. But while this book is not primarily about how to manage remote workers, we believe it is a tremendous resource for managers because of what it *does* discuss: the remote worker, from the remote worker's perspective. To manage remote employees, a manager needs to understand remote employees. In fact, the last section of this book is written specifically for managers, but it will only be completely understood by a manager who has incorporated the lessons from the earlier chapters.

The biggest revelation we experienced while researching this book was that, thus far, little consideration has been given to the thoughts and emotions of the remote employee; the psychology of the remote worker is rarely addressed. But, by definition, a remote worker must confront a number of challenges alone. As we began to structure this book, we realized we had to focus on the psychological world of the remote employee as a definitive element of the experience. Only by understanding this inner world of the mind could the reader make sense of the corresponding physical and functional aspects of working remotely.

This book is written by the employees who made it through Kaplan's radical transformation and thrived. By writing about an experience that is based on the collective realities of many brilliant and sharing individuals, we hope to portray a picture of what could and should be the reality for future remote workers everywhere.

By employees, for employees. Let's begin the journey.

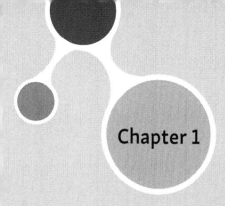

Chapter 1

Secrets of the Right Mentality

Of all the transitions you'll have to make as you move from a traditional office into the remote workforce, the psychological adjustments may be the most surprising. Many people already know that they need a comfortable physical workspace. This chapter will help you think about setting up a comfortable mental space as well.

Settling into Your New Environment

Working in a remote environment is something that you may not have experienced before. There are many similarities between working remotely and working in a more traditional office setting, but there are also many differences. When you're a virtual employee, you shoulder more responsibility to understand your company's culture and ensure you are living up to your commitments.

What do you really know about the company you work for? When you started, what kind of research did you do? If its stock is publicly traded, did you check its performance on the stock exchange? Did you do an internet search of the company name along with keywords like "love," "good employer," and "quit"? Doing this type of investigative work before signing on with a company gives you both a sense of job security and some context for the information your interviewers provide. Gone are the days of a job for life. The best and brightest will likely work for several companies, so it's important to control that process to be in charge of your career. Investigating potential employers is crucial.

Far too often, this investigation, if it occurs at all, ceases once someone accepts a job offer. This makes sense in the short term—after all, the interview was a success, the new job is yours, and if you did that important research before accepting the position, you probably feel that you know enough about the company to rest easy about your decision and how your new role fits with your long-term goals.

In reality, though, you don't know enough about the company. You may know the likelihood of its longevity over the next few years, but you have no idea about the inner workings of the different departments you'll soon be interacting with, what your boss is really like, or why your colleague, who is supposed to be showing you the ropes, is acting in such a cold manner toward you.

In a traditional office environment, a lot of your knowledge about the company's history and culture occurs through a natural process of osmosis. You overhear conversations in the next cubicle. You run into a colleague on the way to the printer and take a few minutes to discuss why they look so frustrated. Lunch provides a great opportunity to learn the backstory of recent changes. While this can easily spill into gossip, it quickly provides a good understanding of why things are the way they are.

When you're part of a remote workforce, that intrinsic knowledge is much harder to come by. It will come eventually, but by the time you have a full picture of the company's history and its major and minor players, a significant amount of time will have passed (more than would have in a non-virtual work environment). There's no point in waiting that long and struggling unnecessarily as you start out. The solution is to take action.

If your company provides you with a relevant company history, it's an excellent sign of a company that cares. If you don't receive such a history, or the one you're provided is superficial at best, then it is up to you to obtain a history you can use. Ask for a summary of recent changes that affected the organizational structure of the company and your division. Ask for the background on any personnel changes that are relevant to you in your new position. Requests such as these are a big part of setting yourself up for success in the remote workforce.

Without this knowledge, you're going to be guessing at how to best perform your duties and maneuver among colleagues and departments. But there is more at risk than just that. As we'll discuss in later chapters, networking in the virtual work environment begins much earlier than in the traditional workplace. Knowing the lay of the land from the past to the present allows you to start mapping out your career right away and avoid falling into the hidden traps created by events that took place before you ever arrived.

If you are in the process of onboarding, you can ask your HR department if they have a video or a manual or other collateral that discusses the history of the company, including when your role or department went remote. If you are not in the process of onboarding, or your HR department doesn't have any materials, then you may be able to gain this information in other ways. You could informally ask people to share their stories—how did they get hired into the role they are in now, when did they join the company, etc. This activity will help you build a picture of recent company history, and help you build your network, all at once.

—Teresa Douglas

Knowledge and trust are keys to success as a member of the remote workforce. Know what you're getting into before signing on with a company, and know what you've gotten into once you're there. There is a baseline level of trust that every employer-employee relationship needs to have, but in a remote workforce, the stakes in this circle of trust are significantly higher. It is incumbent on you, the remote worker, to both understand the implications of this change and embrace the dynamics that now exist. Your company has given you freedom and responsibility, and you must understand both the opportunity and the trap that lie therein.

As you will discover, the world of working remotely can give you greater day-to-day autonomy, more control over your work-life blend, and a greater ability to craft your job in ways that you may have previously thought unimaginable. These are all exciting possibilities. Frankly, only time will tell whether you can do these things well while working from home. In the remote workplace, temptations are plentiful. You will need to manage yourself, internalizing the employer part of the contractual bargain and weighing each and every decision you make throughout the day as both employer and employee.

Until you begin to work remotely, it may be difficult for you to understand the extraordinary trust that your company has placed in you, and it may be hard for you to comprehend just how much effort and thought you will have to exert to understand the implications of that trust. As you begin (and continue) to work in the remote workforce, you must periodically ask yourself whether you are up to the challenge and determine whether you are fulfilling your duties.

It is not unheard of for people to agree to work remotely and then spend their days ignoring their responsibilities until their company inevitably lets them go. In a similar vein, not all managers thrive in this environment, where trust is crucial to success. A lack of trust often leads to micromanaging and, ultimately, the resignation or dismissal of the remote employee. However, these stories say much more about the individuals involved than they do about working remotely.

There are also many workers on the opposite end of the spectrum: those who fulfill all of their work obligations appropriately and use the flexibility remote work offers to lead a more abundant life. There are remote workers who train for marathons, foster children, and fulfill other life dreams they may not have been able to without the flexibility offered by remote work.

It is common for companies to be overcontrolling as workers migrate away from the office. It is equally common for remote workers to initially feel as though they are on the outside looking in as they get acclimated to new communication patterns and new logistical arrangements. Discuss these things openly and honestly with your manager and your peers alike. Work through your tentative feelings as you enter this new world.

Your company has gone all-in on your abilities, your maturity, and your discipline. Seize this opportunity. Fulfill the contract you have made. Build your particular remote existence within the parameters established by your company and reap the benefits that result.

Preparing to Work More

What kind of worker are you? Are you someone who looks for any job that gives you a decent salary? Are you after a particular line of work that you will enjoy, regardless of the financial benefits? Or maybe you want anything that keeps your evenings and weekends completely free. These are important questions to ask yourself before getting into the virtual workforce, because one thing is certain in this environment: You will work more.

This concept can be hard for people to grasp, as from the outside the assumption is that you have more free time. After all, there's no boss in the room to watch over you. You have fewer distractions from coworkers, fewer clients coming in with questions, and just less noise all around. But the reality is actually the opposite. With fewer outside distractions, the right type of worker can suddenly have eight hours of pure work time. It's amazing how much time gets used up with random interruptions that are commonplace in an on-site office environment. Once those are removed, all that is left is for you to work. Granted, there are other potential distractions, but it's important to understand that contrary to popular belief, working from home means working more.

Let's take a moment to consider your new workspace. You now have fewer reasons to get up to accomplish tasks. Things like walking across the hall to get supplies or to the copy room to get a printout are all but eliminated, as hard copies are rarely required when working remotely. In the event that you do need to print something, the printer is usually right next to you. Those couple of minutes spent on the move in a traditional office environment can turn into something much longer when they present the opportunity to run into a colleague or supervisor. Any situation involving leaving your desk—getting coffee in the break room, running a suggestion by your boss, heading to the conference room for a meeting—provides an opportunity for distraction. In the virtual workforce, most of these actions are done with a click or two of your mouse.

The other major difference is that when you work from home, it's much harder to separate your home life from your work life. You no longer go out into the world and enter a different building to start your workday. Instead, work is just . . . there. Switching off becomes much more challenging, and it can be easy to start earlier, finish later, and find yourself working on weekends. It becomes harder to tell yourself that things can wait when in the most literal sense, they don't have to—the computer is right there.

The tendency to work more in this environment isn't necessarily a terrible thing, but you need to recognize and manage it carefully to get the right level of satisfaction out of your job and your work-life blend. Ultimately, you have more freedom in how you work, so use that to your advantage. Schedule regular breaks in your routine: Set an alarm to remind yourself to get up and stretch, walk to a nearby coffee shop, or work on a craft project. The activity you choose is less important than the act of taking regular breaks. Just knowing you have a 10-minute break in your day to do something you enjoy can keep you happy and productive in your role.

When you work remotely, your office is really wherever you and your laptop are. I've learned that this makes my technological boundaries just as important as physical ones in a typical office. For example, I don't have my work email go directly to my phone, allowing my phone to remain a personal device while my laptop is a work device. This helps me to feel unplugged when my work laptop is closed, and sends a clear signal that I'm only available for urgent needs when I've shut down my computer for the day.

—*Christine Terrell*

Identifying what you want out of your virtual workforce job will help establish a base level of satisfaction. Know that you will be working more and recognize what that is: an opportunity. It's an opportunity to immerse yourself more fully in exciting work with fewer distractions than you might experience while working in an office. You can take great satisfaction in helping your colleagues and clients in a more timely and efficient manner and make your job something more than just a 40-hour-a-week way to keep the wolf from the door.

At the same time, recognize that this is a double-edged sword you need to wield wisely. Schedule breaks for yourself and set limits so you don't end up burning out. Walk into this working situation with eyes wide open, being prepared to both work more and reap the benefits of doing so.

Dealing with Reactions of Friends and Family

A month or so after I started working from home, I began getting calls from my mother in the middle of the day. At first I was concerned. We lived on different coasts, and a call in the middle of my workday used to mean that something momentous had happened. Someone was in a car accident, or sick, and I needed to either buy a plane ticket or call a relative in the hospital.

These turned out not to be those kind of calls. My mom missed having me nearby and thought that I would now have time to chat. I would gently let her know that I was in the middle of my workday, but it would still take 45 minutes to get off of the phone, and she would forget and call me again the next time she thought of it.

I found that the only solution was to not pick up the phone during work hours. She always left a message, and I could listen to it right away and decide if I needed to call back immediately. If not, I made a note to call her in the evening when I had time to talk. Gradually the midday phone calls stopped, and we went back to our regular routine of talking after my business day was done.

—Teresa Douglas

No one really understands what other people do for work. We have a much better idea about traditional jobs, the ones children are taught about in school: police officer, nurse, construction worker. But even with those jobs, it can be hard to picture what really happens. When do police file paperwork? How do nurses structure their days? What do construction workers actually do, when so much of their job appears to consist of standing about, waiting? It's not a surprise, then, that it's hard to visualize what a claims adjustor or regional sales director does day to day. Now take that confusion and multiply it by a factor of 10. Welcome to the way friends, family, and even some coworkers view the life of a remote worker, regardless of the job title.

Your home is your place of rest. It's where you raise your family, where you do chores on weekends, where you watch TV and relax. Adding business to the mix, even if you have a designated office area to work from, complicates things. It can be hard for even the person working remotely to figure it all out, so it makes sense that others have a hard time understanding where the line between work and non-work is. Confusion and questions from friends and family are understandable. Fortunately, the trick to navigating these conversations is straightforward: Anticipate questions and comments and take preemptive action, or at least be prepared to respond to the usual queries and misconceptions.

Many people will assume that because you're working from home, you are self-employed and therefore able to set your own hours and work as much or as little as you want. Being part of a remote workforce often means a significant amount of flexibility when it comes to your working hours, but not to the extreme that many people assume. Point out that you have a number of tasks to accomplish each day and that while some things can be moved around, most cannot unless you end up working late into the night to catch up.

Another common misconception is that when you tell an acquaintance you work from home, what that acquaintance hears is, "I'm in between jobs." Providing a bit more detail about your routine can clarify the situation, but having to justify your employment status can slowly wear away at a person's soul: "Trust me! I have a job! I swear it!" The sister reaction to this unemployment assumption is a kind of faux jealousy. This is where the person you're speaking with tells you how lucky you are to have such an easy gig, working from home. Again, a brief description of all that transpires in your day-to-day activities is often enough to educate the other person, but this assumption (like the unemployment one) can make you feel as though you're fighting an uphill battle.

It can be frustrating when friends don't understand your work situation, but it's not something that necessarily requires a lot of discussion. With family, however, it can become a more sensitive topic. A significant other or children living with you need to understand what working from home really means. At the same time, you need to accept that they are not likely to fully understand, so you need to be patient with them. To expect your family members to grasp right away why you can't spend part of the day doing housework or helping with homework is just inviting trouble. There's a flip side to this situation, of course. Working remotely may mean having the ability to arrange your schedule so you *can* take 30 minutes on your lunch break to vacuum. You *can* spend an hour in the evening finishing up work emails in order to spend an hour in the afternoon helping your son do his homework. But family should not assume this level of flexibility or conflict will likely arise.

Lay out the ground rules in advance to minimize confrontations and incorrect expectations. Set up your workplace and time so it's clear, for example, that when the door is closed, no one enters. That until the tie comes off, you're at work. That when the clock turns to 10:00 a.m., the workday begins. Control the expectations of those you live with, and your relationships will avoid dips into disappointment and frustration.

Ultimately, the answer is to be prepared. People who don't work remotely will never fully understand what it's like, and that's OK. You'll likely never know what it's like to be a police officer. In being prepared, however, you'll be better equipped to deal with the different situations you most certainly will encounter. As a bonus, after experiencing the misconceptions many friends and family members will have about working remotely, you're likely to presume a lot less about what the construction worker's average workday is like.

Overcoming Isolationism

Working remotely can be a lonely experience. Even if you are equipped with the secrets we are sharing, you'll likely experience a sense of isolation that can be both overt and covert in its effect on the human psyche. You don't feel the simple joy of stopping by a cubicle to chat with a friend or accidentally bumping into a colleague or high-level boss in an elevator. Even introverts may need interaction, however fleeting or trivial.

The volume of remote workforce decisions can overwhelm even the most diligent and organized person. It can be easy to think that no one in the company works as hard as you or that your team is the only competent one out there. You might lose sight of the big picture—or feel like you never had a grasp of the big picture in the first place. You might be surprised by sudden changes to your business unit or processes. Although not everyone who works from home experiences these extremities of emotion, those who do can feel them intensely.

So here is the secret to surviving these moments: Understand that you may occasionally be overcome by the isolation of the remote workforce life. Make your plan *now* to handle this psychological crisis, because we guarantee that if it does occur and you do not have a plan, you will not have the emotional gyroscope to finesse it when things start to go dark.

Build a support structure that you can lean on during tough times. The savvy remote worker ensures that structure includes people and actions both inside and outside of the company. Sometimes you need to speak to someone on the inside whose judgment you trust, either to vent or to ask for advice. Cultivate friendships now while things are going well so you know who you can talk to when times are rough. At other times, you need to remind yourself that there is a world outside of your home office. Consider joining a book club, or a professional association, or a game night at your local pub or library. Become a docent at your local museum. Volunteer on the weekends. If you have a pet or a hobby or a child, there is a good chance that there is a group out there of like-minded people who meet together socially. Try a few different things until you find your tribe and then attend regularly.

My team enjoys frequent virtual work-alongs that help us both stay connected socially and be more productive. If we anticipate that we will be doing similar work during a given week, we schedule a group video call to chit-chat and bounce ideas off each other while we work in parallel.

—Brian Sabel

Sometimes changing where you physically work can ward off feelings of isolation. It may not be as efficient to do some of your work at a local library or coffee shop, but the act of sitting in a room with other people may help you feel more connected to the world in general. If spending two hours at a library every Tuesday morning can keep you feeling energized about your job, then it is time well spent. Take some time on the weekends to try out new places (and check the Wi-Fi).

If your life circumstances and role allow for it, you might consider taking a class in the middle of the workday. Some employees find that taking time out for a group yoga or drawing class helps them fill the need for human contact.

If you find yourself in crisis mode despite all this, don't do anything rash. Breathe in and breathe out. Seek counsel from friends and family about the issue. Seek counsel from other remote workers. Go for a walk. Wait a preset period of time before making any career-changing decisions. You can opt out at any time, but once you do, it is very difficult to opt back in. We are not saying everyone can and will adapt to the world of working remotely. Many fine employees find that working from home is simply not a good fit. But we are saying you should not leave the remote workforce because of a predictable (and oftentimes transitory) wave of emotion.

Rely on your support network to weather the tough times. With the help of people and activities both inside and outside the company, you can experience the joys and flexibility that remote working provides for years to come.

Staying Engaged: How to Be Social

Connecting socially with your coworkers is a vital part of staying engaged in the remote workforce. But how do you connect socially when you're separated by screens and hundreds (or thousands!) of miles? You may think it's impossible to have any kind of workplace social life as a remote employee, but by using all the resources and technology available, your social interactions can be extremely beneficial and enjoyable.

From this moment forward, be intentional in your interactions. You will no longer walk past someone's office on the way to a meeting or run into them at the water cooler. These quick minutes here and there can build a strong foundation with coworkers. When working from home, the incidental meetings won't necessarily happen on their own, so you need to make them happen.

Take time to just say hello to your coworkers. If your company uses an instant messaging program, periodically use this technology to check in. If you would normally stop in and ask someone how their weekend was in the office, do the same on instant messenger. These interactions only take a couple of minutes, but they can make a big difference in your relationships with coworkers. It can be much easier to work with someone if a social structure is built outside of regular work interactions.

You can also do quick check-ins when you see someone mentioned in a mass email. Promotions, project successes, and even birthdays are often communicated via mass email. Take the extra minute to reach out to the people mentioned and congratulate them. Your support can go a long way.

Stay actively involved in all communication methods set up by your team. If there is a group email going around or a running group chat, participate in it. If there isn't, start one! Adding in a couple of thoughts here and there will not only help your team get to know you better but also help you feel more connected to your team. When you share your ideas, you will feel more involved and have a greater sense of satisfaction with your project work.

Video can be another great way to connect to your coworkers, so don't be afraid of it. Making sure you are always camera-ready from the waist up is a great way to be able to interact with coworkers on a moment's notice. Sometimes, seeing a friendly face is a huge morale booster. Being face-to-face also requires a greater amount of attention, as you likely will not be checking emails, walking around the house, or feeding the dog while video-chatting with someone. This increased attention leads to increased engagement and connection. Being fully present in communications with your coworkers can help them feel valued and show them you care.

There are many other ways to effectively use video with your coworkers. Scheduling time to meet as a group on video can have the same increased benefits as meeting one-on-one on video, combined with the positive effects of group conversation. These group interactions can happen in many different ways and with many different purposes. Work-along sessions are a great way to foster creative development, stay on track, and produce a large amount of work in a short amount of time. Typically, when in person, the focus of a work-along would be to brainstorm and think aloud. While this can happen in a virtual work-along as well, there's an opportunity for a different focus. It can be incredibly helpful to "sit" in a virtual meeting room and work on the same project—even if most of the time it is silent, save for the sound of typing. Not only can you feel more connected, knowing that everyone is in the same mental space working on the same project, but you can also get on your microphone and ask a quick question at any point. If you need an idea for what to write next, or you want the group's opinion on your next step, everyone is there working together. At the end of a work-along, your group will have a large amount of progress to show and celebrate since everyone was putting time and effort in together.

Speaking of celebrating, commemorating group accomplishments and life events can happen remotely just as they would in the office. If your team finishes a successful project, gather everyone on a video call to celebrate. You can even bring in high-level managers to the calls. It can help for these managers to see who was involved in specific projects and for the team to be introduced to the managers they may not have met.

Building connections with group video can happen outside the typical workday and project structure as well. Just as you may have participated in happy hours after work with colleagues, the same can happen in the virtual world, with many added benefits! It is cheaper when everyone can bring their own beverage, there's no risk of drinking and driving when everyone is sitting at their computer in their home, and any accidental uncomfortable physical interactions cannot take place.

On the flip side, it still has the same great benefits that meeting outside of work provides. You can get to know one another on a personal level, again building stronger connections that will improve your relationships inside and outside of work. You also have the ability to loosen up and be your true self. These opportunities are often taken for granted in the traditional office environment but can occur online as well. In fact, depending on the software used, interactions can be much more fun online. For instance, some video programs allow you to add fun backgrounds to your picture and even play games together. Just because you aren't physically in the same space as your coworkers doesn't mean you can't have fun with them.

While building connections in the remote workforce can take a little more effort on your part, these relationships are just as beneficial and necessary as those in physical offices. Participate in activities offered to you and take time to create your own. Over time, virtual interactions will become second nature, feeling just as natural as talking face-to-face.

Chapter 2

Secrets of the Outer and Inner Physical Environment

Working remotely means never having to put up with someone else's office layout. *You* are in total control. Here are some things to think about as you set up the workspace that's right for you.

The Physical Secrets for Ultimate Comfort

> *Changing my vantage point once a week helps bump up my productivity and gives me a variety of options to choose the most comfortable work environment. I'll relocate outside on nice days for a few hours, or visit a local coffee shop. The change in scenery is refreshing and helps keep me energized.*
>
> *I find that even moving to another location in my home can be helpful. When my day is winding down, I can move from my office desk to the couch to begin relaxing while I sort through the final tasks I need to accomplish.*
>
> —*Evan Gaughan*

One of the most underappreciated aspects of working remotely is the very real time and cost savings. Consider your commute time to a traditional office. Let's say, for example, that your commute takes 30 minutes each way, twice a day. With an average of 240 workdays in the year, this equates to approximately 240 hours or 6 workweeks spent commuting. Then there are the additional monetary costs (gas for your car, fare for public transportation, etc.). Add bad weather, road rage, or an accident into the mix, and your commute can be the most stressful part of your day. For many remote workers, getting that commute time back is priceless.

Another benefit to working from home is the reduced wardrobe cost. While business casual or an actual uniform is standard in most workplaces, working remotely often offers you greater wardrobe flexibility. Obviously you still need to be presentable—and ready—for video calls. However, this can mean wearing a collared shirt with your jeans and slippers. Others keep a blazer ready to slip on over a T-shirt. Because your colleagues only see you from the shoulders up, it doesn't matter if you wear the same (clean) shirt over and over again. Of course, dressing for work comes with the benefit of building a routine and getting into the working mindset, but being remote allows you the flexibility to determine some of those standards for yourself. Also, if you only wear a suit jacket for a few hours a week, it lasts longer. This means fewer purchases throughout the year, and your lifetime, to maintain your wardrobe, which leads to additional savings.

Lunchtime is another opportunity where the remote worker can save considerable time and money. When working in an office, generally you're stuck with two options: packing a lunch or eating out. Packing a lunch requires planning, time, and remembering to take said lunch with you to work. Alternatively, if you venture out of the office in search of a reasonably priced option, you're racing against the clock and trying to balance your food budget, all while attempting to enjoy your "break" from work.

Working from home means never forgetting your lunch on the counter again. Full access to your fridge and kitchen also allows for greater control of the health and nutrition of your meals. Some remote workers have taken the opportunity to become locavores, while others have taken up bread making. You're limited only by your own imagination and culinary skills.

If you have children, then child care may also take a significant portion of your income. Depending on where you live, child care costs can potentially eat anywhere between 10 and 50 percent of your monthly salary. This doesn't include workdays lost to caring for sick children. Working remotely, however, offers much more flexibility in terms of the amount and type of child care needed. While this may or may not translate into actual dollars saved (though it likely will), it increases options for care and can allow for more time spent with your loved ones. Some parents have (with their manager's approval) crafted a split schedule—adding a weekend day or some early morning and late evening hours into their work schedules so they can care for their children for a portion of the day. This schedule flexibility has helped some reduce the amount of child care they need to pay for, while others have eliminated this cost entirely through the strategic use of family and friends.

Without a doubt, working from home can add both money and time back into your daily routine. This is but the tip of the iceberg. Take a look at your workflow and get creative. With a little thought, you will soon have the kind of work-life balance that makes you the envy of your friends.

Your Workspace

When you work remotely, not only *can* you have your office the way you want—you *should* have your office the way you want. It needs to be set up in a way that will allow you to be a productive worker. The space should be distinctive for you, clearly identifying itself (to you and to others) as your workspace. This is important because there need to be boundaries that differentiate the space you work in from the space you live in. Where you live is typically your place of rest, a location you don't associate with the outside world, where family and non-work activities traditionally take place. Working from home means carving out a section of your living space and converting it into a working space, both physically and mentally.

Ideally, your home office is a separate room with a door you can close. If you aren't able to devote an entire room to your workspace, consider taking the time to arrange the furniture in a way that creates a clear division between the space where you work and the space where you live. If having a permanent space dedicated to working is not realistic, you can still make your space work-ready by having a routine at the start of your day where you adjust the furniture and lighting and bring your tools for the day out from a cupboard. The end of your workday can consist of your morning routine in reverse, transforming your space back into your personal living environment. It's also wise to avoid lumping your personal "work" tasks and your actual work tasks together in the same space. Ideally, you should not do your taxes or pay your bills in your non-personal work area. Another benefit of having a defined workspace at home is that you may qualify for tax deductions for a dedicated home office. You may wish to consult a tax expert to see if this is true for your home and financial situation and to find out what the government requires to claim the deduction.

There are a few physical items every home office needs in order to function, mainly a good desk and a good office chair. These ingredients are integral to the comfort and success of your work environment, and there is no one-size-fits-all solution. Every chair fits different people differently, and every desk has its strengths and weaknesses.

The best approach to finding your fit is to try different options. Try out multiple chairs, sit (or stand) at every desk you come across, and determine what you need from each. Consider whether you want (and have space for) multiple workspace configurations. For example, perhaps you want to spend part of your day working from a standing desk. Explore all options, keeping nothing off limits. When you find the right setup, be willing to invest in it. You'll likely be spending a lot of time using it, and just like a mattress or car, you want to make sure it is right for you.

I recommend putting together a mobile office. I have a big command-center style setup for my regular office as well as a scaled-down version of everything I need that fits easily in a backpack. That way, I can do big projects that require a lot of hardware at my home base, but I also have the option to easily hit the road and still get everything done. I prefer cloud storage solutions like Google Drive over saving files on a particular computer so that I always have access to them.

—*Walker Williams*

Once you have the basics down, it's time to build your surrounding workspace. As a remote worker, you'll likely spend some time on camera, so it's important that your face be properly lit. Consider a flexible desk light, one that can be turned to light your face as necessary to create a professional appearance on camera. Every aspect of your lighting is within your control—make it work for you.

The décor of your office can paint a picture in your coworkers' minds of who you are and how you work. Be cognizant of the items behind you while you are on camera. Some companies may have guidelines that dictate what should be seen. If your company has such guidelines, follow them. If not, pay attention to the workspaces of your coworkers. Often, following the lead of your colleagues is a good rule of thumb. Even if you are used to whatever is behind you, keep in mind that the person you are calling may not be, and if there is too much going on, it can be distracting. In most cases, keeping it simple is best.

Just as the items behind you can be distracting, so can the items in front of you. Find a view that allows you to maintain focus during your workday. For example, some people work best with a desk facing a wall that allows for full focus when at the computer. Others like to set up their workspace to allow them to look out a window.

Consider the ambience of your workspace. Do you enjoy working to music? If so, it would be worth your time to research radio or internet-streaming solutions to improve your work ambience. Also consider the atmosphere: Think temperature, air quality, and outside noise. Do you need a space heater? What about a desk fan? Maybe a couple of plants to increase the oxygen around you?

You may find that when choosing items to design your workspace, you wonder whether a certain purchase is superfluous. Art, fancy ergonomic furniture, and other items often make this list. As many remote workers will agree, though, you should allow yourself to spend more on the right items (for you). Your workspace is your home for a significant portion of each day. Investing in your comfort and enjoyment while working is truly a case of care of the soul.

Is there a pet in your home? The companionship throughout your workday can be beneficial, but thinking through the logistics is vital to making this work. Set up a space for pets that allows them to be near you while not interfering with your work. Be sure that a system is in place to keep everyone safe from electronics and cords. While some colleagues or clients may enjoy visits from animals, others may not. To be ready for a video call at any time with pets in the room or nearby, have a quick way to turn off your camera and mute your microphone. For example, if you know your dogs will bark at the mail carrier, putting up a gate may not be enough to keep them from disrupting a meeting.

The final thing to consider about your workspace is how to effectively take advantage of the flexibility that working remotely offers. Even if you love your home office, you may want to take advantage of working from a coffee shop sometimes. Or perhaps you have to be elsewhere for family or personal reasons. On a beautiful spring day, you might want to work from your patio. You may be someone who flourishes around other people; in that case, research coworking spaces in your area. On the other hand, some people, without the structure of their clearly defined office space, get easily distracted and find themselves being unproductive. Test the waters to see what your limitations are. Maintain your routines of how you log in and in what order you complete tasks, making these function as the structure of your working environment.

Working *from* home doesn't have to mean working exclusively *at* home. Keep things as separate as you can, both in terms of not working in the space where you live and not living in the space where you work. Nothing is set in stone: When you find things that work well for you, stick with them. If you come up with ideas to improve your workspace, implement them. Mix things up within your workspace to get the maximum value from being part of the remote workforce. Ultimately, your experience working remotely will be not only more tailored to how you work best but also far more enjoyable than any "perfect" on-site office ever was.

Your Tools

It's important to have the right tools for your job. Some tools are so crucial that they are necessary for you to do any work at all, whether in a traditional office or a remote one. When working remotely, the onus is often on you to ensure you are set up with all the tools you need.

Your company may provide a computer. In such a case, you will likely be restricted as to what programs you can put on the machine and have little to no choice about whether the computer is a laptop or a desktop and what operating system it uses. However, you typically don't have to pay for the device or the software. Alternatively, you may have the option to use your own computer, allowing you greater latitude for customization.

Of all your tools, a computer is likely the one you will use the most in your job, so it's important to have it set up in a way that allows you maximum comfort and efficiency. If the monitor is too small, definitely consider upgrading (assuming that such a change does not go against any company policy). A few other things to consider adding include an external keyboard and mouse, an external webcam, an external microphone, and headphones. While this list is not exhaustive, it should give you a sense of the importance of choosing the right technology for your situation.

To the extent that you are allowed, install the programs that you like best. Use the browser you feel most comfortable with and the email client you prefer. Customize other programs so they look and behave the way you like, with your frequently used features readily accessible.

While you may be able to do some work without an internet connection, access to online resources is generally essential. Even if you can complete all or some of your work in an offline program, that work often needs to be transferred to or from somewhere online. Therefore, a fast, reliable internet connection is necessary for most tasks in the remote world. Where possible, choose an internet provider with a good reputation and educate yourself on bandwidth and connection speeds. Depending on the type of remote work you do, you may need a wired connection. Many remote employees need to attend regular video meetings, and a wired connection is more consistent than a wireless one, reducing the risk of freezes and call failures. This becomes even more crucial when dealing with clients. Colleagues may be willing to work through your technical challenges, but a client will likely find the overall presentation and service lacking, and this may affect their desire to stay with your company. Therefore, if you are allowed to choose your own computer, make sure you get one with an Ethernet port if necessary.

Don't take for granted all the resources that come with working in a traditional office building. You may need various supplies to do your job remotely. If you work with paper, do you have a printer and spare ink cartridges? Pencils, paper clips, and a stapler could also be essential. Do you have a way to store important documents? USB drives, cameras, and other electronic equipment might also be items you use every day. Your company may have a list of items you are expected to keep on hand. If so, use this resource. If not, when setting up your office space, consider what you need and prepare the space accordingly.

It's essential that you take care of your tools. Clean your computer regularly, both the outer surface and its hard drive. A computer that is regularly maintained performs better than one that is not. Deleting temp files, defragmenting the hard drive, and cleaning the desktop will help keep your computer from slowing down. Check with your company's IT department, as some performance-boosting tasks may be done automatically, while others may need to be done manually. If the latter is the case, set reminders as appropriate so you can do these maintenance tasks.

You should also be prepared in case one of these important tools fails. Back up your computer on a regular basis so that all your data are not lost if your hard drive crashes. If your internet goes down, know where to go to get online again as quickly as possible. Your phone may be able to function as an internet hotspot to bridge a temporary outage. If your documents are in the cloud and you have mobile versions of the necessary apps on your phone or tablet, you may be able to work on your mobile device, at least for a while. Arm yourself in advance with the know-how to access the content you need on your mobile device and any additional costs for going online through your carrier. It's also a good idea to have a colleague's phone number on hand in cases where you can't easily get back online. You may have important meetings or tasks to complete, and that colleague can let others know what's going on. Being prepared for this situation will reduce your stress and the negative impact on others if it does occur.

I showed up 10 minutes early to a video call I was running to get the virtual room set up, load the PowerPoint deck, and chat with the attendees as they came in. Approximately one minute before the session was supposed to start, my screen went dark. It took a few minutes to figure out that I'd lost power, and with it, my connection to the internet. I grabbed my mobile office bag, stuffed my computer and power cord into it, texted my boss to tell the team what had happened, and rushed to the coffee shop six blocks away, where I was sure to have power and Wi-Fi.

While it was frustrating to have to use my plan B, I was sure glad I knew exactly where to go, and how to communicate, when I couldn't use my workspace as intended.

—Teresa Douglas

Treat all your tools with the respect they deserve and be prepared for any situation in which you lose one of them. Your mastery of the nuances of the remote working environment will help you to maximize your productivity.

Your Physical Fitness

> I am passionate about fitness and making connections with my colleagues, two pursuits that can be challenging in the remote environment. To keep myself accountable, I created an online Health & Wellness Community in which my co-workers and I post recipes, fitness tips, mindfulness ideas, and even funny memes. I lead the group and post once or twice a week, which encourages virtual water cooler talk. We also commit to challenges ranging from posting pictures of our go-to healthful lunches to running races out in the real world.
>
> —Julie Minnich

You may have heard someone say that "sitting is the new smoking." As our lifestyles become more convenient, getting through the day makes fewer demands on our bodies. In our personal lives, we have smart devices that take care of everything from banking to grocery shopping with just the tap of a screen. In our work lives, many of us spend the majority of our day sitting in front of a computer. This is true whether you work in a traditional office or as part of the remote workforce. When we think about the challenges of working from home, we may focus on psychological issues and how to deal with them—situations that involve family, job satisfaction, and the need to connect with others. However, your physical health is just as important, and there is a lot that you can do to control the situation.

The first step toward managing your physical health in the remote workplace is to recognize that you need to actively manage your physical routine. Eliminating the commute to and from work also eliminates some exercise opportunities. Consider the extra steps you get when you commute into the city and work at an office. You might have to walk to the bus, or climb up and down stairs at the train station. If you drive, you have to park your vehicle at a lot and then walk into your office building. Your office might have stairs. The lunchtime food run provides another opportunity for activity as you walk a couple of blocks down the street and then back again. In a traditional office, you have to get up to walk down the hall for meetings or to use the photocopier. After work, you might walk to a pub or coffee shop with a couple of colleagues. All of these built-in movement opportunities go away when you work from home. That doesn't mean that remote workers must resign themselves to being less physically active. It simply means that you'll need to create those opportunities yourself.

Use the greater flexibility of working from home to your advantage. Build exercise time into your routine. Naturally, always check with your doctor before taking on new physical activities. Once you have the all-clear, there are several different things you can do to stay fit. Take advantage of flexibility in your schedule to arrange regular trips to the gym as appropriate. Some remote workers go to the gym in the afternoon, when there are fewer people on the machines, and then make up the work hours later in the evening. Other employees take a midmorning walk to get fresh air along with their exercise, while still others keep a set of weights near their desks. Do some research and try different things. Mixing up your fitness routine can also add variety to your day and help you manage your stress level.

You can also find fitness opportunities during work itself. Look into customizing your desk space to allow you to stand throughout the day (or for portions of it). This will improve your overall health and posture, while also strengthening your legs and back. You can purchase a standing desk, or you can do a little research into DIY standing options. Regardless of the route you go, changing your desk is much easier to do at home than in a traditional office, where company policy might prevent office workers from modifying their office spaces. Even if there is no such policy, some workers might feel uncomfortable about standing at their desks. They might work in an open environment where standing will make them literally stand out amongst everyone else on the floor, and this can be embarrassing. That kind of social anxiety doesn't exist when working from home, so you can protect your health and your dignity all at once.

Consider other modifications beyond a standing desk. You could use an exercise ball instead of a chair, a pedal machine that allows you to keep your legs active while working, or even a treadmill desk. With a little research and some due diligence to prevent injury, you can leverage your remote working situation to be as healthy as possible.

Remind yourself to get up and take mini breaks throughout the day. In an office, you likely had to get up to retrieve documents, talk to colleagues, grab coffee, and go to meetings. At home, make excuses to get up periodically to stretch your legs and move around. Some workers even set a timer to remind themselves to get up at regular intervals throughout the day. You can also do a little research and find exercises you can do while sitting at your desk, for those days when it isn't possible to take an extended break.

Remember: Losing the traditional office doesn't have to mean losing all activity from your day. With a little thought and creativity, you may find that you have even more time to exercise than you did before.

Chapter 3

Secrets of Logistics

Most jobs have a certain rhythm for deliverables, such as calling all clients by the end of the day or closing out the accounts by the last day of the month. This chapter will help you set up the structure for the things you need to do.

How to Find What Works for You

I work a flex schedule, which gives me a strong start in the form of early mornings and the opportunity to connect with my children throughout the day. While uninterrupted time can be built into any workday, it's an automatic part of all my days. I start work before most of my coworkers come online, which allows me quiet time to get a head start on the day's tasks or focus on a special project before email and chat notifications start popping up.

Having this flexible schedule also lets me split child care with my husband. While I am working in the morning, he feeds our kids breakfast and prepares them for school. Before they head off, I get to hug them and occasionally help with a hairdo before continuing on with my work.

I take a midafternoon break to retrieve my kids from school and get to hear about their day on the way back. Once we get home, I hand them off to the nanny and dive back into work.

—Melanie McKay

Employees in the remote workforce can be very different from one another when it comes to how they manage their schedules. Some thrive by working all day, starting early in the morning and finishing late at night, with extended breaks scattered throughout. Others prefer a standard 9-to-5 workweek, with weekends off limits. To be a successful remote employee, you need to understand both your own preferences and the amount of flexibility your have in your role. There are many factors to consider when figuring out what works best for you while meeting the needs of your employer.

Start with considering the needs of the business. After all, if you can't do what is required to make your work a success for your employer, then you should probably be in a different position or perhaps even at a different company. The business you're in may have certain peak times every day or week, and you should be present for them. If you're on Pacific time and the majority of your clients and colleagues are on Eastern time, you are likely going to have to wake up early some days. If you're expected to talk to clients in the evening after they have finished work, then you'll need to include evenings in your working hours. Knowing the ebb and flow of your company's work rhythms will allow you to build your schedule accordingly, leading to professional success.

Once you have a solid idea of the rhythm of the business as a whole, take time to confirm expectations—both explicit and implicit—with your manager. For example, are people in your role expected to be available on the weekends? It does you no good to arrange your workweek in a way that works for you if your boss is not on board with it. Your manager may have certain expectations when it comes to daily or weekly meetings, or how you sign in and out. Your boss's own schedule preferences may also require you to be accessible at certain points in the day. This doesn't mean you'll have no say in these expectations; any good boss will want to meet the needs of remote employees where possible. Treat your schedule as an ongoing dialogue among you, your manager, and the needs of the business and be prepared for it to evolve over time.

With this knowledge as a foundation, you can confidently address your personal schedule preferences. When are you most productive? If you do your best thinking in the morning, then it makes sense to start your day early. Do you lose focus around midafternoon? Perhaps you need to schedule an extended break and return to work in the evening, when you have your second wind. Some remote employees enjoy working during these traditionally "off" hours because with fewer people working, they can focus on a specific task. Alternatively, if you prefer to power through your day with very small breaks, then a more compact schedule is likely best for you.

Expect that your preferences may evolve over time. This is especially true if you have never worked remotely before. Once you have figured out the needs of your employer and the business, try out different schedules. Do a test and see what results in the highest levels of both productivity and personal satisfaction. This kind of experimentation is also useful because the company may need you to be flexible. Besides having peak hours of the day or days in the week, your company may have peak seasons, when you'll have to change your schedule to handle the extra load. Being too rigid with your schedule can cause more frustration than it prevents. While it is good to have a general structure to your day, remember to build in unstructured time for the unplanned events that always seem to crop up.

Many people talk about work-life blend; the remote workforce offers, in many cases, greater control over this blend. If you carefully consider the needs of your employer, your manager, and yourself as you construct your schedule, your experience in the virtual working environment will be a positive one. The beauty is that often those three stakeholders are very much in alignment with each other—it just takes some active consideration to find the perfect fit.

Your Daily Routine

When I first began to work remotely, it was difficult for me to end my day at a reasonable hour. I needed to re-create leaving my work on a computer halfway across town! I learned to actually schedule the end of each day in my calendar. At the appointed time, I wish my team a good evening, close the team chat client, use a separate browser so that I don't receive any more notifications, and stop all work-related activity.

To my surprise, this practice has even made me more productive. That end-of-day deadline forces me to get everything crossed off my list by a specific time rather than dragging it out into the evening or next morning.

—Brian Sabel

If you look at books on raising children, you'll find that the good ones nearly always talk about the importance of routine. It's a big new world for toddlers, and routine creates a sense of security, along with the opportunity to learn through the repetition of different processes. One might think that as adults, we no longer need this tool to survive different and new situations, but we're not that far removed from our younger selves. Just as taking those first steps and being away from mom can be a hard time for a small child, entering the remote workforce can feel equally traumatizing if you're not prepared for it.

We've already talked about the importance of creating boundaries to separate our work life from our home life. The next step is to look at our daily tasks and come up with a process that can be repeated and creates structure. In many cases, it doesn't actually matter what your routine consists of, just as long as one exists.

For most people, starting work each day at the same time will provide a strong foundation for a routine. You may not need to start work at, say, 9:00 a.m., and the ability to start working whenever is convenient for you is a huge benefit for some who work remotely. It can be tempting to sleep in on days when you don't have to meet people right away or complete time-sensitive tasks. That, however, is an advantage you should explore once your routine has been solidified and you are comfortable in the remote workforce. Until then, choosing a start time and sticking to it will provide you with a strong sense of consistency and ground you for the tasks you need to complete throughout the week.

Another approach that works for some people is to avoid checking email as the first task of the day. Email is like oxygen for most people who work remotely: We need it to function and survive. The problem is that many people in the virtual workforce get a high volume of email, and if you work with colleagues and clients who are in different time zones, your inbox in the morning can be quite full. If you check your email first thing, you run the risk of completing tasks in the order in which they appear in your inbox, rather than in order of importance. Over time, that kind of experience can be incredibly draining.

Instead of making your inbox your first stop, it may be more beneficial to have a list of tasks that you need to accomplish that set you up for your day, provide you with a sense of what's new, and allow you to cross off certain to-dos before they lose out to the temptation of working through a full inbox. Depending on your role, these tasks could include looking at the stock market, checking daily company updates, starting the apps you'll use throughout the day, checking in with colleagues, or listening to your voicemail. Your to-do list should be planned the day before or be a regular series of steps built into your routine. Some remote employees have no choice but to check email as one of the first steps in their day. If that describes your role, then you will need to build in a different type of discipline into your morning. Identify those messages that are directly related to the task at hand and mark them for immediate action; leave the remainder to be read and processed later in the day. In this fashion, email sets up your day but doesn't dictate it.

Building in routines later in the workday is also important. Try to take your lunch break at a regular time and for a consistent length of time. Planning smaller (but still deliberate) breaks is also wise—perhaps an afternoon tea, a power nap, or a walk around the block. Such breaks are not just time away from work but also regular activities that have the ability to become habits, giving you consistency throughout your week, every week. Taking a break and chatting with friends or surfing the internet can give you a breather from your work tasks, but unless you have a lot of structure and repetition to these breaks, they won't necessarily strengthen your routine.

It is also important to end the day at a regular time. Finishing at 5:00 or 6:00 p.m. makes sense for many people, as it means they stop working in time for dinner.

The specific end time doesn't matter though, as long as it's generally consistent from day to day. In the remote workforce, it can be difficult to stop working. While at an office, you typically have to leave at some point, at home you never do. There is almost always something more to do, and your work space is always available to you. Having a planned end time to your day is essential for creating stability through routine.

Sometimes setting a planned end time is not enough to pull you away from work. If you have nothing to do in the evening, it can be easy to continue working after you had planned to stop. One way to break this habit is to schedule some activity immediately after work, such as spending time with a loved one, reading a book, eating dinner, or doing yoga. Plan something that you enjoy so that you are motivated to go do it. Creating a routine that helps you leave work—both physically *and* mentally—is vital for anyone who wants to enjoy working remotely.

Building a routine is important for both short-term and long-term success. Sometimes the excitement of a new world can mean that your enthusiasm overshadows the basic need for structure in your day. Suddenly you're a few weeks or months into your new virtual work experience and feeling overwhelmed. By setting a routine from the start, you can avoid the crash when the initial excitement wears off. Situations will come up that require you to vary your routine from time to time, but under this system, they will simply become the odd exception, rather than the way you live your working life.

How to Set Up Your Day

Remote employees often live and die by their calendars, and with good reason: Careful management of your schedule will allow you to be successful in your remote role. There are many calendar programs out there, but your company may require that you use a specific one. None of that really matters as long as you get in the habit of using your calendar to structure how you go about your daily tasks. Otherwise, you run the very real risk of missing deadlines or appointments. You may have heard mixed stories about productivity in the remote workforce. Some people say that they get more done as remote workers, while others have seen their productivity drop off. The difference between success and failure starts with a strategic approach to setting up your day.

Be aware of what lies ahead today, tomorrow, and into next week. Begin your day by checking your calendar. Look ahead and see whom you need to speak with and what preparations you need to make in advance of those meetings. The flow of each day—the balance of meeting time versus task time—will likely vary. Check your calendar regularly to keep up with the flow and to avoid showing up to a meeting at the wrong time or unprepared. Finally, toward the end of your workday, check what's happening tomorrow. Leave yourself a bit of time when you do this; too often, you'll see an early morning task or meeting that requires some advance preparation, and you can wind up working well past your planned end time. Give yourself enough of a cushion to prepare for tomorrow's schedule before today ends.

As you review your schedule for the next day, plan out the tasks and goals you need to complete and then build that time into your calendar. Give yourself deadlines. Don't assume that your tasks will somehow get done at some point in the day. If you haven't allotted time for those tasks on your calendar, it is all too easy for regular meetings, email, last-minute calls, and unexpected delays to fill your work hours. Use your schedule to determine what you do and when.

Don't forget to look at your workday as a whole. Do you have the right balance between scheduled work time devoted to specific tasks and unscheduled work time that can be used for meetings and other work? If you schedule too much task time, people may not be able to find time to meet with you on important issues. If you schedule too little task time, you may not have enough time to complete everything you have to do. When you first create your daily routine, you will have to use trial and error to find the right balance. Once you have been in your routine for a while, you can use experience to decide whether the ratio of task time to meeting time needs adjustment. If you feel overwhelmed by your workload, that may be a sign that you need to schedule more private work time and fewer meetings into your calendar.

Remember that other people's schedules will also have a direct impact on your calendar. A boss who spends most of his afternoons in meetings will likely be available for questions only in the morning, so plan for that situation. Alternatively, you may need to leave evenings free to make outbound calls to clients. For many in the remote workforce, time zones add further complexity to scheduling meetings and workload. When you start working with colleagues in different time zones, finding an appropriate meeting time can feel like a big task. With a little practice, however, you will soon become adept at finding a time that works for most. Find out which (and how many) time zones you have to contend with. Use this information to arrange your schedule so you can be available to colleagues during their work hours. Many calendar programs allow you to view the availability of colleagues on the same network. If the program allows it, enter in your usual business hours so your coworkers know whether they are trying to schedule a meeting outside your work hours. In this way, you can efficiently craft your schedule so that you are in sync with the people you work with the most.

It's equally important to schedule a proper lunch break and other breaks into your day. Just as important tasks can get swept aside if they aren't built into your calendar, lunchtime can easily disappear under the weight of your to-do list. The same goes for breaks. Sitting at your desk and working on the computer all day is not a healthy long-term strategy; you need moments to stretch your legs, get a drink, or go for a short walk outside. These breaks should be part of your regular day. They may not occur at the same time every day, and you may have some days with more time than others, but breaks are an important part of thriving in the remote workforce. Build them into your calendar and consider their timing: A mid-afternoon walk could be the perfect time to get your second wind as the day winds down. Make your lunch break an early or late one depending on the needs of the business so you're available for others as required at an appropriate time. Perhaps schedule another short break when your kids come home from school so you can say hello to them before diving back into work.

I used to feel guilty setting aside time during typical working hours to run to the post office or pop over to the store to get that missing ingredient for dinner, but that changed when I heard a senior colleague talk about getting his hair cut on a Tuesday afternoon because that was when he could fit it into his schedule.

I feel refreshed when I take time to get out of my house at least once a week. Since many of us start early, eat at our desks, and work after hours, taking breaks during the day for personal tasks is sometimes necessary. So long as I keep these personal task breaks to a minimum and complete them efficiently, I no longer feel guilty for making time in my calendar for them around my work responsibilities.

—Jenn Freeman

Working from home will likely cause your personal and professional calendars to overlap and become one. You may have the flexibility to take an afternoon off to catch a child's baseball game or get a massage. If you commit to something outside of work, schedule it into your work calendar so that nothing gets scheduled during the event. The reverse is also true: You need to schedule the time you plan to be working so that the other people in your life know you will be busy. By letting those who rely on you know when you are working and those you work with know when you are off, you will manage the expectations of all the people in your life while maintaining the balance you need.

You are in charge of managing your calendar efficiently. Just as a car needs an occasional tune-up to work well, your daily routine will function at maximum efficiency if you take the time to fine-tune your calendar. Take a look at the meetings on your calendar. Does every meeting have a purpose? Some meetings may be required by your supervisor, others may cover current projects, and still others may help your professional development. Avoid unnecessary meetings by learning how to say no. Saying no does not mean pushing something into the future; the future quickly becomes the present and those delayed meetings arrive before you know it. If your presence at a meeting is unnecessary, speak up! Talk to your supervisor about any meeting requests you feel uncomfortable turning down on your own. If there are valid reasons for you to decline the invite, your supervisor can work with you on next steps.

Of course, taking meetings off your calendar may not be possible. In that case, you can focus on making your non-meeting time as efficient as possible. It can take between 15 and 30 minutes to refocus after an interruption, so try to schedule your meetings in blocks, with small stretch breaks in between. Some employees designate a few days per week as their dedicated meeting days and spend the other days working exclusively on their task lists. Other employees schedule all their meetings in the afternoon, leaving the mornings free for work. If you can't do either of these things, try to schedule your meeting blocks far enough apart that you have one to two hours of private work time in between. This gives you the time you need to refocus and make progress on your task before the next meeting.

Remain flexible—understand that your calendar isn't set in stone. There will be days when four of your five scheduled meetings get bumped back or canceled entirely. This can be a great opportunity to get a head start on tomorrow's task list—or to take a walk around the block to decompress. The reverse can also happen. Your boss could call a meeting during your lunch break or squarely in the middle of the non-meeting work time you blocked out for yourself. Be prepared to shuffle things accordingly.

Whether it's to make your day more efficient, to be available for colleagues and clients, or to get time for yourself to rest, use your calendar to structure your day. Remember, those in the remote workforce who are highly structured are the ones who are highly successful. With that said, don't be locked into your daily and weekly plan when things come up that require you to change. Assume that all will go as planned, but be prepared to develop a plan B when required. Knowing what your day holds for you and when you need to accomplish all that's on your plate will give you a stable foundation and ultimately lead to a higher degree of satisfaction with your work.

How to Manage Your Inbox

> *My colleagues and I are no longer able to simply see whether we're at our respective desks, and it can be easy to think that teammates are always available. I recommend that new managers utilize their out-of-office email auto-responses every weekend as soon as they step into their roles, so they can clarify from day one what their working hours are, how to best contact them, and when colleagues can expect to hear from them.*
>
> *In a role that necessitates quick responses, it can also be useful to take this one step further and set up an "away from my desk" message or a "delay in response" message any time you believe you'll take longer to reply to messages than normal. Technology has many ways to help us be visible the way that we want to be, and your auto-response can be one of them!*
>
> *—Christine Terrell*

Email is a crucial aspect of the remote workforce. In many instances, it is the only contact you will have with some of your coworkers and clients. Thus, the image you portray in your email can be the only image people have of you. As with handling other aspects of working virtually, managing email is best done by creating a system that works for you.

When working remotely, you'll likely receive significantly more email than if you were working in the office. The times when someone would stop by your office to ask a quick question are replaced with emails asking questions. Varying time zones and work hours can make a quick phone call unfeasible; these calls are often replaced with more emails.

Scheduling specific times to check your email can be helpful. If you respond to an email each time one comes in, you will constantly be interrupted and have to shift focus. By turning email notifications off and only checking your inbox periodically, you will maintain focus on projects and complete them more efficiently. Many people benefit from checking email once in the morning and once in the afternoon. You may need to increase that number to three or four times a day, or you might need to check your email every hour. Over time, you will find what works best for you and is necessary for your role. When you do, manage the expectations of those you work with. Let your coworkers and clients know the best time to reach you by email.

If you are in a position that involves a significant amount of email, you may benefit from performing a sweep of your inbox when you start your workday. You can often use the sender and subject information to determine whether an email needs to be answered immediately. By taking care of emergencies first, you can move to the rest of your emails in a way that makes sense for you.

Some messages can be answered right away, while others require detailed responses that take more time. In general, if you can deal with an email in fewer than five minutes, you should answer or delegate it as soon as you open it; it is most efficient to read something once and take care of it immediately while you are thinking about it. For the emails that require more work than you can accomplish in five minutes, determine how much time you will need to properly answer. If you won't be able to compose an answer that day, it is best to send a quick response stating that you received the email and are working on it. If possible, include an estimated time frame for your full response. Then be sure to add that email to your to-do list.

Whatever the volume and urgency of the emails you receive, you should find a way to organize your emails properly. Different email systems have different tools to help with this. Find a simple way to denote emails that require further follow-up. Even though you should have added answering these messages to your to-do list, you still need an easy way to access the emails themselves later. Some email systems have a star function that lets you place a star next to emails to come back to. Other systems have different levels of importance that allow you to flag an email in various ways based on priority. Find a system that makes locating unanswered emails as easy as possible.

If, on the other hand, you have completed an email and no longer need it, many systems allow you to create folders to store old messages in. This can be a great way to clear out your inbox so that you don't feel bogged down. Become familiar with your email system and the features it provides so that you can use them effectively.

You may be in a position that requires you to be on email threads you do not actually need to read. For example, maybe you're a member of a cross-functional team that requires you to have a record of a certain type of transaction. In that case, you could benefit from applying email filters that automatically archive these messages and store them in a designated folder. If you use this system, it's a good idea to make sure the emails are still marked as "unread" so you know which ones you have seen before and which are new. You can then schedule a time once a day or even once a week to look at them. But be careful with this method: It can be common for people to completely forget about these folders and miss an important email that was filtered by mistake. Other people have found success using filters to automatically flag or label emails instead of archiving them. This has the benefit of helping you prioritize without the risk of missing the email altogether.

Another tool many people find helpful is nesting. This functionality automatically groups all replies and forwards of a particular message into one email thread. The benefit is a much clearer inbox: Each subject takes up just one line, and you can see all the responses in one place. This helps you to be sure you are seeing every response to the email chain before you chime in. However, some people find this method confusing, actually making it harder to read the entire chain and catch all of the pieces. This is particularly true if someone replies to everyone on the email and someone replies separately only to you, because both responses will be grouped into one chain. In any situation, it can be helpful to read the most current emails first to be sure you didn't miss a more recent response. Ultimately, the way you use the tools in your email client will be completely customized by you, for you. Try different things and see what works best!

Even with tools in place, the amount of time you need to set aside to answer emails will be very different depending on how many messages you typically receive in a day and how often you check them. Regardless, checking email does take time, so it is something you should schedule. To determine how much time to schedule for answering emails, start tracking how long it typically takes you to do so. Once you know how long it normally takes, you can allocate the proper time in your day.

Emails are a quick and effective method of communication. You can collaborate with multiple people at once, communicate outside of normal working hours, and have a written record of the conversation. Creating your ideal system for answering emails will ensure that you respond promptly and give those you work with a great impression of your ability and professionalism.

Chapter 4

Secrets of Communication

In a traditional office, if your colleague isn't responding to email, you can casually stroll past her office to see what's going on. The remote worker in Florida can't do the same with her colleague in Canada. In this chapter, we'll discuss how to get what you need while maintaining your professionalism.

Basic Etiquette

In the virtual world, there are so many more ways to connect than you may be used to. Unlike the physical workspace, where you can pass someone in the hall, see them in their office, or take them out to lunch, there is a new horizon of virtual communication that allows you many different options for getting in touch. This new horizon comes with a caveat, though: Because your interactions with colleagues may now be fewer and farther between, it is more important than ever to be thoughtful in how you choose to communicate.

One obvious option is to send an email. In a traditional office, email may be reserved for longer communications, conversations with large groups, or exchanges that need to be documented. In the virtual world, all of these aspects hold true, but there is also more potential for quick emails back and forth that result in instantaneous communication. There are also many instant messaging applications. Your workplace may have one such platform or it may have several; it is important to become comfortable with each. Many instant messaging platforms allow you to set statuses or write updates for your coworkers to see—make sure you are using these features appropriately. There are other, more personal ways to connect as well, including voice calls and video calls.

Communicating in the remote workforce is a challenge because there is so much to consider. You need to figure out the right medium to communicate the right message in the right situation. For each message that you are trying to communicate, think about the preferences of the recipient. You may work with someone who hates email and would always rather set up a 15-minute chat. On the other hand, you may work with someone who loves how easy it is to manage email and prefers all communication be sent this way so that there is a record of it. Or, you may work with someone who is constantly in meetings but is able to answer instant messages throughout the day. When possible, communicate with people in the way that is best for them.

Which medium is best also depends on what you are trying to communicate. Some things are better said in a stored written format; an example would be communicating deadlines and deliverables to an entire team. Other content—for instance, sensitive information or difficult conversations—may be better handled over the phone. Often the best medium for conversations like this is a video call so that you and the other person can see each other's facial expressions.

If you have decided to communicate in a written format, remember that the written word creates a trail to follow. There is documented proof of everything you have said. It also forms a mental picture of you in the mind of your colleagues. In the virtual workspace, this may be all your colleagues use to get to know you. Thus, it is important to take the extra time to think about how your words will be translated over text. You may want to avoid slang and informal language so your words are not misinterpreted. It is a good idea to always stay as polite as possible and maintain proper grammar.

When drafting an email, there are many aspects to consider. One important area is the recipient field. Think about whom the email should be sent to. Also think about who should be copied. For example, if you are checking in on the status of a project that is due next week, it may not be appropriate to copy the main recipient's supervisor. Often, copying a supervisor can be seen as throwing someone under the bus or trying to get them in trouble in some way. However, if you are sending out a thank-you email to someone who finished a project ahead of schedule and did an excellent job, copying their supervisor is a great way to make sure that their accomplishment is recognized.

The subject line is an equally important aspect of email communication. The more informative it is, the better. Many companies have a protocol for emails that require special attention. You may be asked to write "Urgent" or "Please Respond" in front of subject lines that are time-sensitive or require a response. Alternatively, your team may choose to start the subject line with the project name and a colon so that everything regarding that project can be easily seen at a glance.

Be conscientious of email length. People you work with may save long emails for later, so be sure that your written word is succinct when possible. You may want to include bullets or numbered lists to highlight the points. Numbered lists are especially helpful when asking multiple questions because they allow the person to respond and answer by number. When you are responding to an email with multiple questions, it can be helpful to do so in another color so that it is easy to see the difference between the questions and their answers.

Throughout all communication, it is a good idea to be as clear as possible and make sure you understand what someone is conveying to you. Never assume that you know what the person means. If you have a question, ask it. Pay attention to the subtle unwritten and unspoken clues often present in communication; you ignore this subtext at your peril. There is a tendency to read written communication as more negative than what is meant. Before pressing send, read your message again to be sure it is conveying the intended tone. While communicating in the virtual world, there are many things to keep in mind. Being thoughtful in your communication choices will go a long way toward building understanding and good working relationships.

Setting Expectations and Achieving Transparency

I start an ongoing conversation about expectations with my direct reports from our first meeting, premised on the idea that what I expect from them is what I should model for them. My reports—and my colleagues—can expect me to respond to their calls or emails within 24 hours during the week, but only for emergencies on weekends. They can also expect that I will value their time: I look at my calendar every morning, and when I notice that two meetings may overlap, I reach out to shift one of them proactively so that I can be fully present in every interaction. This gives me credibility when I address consistent lateness to meetings with my employees.

I am careful not to assume that my remote coworkers have the same availability I do. Just because I do something a certain way doesn't mean I have a right to expect it from someone else, so I learn whether colleagues are available on weekends before depending on them to help me with something urgent.

—Melody Young

One of the major differences between working in an office and working from home is your level of visibility. In an office or any other physical location where you are required to "punch in" (either formally or by virtue of being seen arriving on time), your absence can be quite conspicuous. When you are at meetings or visiting clients, a dark office or an empty chair at your cubicle clearly indicates that you're not present. If someone is looking for you, oftentimes the people who sit near you can tell your visitor that you are in another meeting. On your return, those same people can tell you who dropped by your desk.

Now consider the remote workforce. If colleagues and clients don't get email responses from you or are unable to see you online through various instant messaging programs, it could mean that you are in meetings or visiting clients. Or, it could mean that you are on an extended lunch break. Perhaps you're simply busy with projects and are ignoring communications from others for the time being. In a worst-case scenario, something tragic could have happened, and it could take a long time for anyone to realize you aren't around. Add different time zones into the mix, and you can see that setting expectations about your schedule and providing transparency about your whereabouts is an important part of succeeding in the remote workforce.

The beauty of working from home is that in many cases, you have the opportunity to organize your own hours. That said, your coworkers should have a rough idea of your work schedule. Once you set your schedule, stick to those hours as much as possible so your colleagues and clients can plan accordingly. You could list your normal working hours in your email signature, on your web page, or in other locations where you have a digital work profile. When you will not be sticking to your regular schedule, use the out-of-office reply function to let those who email you know that they shouldn't expect an immediate reply.

Similarly, update your status in relevant messenger programs so colleagues and clients looking for you online know that you are not in the office. Instant messaging programs are very popular for colleagues to quickly and informally contact each other. Many of these programs allow you to display your status, showing whether you are online and available, offline, or online but unavailable. The challenge is remembering to update your status. For example, if your Skype status doesn't change for days, then it will soon become meaningless. Everyone will contact you at all times, because they assume that the "unavailable" setting is not actually true. The same goes for profile updates: If you don't maintain them, they too will lose their power. Make sure that you date your updates so that even if a message is left on display for too long, at least those reading it will be able to make appropriate assumptions about your true availability.

Setting expectations shouldn't be limited to your work schedule. Also make known how and when you will respond to people. There are some workers whose job duties, typing speed, or personal preferences allow them to reply to all emails and messages within 24 hours. However, there are those on the other end of the spectrum who cannot realistically respond to emails until certain days of the week or who much prefer to save responses for meetings. Either approach could work, but only as long as the people you interact with know what to expect. Many companies will have a formal or informal expectation regarding email response time, and that can be sufficient.

Instituting regular meetings can also help you to develop a high level of transparency and trust in those around you. This may not be an option for all remote workers, but where possible, having regular team and individual meetings can be another way to display your consistency. You can take this a step further. If you use a shared calendar program, those with access to your calendar will be able to see when your meetings are and identify patterns of when you are unavailable. Some programs also allow you to set your normal working hours on your calendar so others will receive a notification if they send you an invitation for a time outside of those hours. This can be particularly useful when dealing with people in different time zones who might want to talk with you during what is their morning, not realizing that you might not even be awake at that time.

As an employee in charge of your own schedule, you generally know what you'll be doing each day and what part of the day you'll be working. No one else will, however, unless you tell them. Help your coworkers by being transparent about when you are available and when you are not. Creating habits and patterns in the way you work allows others to learn what they can expect from you and when they can expect it. This builds trust, which is critical in the virtual environment where people can't see what others are doing.

Maintaining Professionalism

I follow the advice of Hall of Fame football player Deion Sanders: Look good, play good. Sure, I could get away with working in my pajamas all day, but I just don't feel like a professional when I'm not dressed as one. Instead, I wear clothes that put me in the right mindset and make me feel like I'm going to the office. This helps me do better work and signals to my teammates that I take their work seriously.

—*Brian Sabel*

The ability to choose whether to work in your office, in a local café, or just outside on your patio is a great part of working remotely. But the freedom to work anywhere comes with a new set of risks concerning the image that you project, as it can be very easy to skew overly casual in your attire and communication style. Most people don't start their remote workforce career wearing their pajamas on video calls or chatting to their colleagues in the same way as friends on social media, but professional standards can erode over time. If you have limited interactions with others, or if you have plenty of interactions but none with someone physically in front of you, it can be easy to unknowingly drift away from professional standards.

A remote worker donning traditional business wear on top, perhaps a suit jacket and tie, with a pair of casual shorts is an amusing picture to conjure up when thinking about the dress code of the virtual workforce. This fashion dichotomy most certainly happens, and naturally it's rarely an issue if it does, since remote workers are almost never seen from the waist down. One thing to consider is whether that lower-half comfort is coming at the expense of the work-home boundaries you've set for yourself. If you can maintain that distinction with only your top half being camera-ready, that of course is not a problem and is just another benefit of working from home. It is important to be aware, however, that there are times when you do need to stand up while on camera. You might need to grab headphones or deal with an interruption that requires you to leave the room. In those situations, if your lower half is not camera-ready, it could be awkward. Master the art of sliding out of camera view, or simply make sure you cover or turn off your camera before getting up. The safest option, naturally, is to be camera-ready from head to toe.

Casual Fridays have their place in the virtual world, though again this will depend on your boundaries, the people you need to interact with on camera, and your company's culture and expectations. It's a smart move to change your Skype status or other relevant indicators to prepare colleagues and clients for what to expect when you come on camera. They won't have the same visual cues as they would in a traditional office setting, where seeing employees in T-shirts and shorts quickly broadcasts the company dress code for the day. In a similar vein, be conscious that clanging jewelry, baseball caps, and loud shirts will not necessarily be camera-appropriate on any day, even if they are distinct from your regular wardrobe. You might have your "work" baseball cap on, but it's not likely to be the best wardrobe choice when conducting meetings. Consider what is appropriate for both your personal needs and what the company expects from you. Acquire an appropriate wardrobe and keep up with your laundry so that what you choose to wear signifies to both you and those you interact with that you are ready to work.

In addition to knowing when to dress professionally and when to dress casually, it's important to know when to be formal and when to be casual in your interactions. For many people, going online and chatting with others over instant messenger or in video calls is rooted in friendly and social interactions. When using those methods of communication in the work environment, it can be challenging to find the right level of formality, as the instinct is often to veer into the casual. Resist this instinct. In the online working environment, it is usually safer to err on the side of being overly formal than to come across as too casual.

Consider how your email and typed chat messages will be interpreted. Who will be reading them? What is this person's position compared to yours? How well do you know them? Is there room for misinterpretation? A wise remote employee carefully considers these questions before hitting the send button and generally saves jokes for calls. When it comes to regular group calls, it can be helpful to set up a list of guidelines at the beginning. Outlining the dress code, the level of formality, and any other relevant points ensure that everyone is on the same page. You may find that the group functions better in an informal mode, but it's better to find this out up front than to make assumptions and risk being surprised.

Are there times when casual is better? Of course. Some organizations will hold game nights online, have virtual happy hours, or allot time for those higher up to mingle and interact with subordinates. Outside of these structured events, talking one-on-one with colleagues you know well can provide you with the chance to relax and have a fun conversation. It's simply a matter of being aware of the people you're interacting with and recognizing that you're talking to colleagues and clients, not friends on social media.

"Be professional" seems like a strange thing to remind an employee to do, but those in the remote workforce should give themselves this healthy reminder from time to time. In an office setting, you receive immediate visual cues when you say something that borders on inappropriate, and you can make a mental note to phrase things differently next time. Clothing standards are reinforced every day when you see what your boss and colleagues are wearing. You can read the signals of your audience when speaking and make adjustments to your delivery in real time.

In the remote world, you often send information out into the ether and then have to read between the lines when you get a response. The opportunity to adjust on the fly is almost nonexistent. Even with video calls, it can be hard to read facial clues when there are image delays and audio glitches or when some participants are off camera. Just being aware of the situation, however, will allow you to maximize your chances of coming across in the way you intended. You can also be transparent about your attempts at finding the right level of professionalism and solicit feedback from your supervisor or colleagues. While it's important to develop your self-awareness, there's no reason why you can't get an outside perspective as well. You'll soon become an expert at projecting a professional air when it is required and a more casual one when the situation calls for it, so you can come across in exactly the way you intended.

Expressing Yourself

I am retiring by nature, but I've found that I don't need to pretend to be an extrovert to work successfully in the virtual world. I have opened lines of communication by simply asking thoughtful questions. This can mean making it a point to speak up in large meetings, inquiring about changing business practices, or gathering input on a project I've been pouring myself into from colleagues with expertise beyond my own. Collecting feedback lets peers and higher-ups see my achievements, demonstrates that I am open to collaboration, and encourages others to feel invested in my efforts and growth.

—Caitlin Duke

Think about a traditional office environment. Now picture the hardest worker in that office. Think of her as she works throughout a regular eight-hour day. This is someone who gets things done and doesn't allow herself to be easily distracted. She produces good work, which takes time, and she likely checks that work before sending it out. A good worker like her is probably too busy for small talk, so she keeps her conversations quick and to the point so she can get back to producing good, quality work.

Now picture this worker in the virtual workforce. But remember, you can't see her because she's working at home, so all your interactions are done online. This person may still be a good worker who produces quality work, but few people will know. This is one of the most interesting and, for some, most challenging parts of working virtually. Hard work that no one can see does not translate into success. It simply makes you a hard-working ghost.

In the remote workforce, you must demonstrate that you are a good worker by managing your persona in a conscious and deliberate manner. The long-standing practice of keeping your head down, doing great work, and being recognized for those efforts doesn't work in the virtual environment. You need to be more visible, even about mundane matters, because otherwise you are quite literally out of sight and therefore out of mind.

So what does this *not* mean? It doesn't mean changing your persona into something you are not. If you are someone who has always let your work speak for itself, you don't need to transform into a self-promoter who is constantly making big announcements about your progress. A transformation is necessary, but not one that radically changes who you are. Instead, you'll need to consider how to be a visible employee in terms of the choices you make in your interactions with colleagues. Consider it akin to dressing for success—only in this situation, you're showing your work accomplishments rather than your new tie.

This also doesn't mean that a great online presence makes up for poor work or poor productivity. Talking a good talk will mean little if the results aren't there to back it up. Virtual workers who lack the substance to support their presence are quickly identified. Indeed, with the greater trust placed between an employee and an employer in the remote workforce, a breach of that trust has greater repercussions. Be honest and be appropriate. Let those you work with know you're working and that you care about getting the job done.

Creating your persona and promoting yourself take effort. You are not visible unless you consciously take action. Your company will likely have different communication processes set up, which could include group instant messenger chats, virtual communities, email chains, and so on. Take the initiative to make good use of those forums to share what you're working on and create a fully realized picture of yourself in the minds of those in your workforce. For some people, this kind of interaction may not come easily, but with time, even quiet individuals can learn to comfortably share what they need to with their colleagues.

Interestingly, someone who is an introvert can actually thrive in this kind of environment. Many individuals who are fairly shy and not particularly adept at in-person social situations can become almost unrecognizably outgoing in their online interactions. Not just through typed communication but even on video calls, these people function quite well in situations where much of their social discomfort is filtered out through the curtain of technology. Thus, if you're concerned that you don't have the outgoing personality one thinks about when picturing a highly visible and chatty employee in the non-remote environment, rest easy. This new world could very well fit your personality in a way that an office workspace never would.

This doesn't mean that extroverts should avoid working remotely. The virtual workforce can expose you to groups of people whom you might not have otherwise met. You could have colleagues in different cities, different states, or even different parts of the world. Office banter, via instant message, can even be better, as introverted colleagues are more apt to join in the witty (written) repartee. While it may not be possible to meet after work for happy hour, many virtual employees have found that an online video happy hour can be just as fun.

Remember, the virtual work environment is an altogether different world, with different rules and parameters. Bringing out your online persona means making conscious decisions to connect with others. Forming your online persona means choosing what you say. You won't need to develop a new vocabulary per se, but rather a different way of expressing yourself. Online communication can be prone to misunderstandings, so using emoticons and keeping comments short and simple are all part of interacting effectively with colleagues. Modulating your message and tone will ensure you are seen as not just a good worker but also someone who is present and engaged with the whole team.

It's an exciting opportunity, working online. You get to craft your persona in a way not typically afforded by working in a traditional office. Naturally outgoing individuals can funnel that social personality into vibrant virtual connections. More introverted types have a chance to flourish and connect with a lot of people in an engaging way that allows them to remain comfortable. Regardless of where you fit on this spectrum, being visible is essential in the remote workforce. Do your work to be seen in a positive light, and you will set yourself up for even greater success down the road.

Working with Your Boss

It's important to know how often your boss wants to meet with you. My boss and I had a standing one-on-one appointment once a week that worked well for us. And then last year, as we were thinking of ways to become more agile, we decided to try meeting for 10 minutes every day instead. We phrased these daily meetings as a pilot, and had even set up the calendar invite so that it would end after a certain number of weeks.

Unfortunately, we didn't have the discipline to stick to a 10-minute slot. The 10-minute meetings quickly became 20-minute meetings, which turned into 60-minute daily meetings. We always had plenty of actual work tasks to talk about, and the conversations were good, but our schedules could not accommodate a standing 60-minute meeting. Once our pilot was over, we agreed to return to meeting once a week, with ad hoc communication as the need arose.

—*Patrick Reagan*

In business, if relationships aren't king, they are at the very least the power behind the throne. Nowhere is this truer than in the relationship you have with your boss. All bosses have the potential to be an advocate and also a gatekeeper. In the virtual workforce, your manager's influence over your brand is much more pronounced. Work hard to get this relationship right; you will be more engaged and effective in your role if the person you report to is your ally. For some companies and many supervisors, managing a virtual team is new territory. It's one thing to manage a single freelancer while working in a traditional office. It's quite another to manage an entire team of virtual workers while also working from home.

If your company is new to the remote workforce, your boss may be grappling with how to manage you effectively when she can't see you. Be persistent—and polite—when asking for what you need. Above all, go into this relationship assuming that the person you report to wants to help you succeed. If your boss doesn't answer your questions in one medium, try another. Do not mistake a lack of responsiveness for a lack of interest. They could be working at the task at hand and just not providing any updates. If you still don't get a response, try reaching out to a more veteran colleague to get the answers you need. If you do get an answer to your question from someone else, be sure to let your manager know. Your colleague in the same role may also lack resources, or he may not. A cross-functional colleague you work with every day may also have that information. You won't know until you ask. Word your requests as neutrally as possible and keep a virtual paper trail.

Conversely, many new virtual managers try to micromanage their way through the remote world. If your manager is micromanaging you, understand that this isn't necessarily about your manager's lack of trust in you; it may be a response to uncertainty. Luckily, there are things you can do to help your manager navigate this unfamiliar territory.

If you are unsure about any aspect of your job, ask! Err on the side of too much communication at the beginning, then gradually dial it down until you get to a communication level that works for both of you. This might mean living with micromanagement for a little while, then calling a meeting to discuss communication expectations now that you have both had a chance to get to know one another better.

We all have a preferred way to interact with our colleagues. Your manager is no different when it comes to interacting with her direct reports. Among other things, you want to figure out where she stands on the formal-informal spectrum. Does your boss like joking with her direct reports, or does she prefer to keep all communication centered firmly on the task at hand? Does she prefer meetings or written reports? While there may be some room for flexibility on these issues, you will get along better if you understand that you will need to adapt to her style more than she will adapt to yours.

Every role has performance metrics. Some companies may post scorecards for each role on the company intranet. Even if your company doesn't do this, you can often figure out what is most important to the person you report to by paying attention to what she asks for and when she asks for it. Ask questions. Make it clear that you want to ensure you give her exactly what she needs.

Ask for feedback. In a perfect world, you would receive thoughtful, balanced feedback about your performance on a regular basis. In the real world, day-to-day concerns can crowd out these larger conversations unless you ask for them. This is especially true in the virtual setting, where everyone works more and you are literally out of sight for most of the day. If, for whatever reason, you don't receive feedback on your performance, try to elicit it by asking specific questions. "How am I doing?" is not a specific question. "On a scale of 1 to 10, how well would you say I get along with others?" is better. If you change the way you do something in response to your boss's feedback, let her know. This sends the message that you value her opinion and want to do a good job.

In almost all cases, you will settle into a mutually productive working relationship. If this doesn't prove to be the case, then try to identify the problem. Diagnosing issues can be challenging in the remote workforce, where it is all too easy to feel isolated if things are not going well. Still, there are steps you can take to get the help you need.

Sometimes the problem between you and your manager centers around differences in working style. It is all too easy for this type of conflict to look like a performance problem. For example, if you are the type of person who needs to think about something ahead of time and your boss needs to talk things out in the moment, your boss may draw the wrong conclusions about your strategic thinking ability. How you handle this type of friction depends on the personalities involved.

In some cases, you can call a meeting and try to address the issue directly. You might do this by saying something along the lines of, "I've noticed that we've had some conflict, and I would love to find a way for us to both get what we need." In other cases, this is not possible. Your network can be a resource here as well. First, a trusted member of your network can act as a sanity check. Ideally, this person is well connected and has a good sense of the company culture and the wider goals of your unit. Are you being reasonable? It can be hard to hear that you are the problem, but if this is the case, then denial does not help you. If your boss is the problem, then your colleague may have ideas that can help you to either endure or change your situation.

There are also things you can do on your own. Make sure that you are doing an excellent job in your role. Do not let your performance metrics dip. This might also be a good time to excel on other projects for other departments. If you are seen as an asset by other members of your leadership team, it can mitigate your boss's perspective of you. You might even be able to use the managers of these other projects as references if you decide to look for a different internal role.

Many virtual employees have found that being managed remotely provides a great mix of immediate interaction and uninterrupted work time. In the vast majority of cases, applying a little patience and doing a little detective work will help you develop a great working relationship with your boss.

Working Effectively with Others

> *I learned the hard way that, especially in a remote workplace, face-to-face video calls promote relationship building better than email exchanges. Though I love writing emails—I can write them at times convenient to me, and I'm able to mull over my words and craft my messages carefully—they don't allow for the multi-dimensional variables that arise in a live conversation. Furthermore, if I find myself saying, "No, I don't want to call; I'll just write an email," I know that I need to examine why I don't want to speak to that person and improve that working relationship.*
>
> *—Yeo Ju Choi*

From the moment you start interacting with a new team, you should begin to form an idea of how the team operates. In a physical workspace, you can casually view the interactions of your coworkers just by being in the same space and observing them. In the virtual workplace, you can do the same thing, just in different ways.

Many teams use some sort of instant messaging app and may even have a group chat. If so, you can join the group chat and in the beginning simply observe how your coworkers interact with one another. From a group chat, you can determine how formal or informal a group is as well as the purpose of the chat. It might be a way for coworkers to engage in fun banter throughout the day to keep things interesting, or it may be a quick way to get questions answered. Knowing the purpose can help you determine how often to check the group chat and how to interact within it.

Your team may also have regularly scheduled virtual team meetings. Again, in the beginning this can be a great way to observe how team members interact with one another. You may find that the interactions in chats are the same as in group meetings, or you may find that the tone is very different. The differences may be due to who the participants are in each format, such as whether a direct supervisor or a member of senior management is present, or due to the format itself. Your team may use the group chat to joke around and the team meetings to get things accomplished, or vice versa. In the virtual workforce, it's not uncommon to have different dynamics on different platforms within the same team. You can facilitate your relationship with your team by understanding which communication medium is used for what.

Responsiveness and frequency of communication are also important. Your team may have standards as to how quickly you need to reply to emails, instant messages, and other forms of communication. When you know the standards, you can follow them. The same goes for following up with team members. If your team has a standard of a one-week response time, for instance, you wouldn't want to follow up after three days. However, if your team has a one-day response time, it would be appropriate to follow up after that time has passed.

You can apply this advice not only to working with your team but also to working with outside teams. If you are selected to work on a project with another group, or if you communicate with another team in general, you will want to pay special attention to how their team norms differ from those of your "home" team and adjust your approach accordingly. When in doubt, ask! If you are still uncertain about what is expected of you, let the outside team know how you will interact with them unless told otherwise. That way, there is no ambiguity about what you are going to do.

Knowing your role within the team itself can also have an impact on how you work with your coworkers. If you have been brought in as a leader, you should pay close attention to how the other leaders within the team act. If you were brought in to replace someone else, it could be helpful to gather information about how this team member worked with others, paying special attention to the things that they did well and learning from the things that didn't work as well.

Getting along with your coworkers in the virtual workforce doesn't have to be any more difficult than getting along with people in a traditional office. In some ways, it can be easier, as you don't have to listen to their choice of music or smell what they had for lunch. With a little patience and dedication, you will soon develop positive working relationships with the people you interact with to meet goals and produce results.

Managing Indirect Reports

When you're interacting with your direct reports, there is a clear understanding of your working relationship. You assign tasks, and your staff completes them. If something doesn't go according to plan, you can set expectations and provide immediate feedback. Guidance and disciplinary action can be applied when you feel they are needed. If you recognize someone on your team is ready to grow, you can directly craft their progress, getting them ready for additional opportunities.

Managing indirect reports isn't as straightforward. This is true whether you are in a traditional office setting or a remote one; the biggest difference between the two is the degree to which you need to actively build in communication points. In an office environment, you might regularly see an indirect report working away at various tasks. A casual glance from your vantage point across the room may tell you how she is progressing or if she needs you to intervene. You may have regular and close contact with your indirect report's boss, so updates can easily and often casually be shared. In the remote workforce, none of these visual cues are present. If you want to successfully manage your indirect report, you need to build in your own feedback loops.

Success in managing indirect reports often comes through developing a trusting relationship. It's best to start by trying to understand the needs and motivation of the indirect report. Does this person want to be doing this work, or have they simply been assigned to fill a need? Is it a chance for them to prove they can do different work and participate on a new team in order to strengthen their internal resumé? Or are they struggling on their current team and potentially going to be transitioned elsewhere? Knowing their situation and any relevant backstory will help you assess how someone is feeling so you can act accordingly. While you don't need to know exactly where this indirect report is coming from in order to have a successful working relationship, having this information can go a long way in helping you understand the best way to work together. By doing the right level of research on who you're working with, you can then make sure you're both operating on the same page.

Piecing together your indirect report's backstory may seem complicated when you work remotely, but a little preparation and thought can help you get what you need. This could include learning how this individual already works with their boss, understanding any recent performance concerns or successes, or researching any other events (past or ongoing) that could impact how they respond to your management style. This person, regardless of whether they are an all-star or someone with performance issues, is going to be used to carrying out duties in a way that reflects the needs of the person whom they report to. You may have different, though equally effective, ways of working that don't mesh well with this person's habitual style, leading to frustration, mistakes, and inefficiency. Recognizing where your indirect report is coming from and then establishing clear expectations with them from the start is crucial. This is especially true in the remote workforce, where you won't necessarily know that something is wrong until a significant amount of time has passed or certain tasks are already completed.

It's also important to consider when and how to loop others in. Is it really necessary to copy your indirect report's boss on every email? Probably not, and aside from filling your colleague's inbox with unnecessary emails, it can also set up a relationship that is not based on trust. A better option is to have regular check-ins with your colleague to provide updates about how her direct report is doing while working for you. Sharing a version of those conversations with the indirect report also keeps things out in the open. This makes the process just formal enough and gives you the opportunity to present any concerns in a safe way with a trail of evidence. This can be especially important if you don't have a close relationship with the indirect report's boss or even if you don't know that person at all. That way, if there are concerns, they won't cause as many problems as they would if there were no warning at all.

You definitely want documentation about your experiences with an indirect report. With your direct reports, you get to know them well and you have a clearer picture in your head about how they are performing. You also don't need to communicate as much about them to others. In contrast, you need to be able to pass on updates to the managers of indirect reports whenever needed. If you don't have good examples of how they are doing, you won't come across very well. So keep notes on how they do and you'll not only be doing everyone else a favor, you'll be doing one for yourself as well.

—Mike Webber

You should feel comfortable providing feedback to your indirect report, but if it's feedback that has implications for his regular work, then that feedback should be given with his direct supervisor involved. This is a sensitive path to navigate, because it can sometimes be seen as getting an employee in trouble by looping in his boss. This is why having a strong foundation of clear communication and regular updates is important. Then, if there is an issue that needs to be raised, it's not going to be a surprise for anyone involved, and it's not going to stand out as more serious than it actually is. If you have already provided feedback to the employee about his performance and you don't feel formal communication with his boss is necessary, then a short, personal update to his boss might be sufficient instead. Human resource issues, however, will likely require the employee's direct manager to take the lead, even if the work is being done for you or your team.

Managing others who don't report to you can be a great experience. You get to meet new people, expand your network, and learn about different management and working styles. But of course the challenges of dealing with indirect reports need to be managed as well. Clear and regular communication with both the worker and their supervisor is key, and if your company doesn't have a system in place for this type of interaction, it will be up to you to create one. Find out what works for everyone involved and then provide a consistent communication experience. The remote workforce thrives on good systems of communication, and these systems are especially important when it comes to managing those who report to others.

Running Virtual Meetings

Test out your audiovisual setup with a trusted friend or colleague before hopping into a larger video call. Virtual meetings require some considerations that in-person meetings don't. For example, when I started my remote role, I often jumped into my team meeting without thinking about the camera angle. I was known as "Wilson" (from the show Home Improvement*) because my camera only showed half of my face!*

—*Kristin Robinson*

When first shifting from in-person meetings to virtual ones, it can seem that virtual meetings are less important or even that they don't really feel like meetings. However, in the virtual workforce, these meetings are often all you have. They are real meetings and should be treated as such.

In a virtual meeting, make sure everyone is heard. Some people feel more comfortable talking in person than electronically. If people are on camera, you can pay attention to physical cues. You may notice that someone wants to speak from their facial expression. If you are in an audio-only meeting, it can be helpful to have a list of attendees to reference. You can then go down the list, asking for each person's thoughts or updates.

There are also ways to make sure that everyone at a meeting is on a level playing field. For example, if three people are working remotely and three are in the office, it can put everyone on more even ground for the three in the office to stay at their desks on their personal computers rather than meet in a conference room together. Grouping some, but not all, people together can create an us-versus-them dynamic in the room. It can also make it easier for the on-site people to have side conversations, which can be distracting to the remote participants and cause people to miss information. By putting everyone in a similar situation, you can help to ensure that everyone feels included and equal.

Make your meeting time count. Some issues are better resolved with an email or a phone call than with a meeting. Additionally, it is best to have a limited number of topics to discuss in each meeting. For example, if you are working on five projects simultaneously with the same team member, it may be best to plan to talk about only a couple of those projects at each meeting. It can also be helpful to send out an agenda prior to some meetings. When everyone knows the planned topics ahead of time, everyone can be prepared, and meetings can adhere to the time frame (and topics) given.

Always prioritize your discussion topics so that you hit the important points before the meeting is over. When there are 5 to 10 minutes left in the meeting, determine whether the remaining items on your list can be covered in that time or if another meeting should be set up. It is often better to schedule an additional meeting than to rush through important topics or potentially cause the meeting to run over. Ending a meeting on time is best for everyone involved.

However, meetings do not always stick to the scheduled time. In the physical workspace, it can be easier to end a meeting on time because you have tangible restrictions, such as other people needing the meeting room. Or there may be physical cues that it is time to end, such as people fidgeting or looking at the clock. In the virtual world, the lines become more blurry. Hopping from one virtual meeting to the next is as simple as clicking a few buttons. However, it is equally important to end meetings on time in the virtual workspace, because allowing yourself to be lax can often lead to being a couple of minutes late to the next meeting without even realizing it. Treating every meeting as though there is a hard stop at the end of it is the best way to be respectful of people's time and ensure a smooth workday.

There are ways to help meetings end on time. If you are the meeting organizer, plan content that will fit in the time allotted. When working remotely, you can't steal a few minutes in the break room or the hallway to quickly catch up with colleagues. Thus, these quick catch-up conversations usually happen during meetings. Plan a few minutes at the beginning and the end of the meeting as a buffer. For example, if the meeting is set for an hour, you can plan 45 minutes of content. This extra time leaves room for catching up, questions, late arrivals, and technical difficulties. Some calendar programs allow you to set shorter run times for appointments—25 minutes instead of 30, or 50 minutes instead of an hour—which builds in a bit of a buffer for team members to take a break or mentally prepare for the next meeting. However, meeting participants will only benefit from these buffers if you adhere to scheduled end times.

Sometimes running late for a meeting is inevitable. When you are going to be late for a meeting in person, often the other person you are meeting can physically see that you are not at your desk. They may even be able to see that you are in another meeting simply by looking through the window of a conference room. In the virtual world, this is not possible. When someone enters a virtual meeting space and you are not there, that person often has very little recourse to find out where you are or what is keeping you. If you are running late for a meeting, send a quick message to the person you are meeting to let them know your estimated time of arrival. This can be short and to the point: "Stuck in meeting—will be 10 min late" is sufficient. If there are other people in the meeting, they may decide to start without you since you will be 10 minutes late, whereas they might have chosen to wait for you if you were only a couple of minutes behind. If you are late to a meeting with only one other person, that person can use the extra 10 minutes to answer a quick email or grab a bite to eat. Keeping others informed shows that you respect their time.

One way to ensure you are on time for meetings is to schedule a true break between the meetings themselves. If you have a meeting from 2:00 p.m. to 3:00 p.m., don't schedule the next one until 3:30 p.m. A half-hour buffer is perfect to account for a meeting running a couple of minutes late. Actually scheduling these buffers into your calendar is a great way to ensure nothing else will be scheduled during those times. Another benefit of scheduled buffers is that they allow you to debrief. Some meetings have takeaways and action items for you to perform. Giving yourself a few scheduled minutes to document your new tasks (or perhaps even accomplish a couple of them) can give you a firm handle on your day.

Virtual meetings can be a great tool for getting a lot of work done in a short period of time. By properly planning all aspects of your virtual meetings, you will find that life in the remote workforce is more productive and more enjoyable—for you and for your colleagues.

Communicating Urgency and Need—and Following Up

Your work doesn't exist in a vacuum: At some point over the course of your workweek, you'll need something from someone, or someone will need something from you. Sometimes the request is easy and your colleagues are willing to help you. Other times, people are busy and resources limited. Communicating the level of urgency of the thing you need—and getting what you need in return—is an art unto itself.

We've all encountered that colleague (let's call him Frantic Frank) who needs everything *right now*. Perhaps you have even dropped everything to help Frantic Frank get something done, only to find out that the "emergency" was all in his mind. Or maybe you've run into his polar opposite, Silent Sally. Silent Sally doesn't tell you that she is overwhelmed or unable to complete a task until her deadline passes, and her lack of communication means you miss your deadline, too. The Frantic Franks and Silent Sallys of the remote workforce soon develop a reputation as untrustworthy or hard to work with.

To be successful in any career, you should do your best to avoid becoming Frantic Frank or Silent Sally and, instead, identify and manage your interactions with these types of colleagues. This requires more than knowing how to do your job. First, you must understand what you need. Most needs fall into one of four categories (information, access, skills, or authorization), and the category of need determines the level of legwork you can do ahead of time. If you need someone to authorize your budget, for example, you can often collate all the relevant data in an easy-to-digest email or spreadsheet so the authorizing person can simply glance at the information and make a decision. If you need information, you can research whether the information is already housed somewhere else before you reach out to a colleague. Once you've done your due diligence, you can feel good about asking for what you need. Your manager, or a more veteran colleague, can often help you determine which department handles the type of request you have and which person in that department can help you. Asking the right person for help is key to actually getting the help you need.

Once you know what you need and who can assist you, you can think about when to approach that person for help. In a traditional office setting, you can swing by someone's desk and, if she doesn't look busy, ask for a minute of her time. In the remote workforce, you can't see people, and you will often have dozens of colleagues in different departments across multiple time zones. In these circumstances, it's vital to develop a sense of your target's work rhythm. Is this person busy with payroll on a certain day? Does she reserve mornings for time-sensitive work? Is she out on the road making sales at the end of the month? You might have better results if you wait for a time that is more convenient for her.

Now that you know when to approach your colleague, you can think about how to approach her. This step is especially important if the person is in high demand. You want to make your request as attractive and as easy to answer as possible. This starts with clearly and succinctly stating your need, followed by briefly detailing the steps you have taken to try to resolve the task on your own. Make sure to include a time estimate as well. Something like, "Hey Mary, can you confirm that sales are up 3 percent this year? Joe said I have to get that info from you. I'm presenting our results to our department next week," is much more effective than an email that simply says, "Do you have a second? I want to pick your brain."

If I need something from somebody, that is the first thing I say, right in the subject line of my email—what it is and when I need it. In the body of the email, I also make sure they understand why I'm asking for it. This leaves no doubt about what I'm talking about.

For my direct reports, I use a formula in the subject line: Action Required: (whatever the ask is) and Due Date: (deadline). For people who don't report to me, I omit the "Action Required" and "Due Date," but still state what I need and when I need it. I have also learned that people's communication styles are different, so it is crucial to find out how people work and reach out accordingly. Some members of my team like me to tell them what I need and then to get out of the way. If what they produce isn't good enough, then we can have a discussion on how to fix it for the future. Other members of my team come to me several times during the course of the task because they need to talk it out.

But even in time-sensitive situations, I try to avoid being so solutions-oriented that I bulldoze over my team. It can be hard in the moment, when everything is coming at you from seven different directions, to pull back and let someone else handle the issue. You have to be open to the idea that they may do a better job of solving the issue, and you will be the one to change your approach the next time that same issue comes up.

—Bobby Amirebrahimi

Communicating what you need and when you need it helps everyone prioritize the work that needs to get done. In the remote workforce, you can't see what people are working on. You can't tell if someone is overwhelmed, or needs more training, or was just handed a project that takes precedence over yours. Because of this, you need to set a follow-up schedule that matches the importance and urgency of the the project at hand. If the task is simple and non-urgent, or your company has guidelines for how long it should take to complete certain tasks, then you might wait until the due date to check in. If the task has many moving pieces, is ambiguous, or has a hard deadline, then you may want to set up multiple check-in points.

This is true whether you are managing the entire project or only one piece of it. As a project manager, the list of things you need to keep track of can seem endless, but the general categories of those things tend to fall into one of four areas: access, information, skill, or bandwidth. Some of the questions to ask yourself include the following: Are things progressing on schedule? Does anyone look or act stressed or overwhelmed? Does everyone have what they need to do the job? Does everyone understand what to do? Conversely, if you're an individual contributor on a project and the project manager hasn't set up check-in points, set up your own check-in schedule. You want to make sure you are doing the work expected of you in the time frame required, and it's far easier to salvage a situation if you catch a problem early. If the project changes scope or you are handed a new, higher-priority project, then you need to discuss and adjust timelines and expectations as soon as possible. As a project manager, you can't assume that the colleague who agreed to spend five hours working on your project can stay on for another 20. Similarly, as a member of a project team, you must communicate proactively if your bandwidth changes.

In a perfect world, your colleagues stay in regular communication with you as you work together on projects. Unfortunately, sometimes your colleagues become unresponsive and you have to loop in others. It is important to remain professional and give people the benefit of the doubt when doing so. Keep your tone understanding and make it clear that you are looking for the best way to proceed, instead of throwing someone under the bus. Whether the person is on your team or a different team, your supervisor is often the best person to reach out to first. Your supervisor may be able to follow up with the person directly or point you in the right direction in terms of who you should follow up with next. When possible, follow your company's appropriate chain of command and established guidelines for whom to contact and when.

Communicating urgency and need in a way that builds trust and doesn't paint you as a Frantic Frank or a Silent Sally takes some thought. If you consistently work at it, you will soon be known as someone who is dependable and a pleasure to work with.

Venting Appropriately

> *Many years ago when I worked for a different company, I spoke to a colleague about how handy I found Skype to be, where I could just Ctrl-F to find information shared by others in our chats. She let me know that wasn't an option for her because she cleared her history at the end of each day, because she spent a lot of time venting there and she didn't want anyone to see it. It was an eye-opening conversation, because up to that point I hadn't thought about filtering the things I type in chat. I never said anything unprofessional, but what you type lasts a long time unless you take steps to clear it.*
>
> —Mike Webber

Even if you love your job and are genuinely excited to begin each day, there can still be parts of your work that frustrate you. It could be problems with a coworker, difficulties with administrative processes, or sudden changes to deadlines and tasks that result in your having to cancel or change personal plans. While taking deep breaths, counting to 10, or getting outside for a vigorous walk around the neighborhood are all effective ways to deal with stressful work situations, venting is another effective technique. However, figuring out the appropriate way to vent in the remote workforce is quite important.

It is crucial to choose carefully the audience for your venting. Ideally, you should have the type of open relationship with your boss that allows you to vent without penalty. This individual is responsible for your development and most likely, in the remote workforce, knows you better than anyone else. It can be easy to assume that you have a close enough relationship with someone else to freely vent about a frustrating situation, but do you? Are your few instant messenger chats with a colleague enough for you to take the further step of complaining about a part of your job that is frustrating you? It's easy to have many short interactions with someone online and feel like you know them reasonably well, but be careful. Consider your position and that of the person you want to vent to. If this person is a subordinate, hearing you express frustration about your job may cross the line into inappropriate territory a lot sooner than if the situation were reversed. While it's important that those who report to you (directly or indirectly) get an accurate view of the work you do, there may be a larger amount of sensitive information you could end up sharing that may color the perspective of the other person in large ways. Keep your venting to those you have regular, in-depth interactions with because they have a broader context for the negative emotions you're expressing. Venting to someone you don't know that well could negatively affect the way they think of you or the organization as a whole.

The medium you choose for venting is also important. A video call may be best, because you can see the other person's reactions better and adjust as needed. You're less likely to cross the line by saying something inappropriate for the workplace when you are actually looking at another person and not just staring at your wall while on the phone. Even riskier is venting via typing. You should avoid putting your frustrations down in a recordable format like email or digital chat. Something in writing has the potential to not only last forever but also be retransmitted to an unintended audience and be easily misinterpreted.

You'll also need to choose the appropriate time to meet with someone to vent. When you're working in an office, it's easy to see when your colleague or boss looks free. Even more conveniently, there are many opportunities to take coffee breaks together or do a shared lunch. In the online environment, especially when dealing with different time zones, you need to pick and choose your moments appropriately. Can you easily take 10 minutes of a call with a boss or coworker to vent and then resume your regular agenda? Is asking someone for a few minutes of their time a part of your company's culture, or does doing so signal that you have something serious to say? Pick and choose these moments carefully so you don't make the venting process seem more formal than it is. Remember also to make these *moments*, not extended periods. Regardless of the situation, venting for over an hour is likely inappropriate no matter the topic or audience.

Finally, you need to consider the proper way to frame venting. In most cases, it's best to let your listener know that you need a few minutes to let off some steam about an issue that is troubling you. The virtual workforce is full of lasting first impressions, so if this is the first time you're venting, you will want to make sure you're doing so in a way that shows you can see the bigger picture and are venting for stress relief, not to just complain for the sake of complaining. This is especially important when venting to your boss but can also be a valuable consideration when dealing with colleagues who may not know you that well outside of regular workplace interactions. You should also be conscious of your word choice and tone when expressing your frustration. A vent session is not a free-for-all but rather a controlled way of expressing your frustration so that you don't let it build up, resulting in higher stress and perhaps the desire to quit. Venting can also lead to productive solutions. A savvy boss will use the opportunity to brainstorm resolutions or turn the experience into a teachable moment once the initial release of emotion has occurred.

It might sound like a lot of work to consider how to vent, which, after all, is an emotionally charged action that wants to be spontaneous. But that is exactly the point. Venting at work has its place, and it should be done in a controlled manner for you to glean its value without experiencing any of its drawbacks. You need the opportunity to vent to your colleagues, because who else will understand the troubles you are experiencing as you work in your remote office? But unlike in a traditional office, you can't hang up the phone after a frustrating conversation, sigh and rub your temples, and have a nearby coworker notice and offer up a sympathetic ear. As with most things in the remote workforce, you need to take charge of the situation to ensure that your venting remains a productive experience.

Chapter 5

Secrets of Professional Development and Growth

There are ways to remain visible and grow your career as a remote worker. This chapter will show you how.

Your Network

Even though a virtual network can have distinct differences from a physical one, there are many similarities, and a virtual network is equally (if not more) important to build. While the remote workforce gives you a unique ability to connect with many people in your organization, it's up to you to do so effectively and frequently.

Effective networkers are organized. Develop a framework that will allow you to make networking a regular part of your week. If you're new to the company, find out how your role fits within the overall business. An organization chart can be a helpful tool to picture how your company delivers its product or service. If your company doesn't have an org chart, ask questions until you can build your own. This will help you not only envision your future career path but also understand how different processes and people in the company interact with each other.

Create a list of people to speak to. This can be as simple as writing down the names and contact information of the people you will interact with the most or as detailed as a spreadsheet, ranking people in order of their importance to your work. You can also take the list a step further: Break it into categories to help you remember whom to contact for different situations. For example, you may have a list of leadership mentors you look up to and whose advice you value. And you may have a list of people you simply enjoy communicating with and want to keep in touch with on a professional level. Whatever segments you break your list into, the ability to easily contact someone when you need to is beneficial.

Once you have your list, schedule a 15- to 30-minute video call to get to know your coworkers. Most people enjoy talking about themselves. Ask your colleagues about what they do, what their pain points are, what they love about their job, and how you can best work together.

Take notes after each conversation. Don't rely on your memory to capture everything. Your notes should include a mix of the personal and professional and should grow over time. Knowing your colleagues' birthdays or favorite hobbies is just as important as knowing their skill sets. Staying active in virtual social circles can also help with this.

If you interact with someone on a daily or weekly basis, it can be helpful to schedule a regular call at a mutually agreeable time. For other colleagues, less frequent check-ins may be more appropriate, and these may be a casual email rather than a phone or video call. Schedule these into your calendar to make it more likely that you will actually keep your connections alive. Ask how things are going. Ask about that project they were working on (which you will remember because you wrote it down). Ask what they are working on next. If you do this regularly, you will soon have the opportunity to be of service to your colleagues. One colleague may mention that she wishes she could be more involved with training and development, while another colleague may say he wishes he knew someone who could help with the latest training project. Connecting these two colleagues makes you a valuable part of each person's network. Communicating regularly with the people in your network ensures you are not forgotten or lost in the shuffle.

 I have two or three informal video calls scheduled per month with coworkers who have become friends. We talk about work, but we can also chat about anything on our minds. It is engaging for both parties and helps keep ideas flowing freely. I know it is time well spent, but even more important, our leadership sees value in us connecting virtually because we are physically separated. Unlike coworkers who share office space, we have to make these touch points happen purposefully to learn from each other.

—Julie Minnich

It is also good to remember that a network isn't a static thing. Periodically reviewing your connections helps ensure that you communicate with each person at intervals that make sense. Take time to assess whom you want to communicate with more frequently and whom you'd like to communicate with less.

Your network is also your safety net. Know whom you can turn to if you need help. Different aspects of your job can require different types of assistance. Some colleagues can help you locate the right person to push a stalled project along. Others can help you navigate tricky interpersonal dynamics. Don't be afraid to ask for help. You will be far more efficient and effective if you do so.

The remote workforce can connect you to people who are within your workplace yet far away geographically. This is a priceless opportunity to gain a different perspective on your business. At the same time, you may have to work harder at maintaining relationships because you will not physically run into people. Conduct your interactions with intention and frequency so that you can grow and maintain your network.

When you aren't limited by your geographic location, you can sometimes more effectively collaborate with people outside your immediate team. Master the art of the casual outreach. If you're working on a project, use that as an excuse to reach out to a stakeholder in a different department to gain his or her perspective. If you ever have an issue arise that you are unsure how to handle on your own, ask a more experienced colleague. Don't overlook more informal ways to connect with people. Talking about a shared love of sports, hobbies, or television shows are all acceptable ways to start a relationship with someone outside your immediate team. Take advantage of these different perspectives to learn new methods and strategies. You can also use your knowledge to contribute to parts of the company you may never have had access to otherwise.

You may find yourself interacting with people who hold a position in the company that is higher than yours but not in your direct line of command. While it's always advisable to maintain a level of professionalism and respect when dealing with others, this can be especially true when connecting with people in higher positions. Avoid complaining about various aspects of your job; instead, focus on positivity and solutions. Showing your best work and ideas to people in higher levels can help increase your visibility and open up new opportunities. Be strategic when taking on new opportunities. Always make sure your manager is informed of and on board with any outside assignments handed to you.

Starting on day one, invest the time to thoroughly understand and cultivate your network. As the weeks and months go on, continue to invest in maintaining and staying active in that network. Doing so will help you in your day-to-day activities and any future career path you choose to follow.

Recognition

> The company I worked for was going through some restructuring and I definitely wanted to make the cut, as other people I knew with more experience than I had were being laid off. I wound up with two different managers over that time period and both gave me advice on developing my brand, something I had never considered before. One suggested I become known as the manager who gets good results but that was quite broad and seemed like a high bar to clear given the state of the markets I inherited. The other boss suggested I specialize and, as one of the few managers with non-American markets, to make myself the reigning expert on all that was foreign. I dug in and years later, after I had moved into American markets, colleagues would still reach out to me with questions about best practices across the border.
>
> —Mike Webber

Gaining recognition for your work yields many benefits, whether you wish to stay in your role or get promoted. You are seen as valuable and trustworthy. You may be given interesting assignments. Valuable people tend to be given more flexibility and autonomy. This can develop into a positive feedback loop, where you are increasingly seen as more valuable by working on the things that most interest you; this helps to build your reputation within your team and the greater company at large. This recognition is even more important in the remote workforce, where you are the sum total of your virtual interactions.

If you are someone who wishes to be recognized for your achievements, be the type of person who recognizes others. Be generous with your recognition. If a colleague helps you out, thank her in an email—and copy her boss. If a teammate spent extra time making your slides look good, make sure to mention that in a public setting. What goes around comes around. The people you recognize today may be the very ones who put in a good word for you tomorrow.

But how do you gain recognition in the remote workforce? While there are many different actions you can take, the basic process is this: First, perform well. Then, promote yourself. Finally, cultivate recognition for your contributions. In the virtual world, it's your responsibility to promote yourself. Don't assume that anyone else is going to do this for you. Perhaps you are the type of person who cringes at the thought of promoting yourself. Fortunately, self-promotion doesn't have to be pretentious or insincere to be effective. Self-promotion simply means making sure other people know about your abilities and accomplishments.

Develop an authentic self-promotion strategy by first asking yourself a couple of questions: Who are you when you are at work? What do you stand for? Your answers develop the basis for your professional brand. Your brand can consist of your attitude, your work ethic, and your skill set, among other things. In person, your brand is naturally communicated through your words, your actions, and your physical presence. In the remote workforce, you must approach your brand more intentionally.

Build your brand around your strengths and personality. Are you someone who values harmony? Then in terms of attitude, you may brand yourself as being consistently positive and focused on solutions. Do you enjoy meeting people and building networks? Then you may decide to build your brand on this skill set, becoming known for being able to help colleagues connect with the right people to get things done. Are you someone who can't leave work until your inbox is cleared out? Then consider building your brand on your work ethic: be seen as the person who will finish a project on time, no matter what.

Make sure that your communication and work reflect your brand. Since you often won't be able to count on vocal inflection or physical expression to communicate your ideas, your written communication should always be drafted with your brand in mind. If you would like to be seen as someone who thoroughly plans out and crafts a response to each query, then make sure you do so. On the other hand, if you would like to be seen as someone who answers emails quickly, then do that. Be consistent in communicating your workplace brand, because consistency breeds trust.

Once you've settled on your brand, it's time to deploy it. As a remote worker, you are likely a member of various group chats or internal company message boards. These are natural places to organically promote yourself by publicly helping people solve problems. For example, let's say you decide to build a brand around your work ethic. If someone mentions in a team chat that they wish the company would provide a certain resource, volunteer to create it. Then share it with the group and send a copy of what you created to your boss. This is self-promotion through service, and it is highly effective.

This leads us into how to make your voice heard so you are visible within your organization. For you to be heard, others must consider you someone worth listening to. Notice that this is different from simply being vocal. First you demonstrate your expertise by performing well in your role and building value for the team. Then, when you communicate, people will want to listen. Of course, you must consider whom you should communicate with, what channel you should use, and whether the communication should be public or private. As you become more visible, your judgment will be valued just as much as your performance in your role. It may be that the best way to get your voice heard is to join a committee or task force. Working on cross-functional committees or projects is also a great way to get to know people outside your immediate team and disseminate your brand. Let your boss and colleagues know that you are available to help with these.

It is possible to cultivate visibility within the remote workforce. Spend time creating an authentic brand. Be on the lookout for opportunities to help solve problems. Over time, you will develop your brand and become known as a valued employee.

Soliciting Feedback

Make giving and receiving feedback an expectation with your colleagues. When conducting performance reviews, my team's rule of thumb is that the outcome should never be a surprise, because we should be extolling excellent performance or supporting improvements consistently. In my last round of reviews, I tried something new suggested by a coworker: I asked each of my direct reports what feedback they had for me. Some were surprised and didn't have much to say, but others gave me specifics about communication and resources. I've had fantastic ideas come from just leaving these lines open, and I plan to continue this practice so that feedback becomes a natural part of all my conversations.

—Caitlin Duke

When you think of feedback, official performance reviews may come to mind. These reviews may affect things such as your future career path and salary. However, there are many other forms of feedback in the workplace. Each time you give a presentation, lead a meeting, or complete a project is an opportunity to collect information on your performance. In the physical world, someone may stop by your desk to let you know their thoughts. In the virtual world, you need to actively seek out that same feedback.

When you present in an important meeting, take note of the people in the virtual room. You can reach out to them afterward to gain their insight. When doing so, be targeted with your questions. In person, it can be easy to ask questions such as "How did it go?" or "What did you think?" and then build the conversation from there. However, these types of open-ended questions can be difficult to answer in the concise way required by virtual communication. Thus, you may not get the feedback you were looking for, or any response at all. Instead, be specific. If you tried out something new, such as using the pen function to write on a slide you were presenting, you can ask about that. If you waited five extra minutes before starting the meeting because you were missing a handful of people, you can ask the people who were on time how they felt about that. Any decision you made while presenting can be an opportunity to gain feedback. One way to collect this detailed feedback is to send out anonymous surveys afterward. If you choose to send out an anonymous survey, let your attendees know one is coming. Surveys are a great way for people to give you their honest thoughts without being concerned about consequences. Surveys also allow people to fill out their opinions on their own schedule.

Of course, there will be times when you want a detailed breakdown from specific people on an entire presentation or project. The best way to gather comprehensive feedback is to do so live. Set up a virtual meeting with the person whose feedback you desire. Be respectful of that person's schedule and bandwidth. Calling someone out of the blue to ask them to comment on every aspect of your performance on a project, for example, will likely not be as effective as setting something up in advance. Ask the person whether they are willing to sit down with you and give you their feedback. As with any other meeting, make the intention of the meeting clear. You will get more helpful feedback when you give people the opportunity to properly formulate their thoughts.

Make it easy for people to give you their honest opinion by preparing yourself to receive it. It can be easy to begin justifying your actions when someone gives you constructive criticism. Instead, take the time to thank them and write their words down to think on later. Accepting feedback in a positive way will build a positive relationship, often leading the person you consult to give you more and better information over time.

Garnering feedback can go beyond your boss, coworkers, and meeting attendees. It can be very helpful to learn what upper management thinks of your performance and why. Learning the opinion of those in higher positions can help you find areas of opportunity to work on and may even lead to resources to increase these skills.

Based on information gathered from others or on self-reflection, you may find that there are specific areas of opportunity you want to work on. Discuss with your manager the best way to learn and improve. Your company may have training videos to cover specific skills, or people in the company may possess the knowledge you're seeking and be happy to share it. Once you learn a new skill, test it out. If you learned a new scheduling technique, such as always scheduling meetings to end after 50 minutes instead of an hour, determine whether the new skill is beneficial and being used properly. You'll often get a sense on your own of how well something new worked, but this is also another great opportunity to ask for feedback.

The process of obtaining feedback never ends. No one is perfect, and there is always more to learn. Practice soliciting feedback; add it into your routine. When working remotely, there are still many ways to obtain the feedback and learning you desire—you just have to be more proactive about it.

Advancing Your Career

I was interested in moving forward with my career and tried a few different approaches to find a new role. I made some time to help out in a small way with a section of the company I was interested in exploring. They had me do some tasks with limited scope, and I enjoyed it and didn't break anything. Then a bigger project came up on the same team and they asked for me to come back and help in a larger capacity. I wouldn't have been asked to work on the bigger project if I hadn't volunteered my time on the smaller tasks. After having success there, when a spot opened up on the team, the manager approached me about the role and I was offered the job on the spot.

—Mike Webber

To grow your career in the remote workforce, you need to consistently keep your eyes and ears open. Be alert for any new opportunities, and be aware of the types of roles you would like to pursue in the future. In many workplaces these days, there are several different paths to career advancement. The road isn't always straight up; sometimes horizontal moves make sense for your professional development and skill set. In the virtual world, you don't have the ability to simply walk by someone's office, read their nameplate, and know their position. People won't pass you in the halls, eliminating the opportunity for other coworkers to tell you who that person is. However, paying attention to all the interactions you have can yield a rich array of information. Treat email signatures like nameplates; read them to find out the position and department of each person who contacts you. From there, you can gain insight into the roles and responsibilities of different positions. By understanding the myriad roles within the company, you can start to familiarize yourself with various teams and think about how you see yourself advancing in the future.

In meetings, pay close attention to the people in attendance and their positions. Their involvement in the meeting can indicate their relationship to the project and with the department as a whole. Matching those aspects with their job title can help you better understand the various responsibilities different positions hold. This information can help you determine how you would like to plan out your next steps. You may also learn about new skill sets you'd like to acquire or new projects you'd like to work on.

One way to get a feel for a role is to shadow someone. Shadowing is when you act as a bystander and observe how someone else completes a task. While this can be a great way to improve in your current role, it is also a great way to test out a potential role. In the remote workforce, shadowing works well if you can share screens and talk through particular tasks.

If you don't know where your company posts available positions, find out. Even if you are completely content in your current role, keeping an eye on current internal opportunities can expose you to positions you may never have been aware of before. You may find out about entire departments that you didn't even know existed. Periodically checking the virtual job board is also a good way to keep track of your coworkers and their progression. Being aware of how others move throughout the company can show potential paths available to you. As you browse job postings, be aware of the requirements of certain roles. Some roles may require you to live in a certain location or work a certain number of hours a week. Before you build a career path for yourself, make sure you understand the expectations of that path.

Taking on additional duties outside of your role can be another way to advance your career and gain visibility. When doing this, it's important not to spread yourself too thin. While visibility is important, the people you work with will be more inclined to recommend you for new things in the future if they see you succeeding at your main responsibilities.

Discussing your wants and needs in relation to your work responsibilities can have a positive effect on your career growth. The position you would like to move into may not be available right now, or you may apply for an opening but not be selected. Even in such cases, however, you have alerted people to the type of position you are interested in moving into. This can expand your visibility to other departments of the company that may not have interacted with you before.

If you do find a new job opportunity that speaks to you, speak up. Don't assume that someone will reach out to you or that your supervisor will contact you to let you know. It is your responsibility to let it be known that you want the new position. In most scenarios, you will want to talk to your immediate supervisor first before planning to apply to any new roles. This allows you to discuss with your supervisor your motivations for applying for the role and to be transparent.

Most importantly, consistently discuss with your supervisor the aspects of your job that you enjoy and any new aspects you are interested in. This can affect the assignments your supervisor gives you, which can improve your career path even within your current role. In some cases, this job crafting can lead to a completely different role created just for you. By continuously adjusting your current role to include more of the activities and projects you are interested in working on, you can slowly transform your current role into something more in line with your interests and goals, creating new directions for your career.

In both the traditional and virtual workplaces, you are responsible for your career and personal growth. In the virtual world, it can take more research to discover all the facets of your company and available opportunities for growth, but learning what you need to know is still doable. In fact, it is necessary for you to take charge of your career path and shape it to be exactly what you want.

Chapter 6

Secrets for Special Circumstances

The majority of this book deals with issues and opportunities that are true for most remote workers, regardless of the configuration of the team. This chapter will discuss some of the more common *uncommon* situations some may find themselves in.

Meeting in Person

Even though we chat nearly every day, it can still be intimidating to meet a colleague from the remote workforce in real life—we've never eaten lunch together or even sat next to each other.

On the whole, though, I consider my relationships with my remote colleagues to be stronger than the relationships I've had with in-person colleagues precisely because we don't have physical proximity built in. We are forced to make that extra effort to go beyond the surface, effort that we wouldn't expend if we saw each other every day around the office.

I have made it my mission to meet every person on my team in the flesh. I've found that I fall right in step with my virtual colleagues because we have spent so much time building the foundations of our relationships through our daily team chat. We know all the facets of each other's lives, so it's natural to call these colleagues my friends. Meeting them in person just makes them friends with legs!

—Chrissy Damasco

Remote employees can build strong working relationships with colleagues they never see in person. This is fortunate, as many remote workers will only ever connect through email, video, and instant messaging programs. There are others, though, who occasionally get to see their colleagues in person. If you have such an opportunity, take it. If you are a leader with the decision-making power to plan an in-person gathering, consider doing so. You may find that your employees leave in-person events more engaged with their company and teams.

A certain subset of people don't believe that in-person meetings are meaningful. These people reason that they already have meaningful working relationships with their colleagues via remote channels and that meeting in person adds nothing to their engagement level. This may be true for you. However, it may not be true for everyone in your company. The colleague who takes everything you say the wrong way may understand you much better after sitting next to you at dinner. The manager who is about to create a new role on her team may suggest you apply after chatting with you in the breakfast line. That isn't to suggest that you need to have something brilliant and innovative to say to everyone you meet, but to make the most out of this opportunity, you will want to do some advance preparation.

In a perfect world, your employer will arrange for you to meet with your colleagues virtually before an in-person meeting. How this occurs will depend on the size of the meeting and the relationship of the individuals getting together. A team of 10 people who spend every week working closely with each other will likely not need any prearranged conversation time. Bringing together a couple hundred employees, however, will. If your company doesn't arrange for you to meet colleagues in advance of an in-person meeting, you should consider doing so yourself. This may seem awkward at first, but it will be hugely valuable. Choose a few individuals and arrange a video call. Set the expectation that you can discuss anything you want: hobbies, current events, upcoming plans, or even work. The point of the call is to make it easier for you to walk up to your colleague and strike up a conversation at the in-person meeting. That's a little hard to do if, for example, you aren't sure what he looks like.

If you consider yourself an introvert, you might worry that you will struggle to be social and communicative in person, but there's no reason why you have to have a challenging experience. A little preparation can help you be successful at mixing and mingling in between formal meetings. Plan out your small talk. In some cases, you'll be able to discuss work, but you should also have some non-work topics ready: Did your colleague have to travel far to get to the meeting? How is he enjoying it thus far? Has he had a chance to explore the area? In large meetings, social mixing can almost feel like speed dating, bouncing from person to person; if you don't have a default list of topics to raise, it can be easy for two people who only have a few virtual tasks in common to suddenly go from greetings to silence. Look up relevant topics of interest and be prepared to discuss them to keep the conversation moving. This can be as simple as looking up touristy facts about the area you're staying in or as time intensive as reading articles related to your business or meeting theme and crafting bite-sized ideas to talk about.

Being prepared with a few go-to conversation topics is important. Equally important is to identify the specific people you want to interact with and what you want to accomplish in those interactions. Again, in a smaller meeting of a dozen employees, such planning might not be as crucial, as it is likely you will be able to get face time with each individual. With larger meetings, however, you will need to seek out those you wish to connect with to further your career or to strengthen a relationship. Make a list of whom you want to meet and why; then plan out how you will introduce yourself to them and what you will talk about if they don't take the lead in the conversation. In many instances, the opportunity to talk to someone important to you can come with little notice. You might see the person walking out of the elevator or standing in line for the buffet. If you don't grab them right then, you might not have the opportunity for the rest of the event. In that kind of situation, having prepared what you want to say in advance means you will create a strong in-person impression.

These opportunities can be random and infrequent, so it's also important to be prepared to create your chances. Again, you may need to work harder to create these opportunities in larger meetings. The worst thing you can do is put off chatting with a person on your list until later, as that time may never come. Take advantage of opportunities as they come up and seek them out as well. At a convention, it is perfectly fine to walk up to people as they are talking to see if you can join the conversation, which may easily enlarge to include another person. Pay attention to body language for cues as to whether you can jump in. Often you will be able to chime in on the subject at hand. In other cases, you may wish to use one of the conversation pieces you prepared ahead of time.

Remote workforce employees can be somewhat starved for these social opportunities (You can shake someone's hand! You can see how tall the other person is!), so casual interactions are very important for deepening colleague relationships. The remote worker has to be careful, though. In the world of video calls and home offices, it is entirely possible to know someone very well before ever meeting in person. This can lead to awkward situations. The colleague you banter with all day long may not be a hugger, for example. If you are, it's best to play it safe and settle for an enthusiastic handshake. You don't have enough information on which to base the decision to hug or not. If you are on the receiving end of an unwanted hug, you can sometimes forestall it by leaning back a little and quickly putting your hand up for a handshake. You can take the sting out of your refusal by making the handshake extra warm, smiling, and saying, "It's so great to finally meet you in person!"

Equally important, of course, is the way you interact in structured activities. Presentations, meetings, and discussion groups will likely occur, and success at an in-person meeting in this context relies on one thing: participation. Your colleagues, direct reports, and supervisors will have a certain way of looking at you based on the type of virtual worker you are; this impression may change when they see what kind of worker you are in person. This is your chance to make a lasting, positive impression on those around you. During presentations, take notes. In meetings, ask questions. In small discussions, take the lead where appropriate. You should plan to be visible in your participation at least once during each event of the overall meeting.

Ultimately, these in-person meetings are a chance for you to recharge your batteries. Working remotely is still a new thing for some people, and as more of our experiences are moved to the online world, maximizing the in-person interactions that remain becomes even more important. Where possible, companies with virtual workers should actively create opportunities for their people to meet in person. Employees need to do their part as well, taking active steps to make sure that these opportunities are as useful as possible. The work you do to prepare for in-person meetings will not only help you enjoy them more but also help you enjoy your virtual workplace more when the time comes to go back home.

Managing Past Peers

In today's ever-changing world of advanced technology, the pace of work is always increasing. Not only are jobs and responsibilities often shifting rapidly, but entire organizational charts and reporting structures reshuffle frequently. This is even more true in the remote workforce, where change doesn't mean physically moving someone's office from one place to another or creating new nameplates with new titles. In the virtual world, a big shift can often be accomplished with far less effort. This means that your colleague one day could become your supervisor the next, and vice versa.

Therefore, build relationships with your colleagues now as if a shift will happen in the future. This isn't to say that you should act like someone's supervisor or their direct report when you're not; rather it's advice to maintain your professionalism and be aware of your image throughout your interactions. It is also helpful to be aware of the strengths and weaknesses of those around you.

When you make the shift to supervising people who used to be your colleagues, you can use the good relationships you have already formed with them as a foundation for a good working relationship as their supervisor. The types of conversations you have will likely change as you move from colleague to manager, but the knowledge you gained as a colleague can help you build a better team. By knowing the strengths and weaknesses of your team ahead of time, you can work to distribute tasks to the correct people, based on what they do well or what they want to learn, ensuring the success of your team and helping your people succeed and grow. However, be careful not to pigeonhole someone. Just because you know a person very well as a colleague doesn't mean you know how he performs specific tasks. The colleague who told you an amusing story six months ago about a spectacular failure with spreadsheets may have spent the last four months increasing this skill.

Many of my old teammates and I have moved into different roles within the company, and I know that we may end up working together again in new formations. Just as with my in-person friendships, I make it a point to keep in touch with my former peers. Scheduling occasional check-in conversations with past colleagues can not only make for nice breaks in the day, but also keep our connections strong for any future collaboration or new managerial relationships.

—Elle Mastenbrook

When new roles open up, many of your colleagues may apply, and you may wind up being managed by a colleague who received the role you wanted. Your prior knowledge of your colleague can give you insight into how your strengths and experiences can help the new team get a strong start and define your role within it. Be prepared to give your new manager a break—she likely feels as awkward as you do in the new relationship.

In the continuous change that is sometimes present in the remote workforce, you may even experience a shift back and forth. Someone who managed a project you worked on could become someone you manage on the next project. Or it may be the case that these two projects are going on at the same time. In the span of a single workday, you may find that you have to address the same person as your colleague, as her indirect project manager, and as an indirect report for a project she manages. In these cases, building in cues can help you shift roles. Some have found that simply saying, "I'm putting on my project manager hat for a moment," can help everyone effectively switch gears.

From the very beginning of your time in the remote workforce, maintain your professionalism and treat everyone you work with with respect. Build good relationships with your colleagues and learn their strengths and weaknesses. All of this information will help you in the future, whether you remain colleagues, begin to report to them, or become their manager.

Dealing with People Who Take Credit for Your Work

> *My team shares email templates, tools, and ideas on a weekly basis, and we take care to model proper attribution when talking amongst ourselves or with a wider audience. We make sharing credit a regular practice to help avoid misattribution or confusion in the first place.*
>
> *In management, and even in the remote workforce more broadly, attributing ideas and work to others where appropriate demonstrates that we collaborate with our direct reports and colleagues, and that we recognize and act on constructive feedback. When I bring an idea to my director from someone who reports to me, it reinforces my credibility as a manager, someone who builds up my employees and recognizes strengths.*
>
> —Caitlin Duke

Popular culture often presents working in an office as a cutthroat affair, where it's everybody for themselves as they attempt to climb the corporate ladder. While reality is typically more mundane, sometimes people will take credit for other people's work. Office politics and misinformation have always existed, but in the virtual work environment, things become even murkier. You need greater vigilance to make sure others don't take credit for your contributions. You also need to be aware of how much easier it is to accidentally attribute credit to the wrong person and to be wary about unintentionally receiving credit for the work of others.

The main challenge in properly crediting work is the high volume of information that remote employees have to process every day. In a more traditional office, the pace tends to be slower, and there are more opportunities for face-to-face communication; therefore, when information is written, people can more easily pay attention and keep track of it. But in the remote workforce, the high volume of written information can make it challenging to find the original source of an idea. If someone steals your work, will you even be able to remember whether you first brought up the idea in a conversation over video, typed it in an instant message, or sent it through an email? The amount of information you need to process is the first major stumbling block when it comes to protecting your ideas from theft and protecting yourself from inadvertently stealing someone else's idea.

The other major obstacle is multitasking. While traditionally the ability to multitask has been something to praise, in the remote workforce attempting to multitask can be a weakness. Checking email during a meeting, bouncing from one instant messenger conversation to another, and having several open tabs in your browser is incredibly commonplace in the virtual world. Unfortunately, we know that in many cases when you multitask this way, you are more likely to produce lower-quality work. It's easy to see how this can lead to incorrectly giving credit for ideas and work: An idea gets brought up in a fast-paced email chain. A few messages down, someone accidentally attributes that idea to someone else. The person who came up with the idea might not notice, because he is also multitasking. With no objection and clarification, the ownership of that idea becomes widely attributed to the wrong person. It's possible that this wrong person takes advantage of the situation in an unethical way and doesn't point out the error. However, it's equally possible that this person has forgotten what happened earlier in the email chain, and because everyone assumes he came up with the idea, accepts it as his own.

Technology blurs the lines of ownership further. While this is something that all modern-day workers must contend with, it has a much greater impact on remote workers. When asking for help from a boss or colleague, you often end up with a written response that you can cut and paste to pass on, perhaps to answer the question that prompted you to reach out to your coworker to begin with. While many employees will not blatantly lift ideas from someone else for a high-visibility project, casual plagiarism is more likely. How are you to know whether an email you receive is one that was crafted especially for you? Perhaps your colleague simply copied the majority of it from another person in order to save time or appear more authoritative or knowledgeable. Maybe she didn't want to make a mistake interpreting a policy, so she used language from another source that she knows is accurate. In many cases this is not an issue, but it does muddy the waters of what information is original and what has been borrowed from another source. When it comes time to collaborate on projects with others, this habit can result in pinching ideas, whether intentionally or not. Be aware of this trap to avoid falling into it.

What do you do if you realize that your idea has been taken by someone else? First, look for proof. After all, you could be mistaken. Do the due diligence to find the source of the idea. You can then choose whether or not to raise the issue. Although you don't need proof to do so, addressing the issue without hard evidence to back it up increases the potential of an awkward conversation. In many cases, you won't want to confront the person who took your idea. It might not be worth it, depending on the value of the idea. Simply telling your boss may be enough. In other cases, you will need to be vocal to a wider audience to get credit for your contributions. Escalate your concerns as appropriate. Before you do so, be clear on how the theft occurred and what you hope to accomplish by pointing it out. Take into account the fact that you may be dealing with someone of a higher rank, that raising this concern might not result in any changes, and that if you wait too long to raise your concern, there may be little anyone can do to rectify it.

The situation is slightly less murky if you are dealing with an incident in which the wrong person has been given credit for actual work done instead of just an idea. In those cases, it is often, but not always, easy to establish who did what. If you weren't given credit for the work that you did, it is often best to assume that this was a simple mistake. What you do about it depends on the situation and the people involved. In some cases you can quickly correct the statement. In others, you may need the help of your boss or another, higher-ranking person. Furthermore, if someone wrongly gives you credit for work you did not do, be quick to call out the right person. It is often easier for the person who has wrongly been given credit to rectify the situation than for the wronged party to call it out.

The virtual work environment dramatically affects how we receive and process information. It brings to mind the stories of how multiple eyewitnesses will see the same event in dramatically different, even conflicting ways. Slowing down will help you avoid missing information. Taking the time to record and organize your ideas and projects in a coherent way will allow you to give credit where it is due and determine whether someone has taken credit for something you created. With vigilance and persistence, you can keep better control of your work and what happens to it.

Parenting in the Remote Workforce

Working remotely has allowed me to be very present in my daughter's formative years while still maintaining a meaningful and successful career. I shop for groceries on weekday mornings between school drop-off and the start of my workday and volunteer for lunch duty in the school cafeteria once a month. I take my daughter to school every morning and pick her up every afternoon, and I am here to help her with homework questions in between my afternoon meetings.

I also keep solid boundaries between my work and home lives by planning in advance when my workday will end and sticking to it. This means I not only get to structure my day to be available to my daughter while also being productive, but I also enjoy uninterrupted time with my family every evening.

—Dru Ciotti

Although there are remote workforce positions that allow you to complete your work while parenting your children all day, there is a very good chance that you do not have one of these jobs. If a company's workforce is primarily remote, then it may even have guidelines that explicitly state that parents must arrange child care during work hours. This chapter assumes that your company has such a policy and that you have taken steps to arrange appropriate child care.

Having children adds an additional layer to all aspects of life, including the remote work experience. You work from home. You live at home. Your children also live in your home. As a worker and a parent, you have to deal with not only the logistics that come with this reality but also the assumptions that others in your company may make about you and your work ethic.

No matter how well you have arranged your child care and workspace, at some point your child is going to intrude into your work life. If you have a small apartment and child care in the home, kid noises in other rooms may be loud enough to be heard on a call. Some remote workers have had children knock on locked office doors, loudly demanding justice or juice. It does not matter that their caregiver was closer and available to deal with the situation. It does not matter that you told little Sophie that when the work door is closed, Daddy can't talk.

At some point, children forget that work hours are for working. You will always be their parent first.

You are not immune to this issue if your child care is outside of your home. Employees work across multiple time zones in the remote workforce. Inevitably someone you can't refuse is going to ask for a meeting outside of your work hours. Since the call is outside your normal workday, you may not be required to have child care, but you likely still want to maintain a professional space for your professional interaction.

While you can't eliminate all child intrusions, you can take steps to minimize them. Many parents have found that sound-canceling headphones help with noise. If your child is preschool aged or older, strong visual cues can help. Some parents have put a line of tape on the floor to denote where children have to stop in Mommy's office in order to not be on camera. Other parents have installed locks or stop signs on an office door. If the problem is noise in an echoing hallway, consider ways to muffle the echo. Perhaps a few small rugs can help. Consistent reminders and role-playing can also help children develop the habit of leaving you to your work during work hours.

Dealing with children's intrusions is straightforward, and although you may have to spend some time thinking through a workable solution, you can tell when you arrive at one. The same can't be said about other people's assumptions. A small percentage of people will assume that you are watching your children instead of doing your job. It isn't always clear who may think this, but the assumptions largely come from people who have not dealt with similar intrusions themselves. This could be people new to the remote environment, traditional office workers, or those who are childless.

It can be disheartening to have your professionalism called into question, but fight the impulse to say something intemperate. Often these accusations come as a surprise, since you know you followed the rules. It's important to realize that accusations often come from a place of ignorance. A director in an office in a different time zone may not have thought through the logistical consequences of calling a last-minute meeting at 7:00 a.m. your time, if it is 10:00 a.m. for everyone else. You may have told your boss that your children will be home during the meeting, but the director heading the call may not have received that message.

Where appropriate, you may wish to reach out directly to explain that you can attend said meeting at the designated time, but that the meeting is outside of your normal work hours so your children will be at home. While you have plans in place for your children during your regular work hours, those plans do not extend to your personal time. Your home office is your only office, and the children live in the home. If it is not appropriate for you to reach out, then make sure your boss or another appropriate person does so in your stead. Seasoned remote workers will understand that the personal side of an employee's life sometimes blends with the professional. Traditional office workers will not automatically understand the consequences of meetings held outside of work hours. If you assume that you need to make this clear, then you can minimize the number of misunderstandings and rude surprises.

If the person making assumptions about your work ethic holds a higher position in the company than you do, it is often most effective for your manager or someone of a higher position to act as your advocate. This is especially true if your advocate has a positive relationship with the person making assumptions.

Your strategy needs to be more nuanced if your boss is the one who thinks you are watching your children all day instead of working. Take some time to stop and think about why your boss may believe this. Perhaps you recently became a parent. Perhaps a child intruded on an important meeting. If this is the case, did your boss know you had a child before the child intruded? This may seem like an absurd question, but if you're very good at keeping your children separate from your workspace and you don't speak about your children at work, then that intrusion may have been the first indication your boss had that there are children in your home.

No matter the reason, data can be your advocate. Does your boss agree that your role requires an employee who is focused on the work, rather than watching children? Does she agree that you get your work done on time? Are you finishing things slower than your colleagues or generally at the same rate? Do you turn in quality deliverables? If you were secretly watching your children instead of working, wouldn't that become obvious in your performance? You may also wish to explain your child care arrangements. It's worth reiterating that your child care plans cover your normal working hours, and while you may be willing and able to take calls outside of those hours, your current lifestyle does not support live-in, continuous child care. Above all else, keep your temper and lead with patience.

The remote workforce can present challenges for the working parent. Fortunately, the benefits far outweigh the occasional misunderstanding. The majority of remote employees understand and celebrate the flexibility that comes with the remote lifestyle. Many parents have found that they can more easily attend a school play or field trip because they have the power to make up those hours in the evening after the children go to bed. Eliminating the long commute to and from the office may mean that your family can eat dinner together during the week. You may see your children more often. Enjoy your flexibility, and remember to be transparent with those who may see or hear your children. With some forethought and communication, you can enjoy the benefits that the remote setting has to offer parents and minimize any difficulties.

Staying in the Loop

In any workplace, it's important to keep up with the latest news. This isn't about gossip but rather the important updates and announcements that come with working at any organization. People change roles or leave the organization all the time. Policies, rules, and standard operating procedures can change just as often. In a traditional working environment, you can often absorb this kind of information just by being in the same room as others: It's easy to make announcements to large groups of people at once, and open floor plans allow for quick and easy movement of information.

In the remote workforce, however, it's not as easy. Information comes in many forms, and it usually has to be formally shared to ensure that everyone is updated. The volume of communication in the virtual work environment is such that it is relatively easy for employees not to process new information in a timely manner. While this can be limited to employees feeling surprised and perhaps a bit left out, it can also lead to significant mistakes, miscommunication, or even accidental security breaches.

To avoid being the last person to find out important company news, you need to be proactive. Build into your schedule a daily or weekly review of your inbox, group communications, and any other location where updates are shared. Set aside 30 minutes at the end of your week to sift through announcements to make sure that you have not missed anything important. Prioritize emails that come from individuals who often make important announcements so you read those messages before they get buried in your inbox. Your inclination may be to first take care of tasks that have more action associated with them, but reviewing these info-laden emails in a timely manner can greatly help you in the long term.

It's also important to start wide. Make sure that, where possible and appropriate, you are part of many mailing lists and online work communities related to your position to get a sense of what value each provides. Then trim the fat, removing yourself from those that are not as valuable or that provide duplicate information. It can be tempting to avoid signing up for another group to keep your email volume down, but that new group might actually do the job of two other groups you are already a part of. Test out new information channels as they come along and then pragmatically cut loose the ones that don't provide timely information.

One of the best ways I've found for keeping myself in the loop is to stay curious about other departments, and news that affects them. I try to take a regular look at the current openings posted on the company's internal jobs website. I also make it a point to read the articles people post in the different distribution channels at work, and sometimes post comments and follow-up questions in the thread. I try to act as if I might have to work in that department some day. Doing so has led to a couple of positive outcomes. First, it helps me to remain nimble— when territories and duties change at work, I've already taken that first step toward familiarizing myself with my new tasks. I also have a high-level handle on some of the issues I may have to deal with. Secondly, people are more likely to talk to you if you've been an active participant in a shared chat. This helps me to have a sense of who to reach out to for different things, and because my name is familiar, they are more apt to open my email!

—Teresa Douglas

Information also comes more quickly to those who have opportunities to communicate with others. If you are always on the passive end of a relationship, there's no reason for you to get news outside of highly formal channels, which can often be the last ones to share changes and updates. Being an active communicator is important in general in the remote workforce, but it's especially important if you want to find out information first. Talking to different individuals on a regular basis will allow you to find out what is happening on their end, and news will travel to you more quickly. Regular communication will also help you home in on those select individuals who are privy to the most up-to-date info.

Information is a valuable commodity in any workplace. If you stay apprised of what's going on, then you are more likely to be approached with requests for help, viewed as an important member of the team, and considered for promotions and other opportunities. You are also more likely to feel equipped to handle times of change and transition. Be proactive and engaged, and you will not only know more before others but also become someone others go to for updates and clarification.

Working with On-Site Team Members or On a Partially On-Site Team

The more a business grows, the more potential there is for conflict. Even the best-run operation will see some level of conflict, because human beings are very good at drawing lines between themselves and others, and this tendency exists in the remote workforce as well. Perhaps the most interesting dynamic in the remote workforce occurs when an organization has a set of employees who only work from home and a set who always, or nearly always, work in a more traditional office environment.

People who work from home need to be sensitive to the fact that their on-site colleagues will likely assume that the grass is greener on the other side. They may picture their remote colleagues as living the good life: working in pajamas, sleeping in, and taking as many breaks as they want because there is no boss watching from across the room. Although some remote employees take advantage of one, some, or all of these perceived perks, making the assumption that those who work from home are lazy is incorrect and unfair. That said, it's important to recognize that many on-site colleagues will assume the worst, so try not to take offense when they do. Conflict arises when both sides start accusing each other of having it easier.

Along the same lines, remote workers should resist the urge to talk about the advantages that working from home brings. Seemingly innocuous comments, such as "I did the laundry on my lunch break," can come across as bragging. While in a perfect world, people wouldn't have to be this concerned about what they say to colleagues, savvy virtual employees will choose their words carefully and be aware that any resentment that on-site coworkers display is likely not personal.

This kind of problem can also occur when individuals vent about the frustrating elements of their day. While venting is an essential part of managing one's work life, you have to choose the proper time and place and be aware of the people you're with when sharing your frustrations. Even when those frustrations may sound to your ears like reasons why working from home is not always desirable, they can be interpreted in the wrong way. A complaint about the noise your family has been making all day while you're trying to work is a valid concern, but to an on-site coworker's ears, it may simply serve as a reminder of how little time he gets to spend with his family. Instead, focus on the work itself and the projects at hand to avoid misinterpretations. When it comes to casual conversation (the kind that usually occurs at the start of calls), keep it more neutral and avoid using your place of work as a talking point.

In meetings where there is a mix of virtual and on-site employees and the responsibilities of the two groups differ, it's important to be mindful of meeting topics. If a discussion is only relevant for one subset of the group, it can serve to deepen the divide between on-site and off-site workers. In general, people shouldn't be forced to sit through large portions of meetings that don't apply to them.

There are other steps to take during meetings to ensure everyone's participation is balanced. Something as simple as how the meeting is set up can greatly affect how the different teams see each other—literally. Set up ground rules in advance to avoid dividing the teams in obvious ways. All team members should be on camera if possible, regardless of whether they are on the call from the office or not. If all the remote workers are on camera, while on-site colleagues are together in a conference room and only on audio, it creates two distinct groups. Similarly, it's just as problematic if all on-site workers are together and on a single camera. Aside from the volume and visibility issues this setup can create, it again highlights the difference between the two groups; it sends a visual message that the on-site team is a separate group, rather than several individuals who are part of the larger team. The point is to avoid distinguishing different types of people on the call and to ensure that everyone can hear and participate so that the meeting is as efficient as possible.

There is an art to contributing in meetings where some people are remote and others are on-site. No matter how deeply committed your colleagues are to including you in the discussion, the on-site group will unconsciously bias toward listening to the people who are on-site. You have to be quick with your unmute button and take advantage of any micro pause in the conversation to add your contribution. There seems to be a larger cognitive load attached to listening to the person who is on-screen. The clearer and more targeted you can make your words, the more chance you have of being understood and integrated into the conversation.

—*Sascha Strelka*

As a remote worker, it is wise to be prepared for situations that exclude you. For example, there may be a party upon the completion of a project that includes food or drink, which you cannot participate in because you are a virtual employee.

Someone may have a baby shower and forget to invite the virtual employees. Do your best to not be offended and instead focus on solutions. If you know there will be a celebration that virtual employees are not invited to, reach out to the meeting organizer to discuss ways virtual employees can attend: Maybe the party can be held in a conference room with video calling set up. Maybe food or drinks can be sent to the virtual employees who participated in the project, or they can buy their own and then expense them. Don't be afraid to reach out after the fact as well, to discuss ways virtual employees could be included in the future.

It's equally important to establish with your on-site colleagues that you, as a remote worker, are still very much part of the team and whatever projects are underway. To this end, make sure you are a part of all meetings that are relevant to you and your role. It's easy for on-site project leaders or supervisors to grab employees who are physically in front of them for an impromptu meeting on something that a remote teammate would also find useful. Be proactive: Talk to these leaders so this doesn't become the norm and so you are looped in as a full participant, in whatever way makes the most sense. Ensure that assignments are set with clear deadlines, or at the very least, tell your on-site counterparts what you'll be doing and when you'll have your work completed. Even though they can't see you working, they'll know you're getting your share done and hitting your deadlines. You may also need to compromise when it comes to your schedule, making sure you're available and online when your colleagues in the office are working on your shared projects or tasks. That way, they can easily reach out to you with questions and requests and get a response right away, just as though you were down the hall. The goal is to reduce the impression that you, as a remote worker, are somehow different from everyone else in ways that matter to the team.

When an organization goes fully remote with its workforce, employees face many challenges. But when a company has a workforce split between off- and on-site, there are additional and slightly different considerations. Fair or not, those who work virtually will often have to make the majority of accommodations. Most remote employees have worked in an office, whereas most on-site folks have not worked remotely. That means the onus is on those who work virtually to be sensitive to their colleagues' potential lack of awareness of what it means to work from home. The result will be a more harmonious workforce, which can only be a positive for everyone involved, regardless of the physical location where they work.

The Person Who Has the Option of Working from Home

Some employees work at a physical location that they need to commute to every day. Others work from home and never need to go anywhere as part of their work. Yet other employees work from home some of the time and spend the rest of the time out in the field, visiting clients, performing inspections, and doing other tasks that can only be done in person. There is still another group of workers: those who have the option to work either at home or in an office. This group can potentially be seen as having the best of both worlds. They can take advantage of the benefits of both types of work life while avoiding some of the negatives that each side can bring. Naturally it's not as cut-and-dried as that, and there are many factors these workers need to take into account to do what is best for them and the company they work for.

When deciding whether or not to work from home on any particular day, it's important to understand your supervisor's (and company's) expectations. There may be official rules, which of course make the decision much easier. However, in most cases expectations are unwritten or very general. Learn how much time a person in your position can acceptably work from home and make sure you understand how to notify your supervisor about where you'll be. The last thing you want is for your boss to feel that you're not in the office enough, which can result in distrust. The same goes for coworkers' expectations. If you're working remotely four days a week, while all your colleagues are working from home just one day a week, you may be sending the wrong message. "He's just never here!" is not something you want your supervisor or your coworkers to think. Following both official and unofficial policies helps avoid this issue.

Some of the reasons why you may want to work from home are better than others. Maybe there are personal reasons that keep you from the office but don't require you to take a personal day or time off. Perhaps there's a delivery that you need to be at home to receive. Or maybe your teenager is sick and needs someone to remind her to take her medicine every four hours. These reasons are generally accepted by colleagues and supervisors back at the office but can cause problems if they occur on a regular basis. Making sure that colleagues and supervisors know not just where you are but *why* you are out of the office is important to keep your working relationships harmonious.

One important reason to work from home is to increase productivity. While many people might assume that when you're at work in the office, you're getting more done, working from home usually provides an environment free from interruptions. Think about all the times when someone stops by your office or cubicle to chat and how that can interrupt your flow. You may get called into meetings you feel obligated to attend, even though they are not as pressing as the deadlines you have to meet. Many employees who have a balance of on-site and off-site work locations comment on how much more productive they are when working from home. They can clear their inboxes and work on projects for long stretches at a time, rarely putting tasks on pause.

Timing is also key when deciding which days to remain in the office. While there may be pressing reasons to work from home at certain times, there are also strong reasons to be in the office at other times. There could be important visitors coming to your floor or building, making your physical presence advantageous. Maybe these visitors are a big part of your work duties—collaborators on a project, for example—or maybe they are senior management and you want them to see you working hard. If you're at home, they won't be able to see you in action, and your absence could even be viewed in a negative light. This is especially true if the visit was planned in advance, as most such visits are. Your absence easily raises the question "Why isn't she here on this particular day? Didn't she know we were coming?" It's also important to be present for meetings about big projects you are directly involved with or that you will indirectly be affected by. For situations in which several colleagues or teams often work remotely, there is real value in making sure you are in the office when they are on-site as well so you have the opportunity to interact in person. On the other hand, it may make more sense for you to be in the office when they are gone to provide any needed support in their absence. Make sure you not only have good reasons for working from home but also understand the appropriate times to work from the office.

I used to make it a point to attend all big meetings in person, even though I worked from home.

Home was under two hours away from the office, and it was easier for me to feel socially comfortable actually meeting people in person instead of over a video call. Once I knew a number of people in the office, I didn't feel the need to be physically present at all of the meetings anymore.

—Sascha Strelka

Another important reason to show up at the office on a regular basis is to take full advantage of the "water cooler" moments you can miss out on when working from home. In an organization that is completely remote, your colleagues will probably work together to intentionally re-create such moments, but in an environment where people can choose to work virtually from time to time, you are unlikely to have any sense of the atmosphere of the office while at home. Therefore, it's imperative that you take opportunities to go into the office to get a sense of the organizational culture and strengthen your connections with colleagues through informal interactions. Eat your lunch with others. Visit your colleagues in person and discuss current projects. Have an actual "water cooler" moment at the office's water cooler. Really consider what you want to accomplish by coming into the office. Perhaps a coworker is giving a presentation and your presence, though perhaps not business-critical, would show moral support. Make sure you have a list of important dates for the people you work with. Recognizing birthdays or a colleague's return from an extended leave can strengthen the bonds among you. For someone who more often works from home, being strategic about on-site visits is an important part of being a successful employee.

With the right mindset, employees who have the option to work both in the office and from home can make their jobs extremely rewarding. They can more easily manage the work-life balance that many remote workforce employees sometimes struggle with. They can increase job satisfaction and productivity. They can truly achieve the best of both worlds. That said, there is no default setting. These types of employees need to make careful decisions about when and where they work and how to present the right image to their colleagues and supervisors. If they accomplish this, their careers will greatly benefit.

Chapter 7

Secrets for Managers

This chapter is written for managers with remote direct reports. It contains the hard-won knowledge of those who came before you. These are the things your employees wish you knew.

Is It Really So Different?

> I quickly learned that relationship building is of primary importance in remote management. When I started in this role, I focused on clarifying key responsibilities and setting goals, which in my previous experience had been the definition of successful management.
>
> While those steps are still extremely important, I found that as the manager of remote employees, I did not naturally have the relationship with my team to bring out the best in them. I didn't learn about their lives outside of work the way I might have just by being in physical proximity. In a shared office, you see photos of families on desks, have small talk around the water cooler or vending machines, and exchange stories while grabbing coffee or lunch. In a remote environment, I was missing the personal context to help me understand my employees' challenges and priorities.
>
> That's why I now start every new managerial relationship by asking about my new employee's life, family, and interests, and take the time to share about myself, too. This relationship building gives me a firmer basis for challenging my employees—they know I care about who they are as people, and not just how their output benefits me and our organization.
>
> —*Dustin Semo*

One of the trickiest parts of managing in the remote environment is that it can seem so similar to a traditional office. There are still meetings to run, deadlines to meet, and company initiatives to implement. The sales team still needs to meet its targets, operations employees need to make sure everything runs on time, and someone in finance needs to pay the bills. All of these similarities can lull a manager into thinking that a managerial style that works in a traditional office will translate well into the remote world. However, the savvy manager will realize that the two environments are not the same and take steps to manage effectively in this setting.

To even begin to understand the enormity of the differences, consider this: In an on-site office, managers constantly receive feedback (both overt and subliminal) without even realizing it. Let's say Joe is managing a team and makes a bad decision about something (or maybe the decision is right, but the delivery is poor). The office goes quiet. People look down or start to fidget. Joe's discussions with team members are met with shorter, clipped responses. Employee Sally, who never goes to lunch and is always the last to leave the office, not only goes to lunch with five others but also leaves work an hour early claiming to have a headache. In short, Joe is handed a mass of tacit feedback from his employees that the decision is not being accepted well.

Now let's look at the same situation in the remote world, where management is still operating in an office-traditional way. Joe in Hartford calls Sally in Chicago and makes the same announcement as in the above example. In a remote office, what will Sally do? She'll likely feel isolated, without any colleagues with whom she can blow off steam. She might tell her significant other or a family member about the frustration she feels, or perhaps she'll take a quick walk around her neighborhood to cool off. At some point, though, she'll likely call her friend and coworker Larry in Seattle to consult or vent a little. More than likely, Larry then calls Lynn in Denver, who calls Jane in Memphis, who . . . You get the idea. Potentially in just a few hours, 20 people in the organization know that Joe has a problem. But who is the one person in the country who doesn't know? That's right: Joe.

This is just one example of the new order and new understanding that are necessary to ensure a happy, engaged remote workforce—not in terms of the need for a different hierarchy or reporting matrix (which we take as a given), but in how that hierarchy or matrix needs to function. Information flows in new and sometimes unpredictable ways in the remote world. Conversations in this environment are fundamentally different from those that occur in an actual office, where follow-up and context can be provided as necessary. Interpersonal relationships are crafted and developed in unique ways remotely. Career pathing for individuals has to be inspired and discussed differently. Company culture is not absorbed as it is in the office environment, so hiring and training must incorporate and reinforce this explicitly.

The old management guidebook might have been great in a Madison Avenue office, but in the remote workforce, we need a different map.

To Be Heard

When I first started as a manager, one of my colleagues told me how important it was to check in with each of my direct reports every day. I looked at my packed calendar, which had maybe 10 minutes of free time on it almost every day of the week and asked, "How?"

She said, "It's easy. Just send a chat. 'Hi, how are you? How's your day?'"

It was such a simple piece of advice, but so important. I get incredible energy from time with my own manager. I love the opportunity to talk about what I'm working on, get their perspective, and gain more confidence. The result is that I do my best, and I feel great about it.

So, I made it my mission to check in with everyone in some way every single day. Sometimes it's because we have our regular one-on-one meeting scheduled. Sometimes, it's just a quick chat to say "Hey, how are things?" Sometimes it's meeting with two or three of my reports as we work through a problem together.

One day, I started what I thought would be a quick check-in chat and quickly got 15 messages in response. I immediately told my next meeting that I needed some time to talk to my team member. Once we hopped into a video chat, we solved our problem in the first five minutes, and spent the rest of our time catching up about her life outside of work.

By making myself fully available to my team, I frequently catch needs like these before they balloon, and also get to know my direct reports better.

—Kate Mitsakis

For many people, the idea of an absent or mostly silent boss sounds like an ideal situation. For the remote worker, however, a silent boss isn't a positive thing. When you don't have the opportunity to see your boss roaming the halls, to notice her talking to another employee who works in a nearby office, or even to run into her while grabbing a coffee, communication becomes much more important. Your employees don't want you as someone who only exists to rubber-stamp payroll; they want to have a relationship in which their thoughts and opinions are heard and acknowledged.

The virtual workspace doesn't lend itself to silent forms of approval or recognition. Your direct report can't see you smile and nod as you read the email he sent. Without some kind of reply, he won't know whether his contribution is a good one, has some flaws, or was even seen at all. It can be disheartening for an employee to share his thoughts and never receive any acknowledgment from his boss. While providing a quick response to messages you receive from your employees is a great place to start, it's also important to really listen to what your people are asking of you. To truly be heard means more than just getting a "Thanks!" in reply. While such replies are appreciated, it's also important to sometimes send longer, more articulate responses so your people know that you are listening to what they are telling you.

Every manager knows that her employees will sometimes find themselves together and use that opportunity to talk to each other about work. They'll discuss the good parts of their jobs and the bad parts; this will be an opportunity for them to raise their thoughts and opinions of their work life and receive validation from their colleagues. This scenario is harder to come by in the remote workforce, so as the boss, you will need to take proactive steps to ensure that it occurs. A boss in an on-site office can lock herself away behind a closed door and at least know that her employees will be able to talk to each other without too much effort. A remote boss who does the same thing risks isolating her employees. Fortunately, there are many things you can do to help your employees feel heard while getting your own work done. You can provide discussion-based opportunities for team members to raise ideas. For example, you could set up a system or program for your team to share ideas and brainstorm through an instant-messaging platform, or you could hold "coffee breaks" online, where you meet an employee or a group of employees for a short period to chat about any topics (work related or not).

It's also important to make sure your direct reports have the tools to communicate with you in more formal ways, if appropriate. A program that allows the sharing of documents can be useful for some remote workers. It makes your communication with your employees a more collaborative one, so they can see how their contributions are being recognized and used in the context of bigger discussions and projects. Many programs that allow you to share documents will also provide you with tools to make comments on contributions, further strengthening the dialogue you're building with your team.

You are your remote employees' most important link to the company. Feeling that you hear them will be a driving force for high engagement and job satisfaction. Use online tools to foster a collaborative and communicative environment where all contributions are recognized in one form or another. By doing this, you will ensure that your employees show up ready to do their best work, confident you are there to guide them along the way.

To Be Recognized

> *At the beginning of every division-wide meeting, we take 10 minutes to learn about the "movers and shakers" in our work community.*
> *Each individual who has moved to a new area of the company is named and celebrated, and we hear testimonials about the people and teams who have made a difference in the business over the previous quarter. This practice is a fixture that allows all of us to publicly recognize one another's accomplishments, and the commitment of time demonstrates that our place of work values us and our contributions.*
>
> *—Caitlin Duke*

One of the most important things to know about managing employees in the remote workforce is that you need to actively show that you hear them and recognize their contributions. But to be an effective manager, you have to go one step further: You need to sing their praises. Like most people, employees want to have that pat on the back, and often they want that recognition to be public to some degree. Remote workers in particular may crave this type of recognition because so often their hard work is only visible to themselves. As a manager in this environment, you need to take more overt steps to show recognition than you would in a traditional office setting.

When considering the best ways to recognize your employees, remember that large- and small-scale rituals are equally important. Examples of large-scale recognition are taking part in a formal awards process or highlighting your employees' significant accomplishments during an all-in meeting. Small-scale options include taking the time to celebrate a minor success during your one-on-one call or a smaller group meeting. If you only focus on the large-scale recognition, your opportunities will be fewer and further between. You may also find yourself lumping together several examples of success by multiple employees in order to cover everyone, which diminishes the value of the recognition. Similarly, if small-scale recognition is the sole avenue of delivery, you risk your employees feeling like their contributions are not worthy enough to be shared more widely. The solution is to provide a mix of both approaches.

It's also important to realize that different people like to be recognized differently. You may have someone who truly feels uncomfortable in the spotlight and may not appreciate being called out in the middle of a large meeting, even though the news being shared is positive. Another employee might appreciate the value of small-scale recognition but yearn for his exploits to be more widely broadcast to his peers. Without that, he may feel like he's not getting his name out there and that he doesn't have the chance to build a network or create a viable career path with the company. Consider individual preferences and weigh the type of recognition you show toward those preferences when possible.

In the remote workforce, you have to consciously bestow praise more than you would in an in-person office environment. There are fewer casual interactions and, as a result, fewer unplanned opportunities to recognize your employee for a job well done. It's easy to think, "Didn't I just praise this person last week? Do I really need to look for something else to say about how well they're doing?" The answer is yes. While it may seem forced at first, you're helping to build a better work environment for your employee by filling in the gaps in interaction with positive recognition. It's also important to note that in the remote workforce, a lot of your communication with employees is likely to be in the form of writing, and while praise in the written word is certainly powerful and people appreciate having their successes documented, hearing the recognition directly from one's boss through a video or audio meeting can be even more powerful.

Recognition is a must for the success of any manager of remote employees. If giving regular, consistent recognition isn't second nature for you, develop a system to help you to remember to do so. The more you practice giving praise, the more naturally it will come. You will find the increase in happiness and productivity of your employees will make it well worth the effort.

To Be Given Flexibility

Nothing makes me feel like I've won the job lottery quite so much as running in the woods on a Tuesday afternoon. While other office workers have to stare out the window at the rare sunny days we get in Vancouver, I get to pound through forest trails, surrounded by old-growth Douglas Fir trees.

A portion of my work can be done at any time of day or night, allowing me to create extended breaks on certain days. I know that my running break makes me a more empathetic colleague and a better problem solver. It's also a great way to ward off the afternoon slump.

Even more importantly, my director recognizes and celebrates the flexibility of the remote workforce by taking breaks himself. If he is going on a field trip with his son, he'll tell us about it in the team chat. If he has a doctor's appointment, he'll tell us when he's coming back. This kind of transparency creates an environment where the team feels safe to take breaks and talk about what we do outside of work.

—Teresa Douglas

One of the biggest selling points of working remotely is the flexibility that it can offer. Different teams have different needs that will determine the extent of flexibility that is realistic, but generally speaking, the remote world allows for more flexibility than does an on-site office. If that flexibility could exist but doesn't, you may end up with employees who are frustrated with their work situation. Even if you tell them (and yourself) that the rules you're laying down are no different from those that employees in a traditional office environment need to follow, your remote employees will soon realize that it's not the same at all.

The first step is to simply accept, allow, and encourage flexibility in your workforce, as appropriate. This doesn't mean that there are no rules and no accountability, though you will have to relinquish some control. To promote appropriate flexibility, you need to be transparent with your reports regarding what is allowed and how they should keep you informed about managing their own time and deliverables. If you provide clear communication and firm expectations about the flexibility your team has at its disposal, then you should not experience problems. If you are not firm about your expectations or are too firm about limiting flexibility, then you will struggle to manage your remote team.

The biggest contribution you can make to your employees' flexibility is being open to a nontraditional work structure. Expecting your reports to always sign in by a certain time and work a set number of hours per day, even if they are nonexempt employees, is going to make your remote workforce feel stifled. Working remotely comes with its own set of challenges, but it also comes with unique benefits, a big one being a flexible work schedule. Denying your employees this flexibility makes no sense and will actively lower their engagement. The focus should be on getting tasks done in a timely manner and less on precisely when those tasks are being accomplished.

Your actions should also back up your words. It's not going to work to say that your team has the flexibility to arrange their schedules in ways that make sense for them, but then set things up so they effectively lose that flexibility. Scheduling meetings is a big issue here. In a traditional office setting, the boss can walk into a shared workspace and see that all of her reports are present and not currently on calls. She can then announce a quick meeting and ask everyone to go into the boardroom for updates. While one can argue about the value of ad hoc meetings even in a traditional office environment, it's far worse for remote workers. You cannot see what all your employees are engaged in, so you should avoid last-minute meetings. If you regularly call last-minute meetings, then your team will feel obligated to make themselves available at all times, thereby reducing their flexibility. Even providing a day's notice is not ideal unless you have pressing matters that cannot be effectively conveyed in another form of communication. Your employees likely have existing meetings set up with clients or perhaps their own direct reports, so sudden requests for meetings can impact your organization in larger ways than you might expect. Plan your meetings out in advance and make good use of a system, such as a shared calendar app, whereby you can see your employees' availability. This will ensure regular meetings happen at appropriate times and the occasional emergency meeting happens with minimal inconvenience. Finally, make sure your team knows it's OK if they can't make these sudden meetings; provide them with notes or some other form of a recap so they don't feel like they're missing out.

You should also make sure that you are honoring the spirit of the flexible work schedule. It doesn't work to provide your employees the option of taking the afternoon off to pick up their kids from school if during that time you're sending messages marked "urgent" or calling them with questions that could wait until they are back in the office. Your employees should feel like they are truly able to flex their schedules without being tied to their phone or laptop to meet your needs. This may require you to adjust your own schedule to ensure you can ask any pressing questions before your employee leaves for the remainder of the afternoon. Additionally, you should demonstrate how you yourself use the flexible work schedule as a way to encourage your employees to do the same. Provide quick updates on how you're leaving "the office" to pick up your child from school and how you'll be staying later in the evening to catch up on anything that needs to be done.

Recognizing that your employees in the remote workforce need flexibility in order to get the most out of their job is crucial. It ultimately comes down to trust. You should trust that they will get their jobs done based on the expectations that were set when they were hired or when your organization went remote, as well as the expectations that you set every time you talk to them about the team's goals. Make flexibility a selling point and then commit to it. Not only accept but encourage nontraditional work schedules, and support them by making the meetings and deadlines you set for your team fit within this framework. You may initially feel like you're losing control over your employees, but you're actually gaining far more—their trust, their commitment, and their longevity.

To Be Engaged

Engagement in the workforce has steadily become a more visible and important topic for businesses. The correlation between a happy and engaged workforce and a company's bottom line is a strong one, so many businesses are putting more effort into ensuring that employees are having a good experience with their jobs. This activity requires a fair amount of energy and attention from those in management, and when it comes to the remote workforce, it requires even greater vigilance.

It's not just company profits that are at stake; the fact is that virtual employees can move to another company more easily, taking their expertise with them and forcing your company to incur the expense of replacing them. If your employees have experience working remotely, they can look for other jobs without being restricted to a particular city or even a country in some cases. While you should be invested in your people enough to want them to be engaged simply because you care about them, the fact that many of your employees are less locked into their job than those in a traditional office should weigh heavily in your consideration as well.

So how do you engage your remote workforce? Stay in contact. There's more to it than just that, of course, but if you make it your goal to be in regular contact with your people, you will be more likely to ensure they feel engaged. This contact is best achieved through consistent check-ins. You can arrange it so that you have a daily, weekly, or biweekly call with your direct reports, or you can use key events in your business to determine the appropriate timing (e.g., after certain sales cycles end). During these check-ins, you should find out what parts of their work your employees enjoy. Conversely, what type of work do they want to reduce? This information will allow you to figure out the best way to keep your team engaged, because it will allow you to modify work responsibilities where possible, based on the preferences of your employees.

The trick here is to be consistent in your connections with your employees but not to slide into the realm of micromanaging. While it's frustrating enough to have a boss who micromanages in a traditional office environment, in the remote workforce it can feel even worse, despite the lack of a physical presence. In part, this is because your remote worker expects to be trusted to do their job, so micromanaging is a violation of that trust. It's also because a ton of formal calls and emails from the boss combined with the random but always-present pings through chat and instant messages can make the employee feel like you are in their head and there's no escape.

A new member of your remote team doesn't have the ability to knock on your door for quick check-ins throughout the day the way she would in a traditional office. I create that opportunity to check in by scheduling a 15-minute daily stand-up with each new direct report. Any questions that came up in the last 24 hours are resolved quickly, and my new employee gets a sense of how I work in real time. By the second week, the team member tends not to need the full 15 minutes, increasing her confidence that she's understanding the role and meeting expectations.

—*Dustin Semo*

With that in mind, a savvy manager of remote workers will assume the best of his employees. It may seem counterintuitive to keep your staff engaged by not always being there to check on what they are doing, but it will actually increase their engagement to know that their boss trusts them, especially in an environment where nobody actually sees them in action.

It's key to find a balance between consistent check-ins and micromanagement; you need to ensure that your team doesn't feel abandoned due to your efforts to show you trust them. Finding that middle path will create a greater sense of engagement for your team. Make sure your employees have ample opportunities to raise any difficulties they are facing. Remember, they won't have the convenience of running into you at the office, so you need to provide them with the opportunity instead.

It is also important to be selective about the number of initiatives you create for your employees. While part of the joy of managing people is identifying new and interesting ways to develop your team, too many initiatives can leave employees feeling pulled in too many directions, with too little time to complete their daily tasks. Especially if these initiatives regularly peter out, duplicate existing work, or fail to create change, your employees will feel the frustration of busy people who were obliged to waste their time. This can also make change management harder for you and your company. Your reports may become reluctant to fully invest in a new procedure because there is a decent chance that procedure will soon become part of the wasteland of abandoned projects and resources. In the remote workforce, evidence of those failures is more obvious and therefore easy for your direct reports to call to mind.

Employee engagement is a crucial area for any manager to master, but the manager of a remote workforce needs to find success in this area sooner than the manager of a traditional workforce. If you can find the right level of engagement, you will not only gain the financial benefits of an engaged workforce, but you'll also feel a tremendous sense of emotional satisfaction.

A Sense of Community

> *Within my team, we have transitioned from top-down weekly group calls into meetings led by our peers. We rotate this responsibility, which gives us a chance to focus on a wide variety of topics. And just as important as the business-related content of each call is the 10 or so minutes we spend responding to a thoughtful icebreaker that helps us continue to know one another as people. Before one team member departed for maternity leave, we threw her a virtual baby shower with a quick game, sent her an e-card we had all signed, and gave her a gift card—we had everything but the cake.*
>
> *—Caitlin Duke*

Remote workers lose so much when they leave the traditional office: long commutes, rigid work schedules, inconvenient office spaces. The list of positive losses goes on and on. As a manager, however, it's important to acknowledge the aspects of a traditional office that many workers miss. Remote employees, who for the most part have grown up associating work with leaving home and entering a ready-made world full of acquaintances, no longer have that world waiting for them when they begin their workday—unless you, as their manager, help them create it.

This sense of community is different from the relationship that your employee has with you. Your direct report needs to feel, as much as possible, that he is part of a larger team of people working for the same company and toward the same goals. In a traditional office, this occurs naturally with little effort from you: Workers are thrown together for 40 hours a week within the same physical space. In the remote world, your team may be scattered across the country—or the world—and each of them may work alone. Unless you take steps to create a community, your reports may feel as if they are freelancers working for an imaginary company.

You may already have a regular, one-on-one meeting scheduled with each of your direct reports. While that is important, it isn't sufficient for building a larger sense of community. Many managers have found that a weekly team meeting is a useful vehicle for connecting their direct reports to each other and the company at large. At the most basic level, a team meeting can help your team get to know one another so they have someone to talk to during the day. If you bring in special guests, your team can also learn more about different departments in the organization. This is helpful, as it often gives people a face to associate with the emails in their inboxes.

While a team meeting is an important first step, it's also valuable to have unplanned interactions that mimic the casual encounters employees experience in a typical office environment. Instant messaging is great for this, especially if you can set up a team chat. Take the lead and initiate greetings at the beginning of the day. Start group conversations throughout the workweek—this will help encourage others on the team to do the same. Logging on and starting your day with a round of online hellos and stories about the weekend helps build the sense of belonging to something bigger than just your laptop. Even if it isn't practical for your direct reports to work together on a project, those greetings and conversations can make them feel part of a close-knit team.

Structured fun is another way to create a sense of community for your employees. Find a lull in the workday to get your staff doing something interactive that is non–work related and fun. You may need to try different things, since what one group thinks of as fun may be awkward and uncomfortable for another. If your first efforts don't work out, keep trying. Some people hold game nights, others pair up employees for short conversations (à la speed dating), while still others get the group together and ask each other a set of questions. A little research will yield a workable list of activities to try out: Search online, brainstorm with colleagues, or ask other managers for ideas. While these activities can be awkward at times, they do bring workers together and make them more than colleagues in name only. While some employees might be resistant to this type of interaction, most will appreciate and understand what you're trying to do. You are creating shared experiences.

Building a sense of community is vital, and it isn't hard to do if you go about it intentionally. Even unsuccessful team icebreakers build community—at the very least, they give your direct reports something to talk about among themselves. Take the time to bring your team together as a group and to introduce them to members of the wider company. Your efforts will build a team that is engaged and productive as it interacts with the broader company community.

A Consistent Experience

One Monday morning in August 2017, I sat down to work in my home office as usual. I reported to my boss that even though Hurricane Harvey had hit Houston that weekend, my family's house was intact, and I anticipated business as usual that week.

Two hours later, as water rushed down the street and into our neighborhood from a nearby reservoir, I quickly chatted my boss, packed up a few things including my laptop, and headed to higher ground.

The next morning, when I learned that my house had over four feet of water in it (goodbye, recently redone home office), I spent about 15 minutes in shock and then powered up my laptop and started to work. This was the day that I would begin expanding my team to include five new members. I would be the third or fourth manager our new teammates had had in just a few months, so we had a lot to discuss.

I spent that day having individual conversations with each of them to better understand their feelings: anxiety over having a new manager, confusion about the change, and excitement about the opportunities ahead of us.

Over the next several weeks, as I moved from house to house and spent my nights figuring out my next moves, I prioritized my time with my team—not out of a sense of obligation, but because I wanted to do it. Change is one of the most important times to harness strengths, seize the opportunity that comes with new beginnings, and foster engagement. My role in this organizational change was the most important thing to me in those crucial weeks, even as I was personally dealing with some major changes.

—Kate Mitsakis

Change is the new constant, and nowhere is this more true than in the remote workforce. Brick-and-mortar companies are constrained by geography and building leases; remote companies have no such limitations. While this ability to change rapidly can create a company that is agile and resilient, it can also lead to feelings of instability among your direct reports unless you take steps to provide a consistent experience.

Consider what might happen in a traditional office before a large change: Your employees might overhear their colleagues on the other side of the office complaining about a clunky process or program. Or perhaps a series of well-dressed strangers are ushered into the big boss's office. New job descriptions might appear on the company intranet. Even if a large change takes your employees by surprise, most employees upon reflection can realize after the fact that they saw the signs of a change coming. The remote worker, however, doesn't get these same clues. Your employee may not even realize that the company is solving a problem or addressing an opportunity until his work responsibilities change.

While you can't stop the rate of change in your company, you can help your employees weather the storm by providing stability where you can. Keep meeting with your reports on a regular schedule, with a consistent agenda. If you have to create additional points of contact because of the change, make sure your team understands that these are temporary and outside the norm. Your employees should know to expect certain topics to be covered in each meeting so they can prepare. This not only makes the meetings more effective and efficient but also provides a sense of stability when things start changing rapidly.

This doesn't mean that you should run your usual meetings as if nothing has changed. Rather, you should demonstrate that business will carry on, even through the change. Make sure you are as knowledgeable as possible about the upcoming changes. This allows you to speak confidently and firmly with your direct reports. Your employees will take comfort in knowing that their boss understands what's going on and will help them through it. This will allow them to adjust to new processes more smoothly. By the same token, be transparent about what you don't know. Especially when change is large-scale and complex, even senior management may not know for some time exactly how each team will be affected. In the absence of information, employees may suspect that their leadership is hatching some grand plot with nefarious consequences. Reassure your people that the implications of the change are being thought through carefully and information will be shared as soon as possible.

Clarity is also very important. If possible, provide your employees with a clear end date for the old process or structure and show how the new process or structure will work. Make sure that the reasoning around the change is clear to everyone. Without that clarity, speculation will run wild, and virtual employees will be bouncing from one colleague to another, fueling uncertainty and making the experience of working in this fast-paced environment more erratic.

Proper follow-up is important once changes are announced so you can guide your employees through new initiatives. It will be harder for you to see whether or not your employees are struggling, as you are likely to see only the end result of their work rather than the employees in the process of completing their new tasks. Check in more often with your staff and make sure your regular meetings include a section on dealing with change and new information. Even in the absence of radical change, companies are always updating policies and adjusting operating procedures. If you make these updates a part of your regular meeting agenda, your employees will feel up-to-date instead of lost.

Sometimes the company change is a reorganization, and some or all of your direct reports will soon report to someone else. It may be that the entire team will be broken up and sent in different directions. If this is the case for your team, then there are still things you can do leading up to and throughout this change. You will, of course, want to continue to hold your regular meetings while the team is still engaged in its old work. If you can, help your direct reports get to know their new boss. If you know the new boss prefers instant messaging to email or afternoon meetings to morning ones, for example, share this information. Depending on the circumstances, you may also want to hold one last team-building meeting so your employees can have closure. Your team may continue to work for the same company, but the team itself is going away, and it is important to acknowledge that. Finally, once the changeover has happened, consider sending a brief email or instant message after some time has passed to check in with your former reports. This may not be appropriate in all situations, but this level of human care from an old boss can create a feeling of stability. At its best, reconnecting with former reports underlines for them that change can mean broadening their networks. Change isn't always about loss.

Change is inevitable and necessary. As a manager, you have the power to help your direct reports navigate uncertainty by being a rock of stability. They will look to you, either implicitly or explicitly, to keep the change manageable. If you provide a consistent structure in your interactions with employees, implement steady transitions when change does occur, and focus on well-considered initiatives, you will have a team of people who can survive significant change to their work lives.

A Partner in My Professional Development

At my first annual review, my director walked through my self-selected goals with me, beginning the process of breaking them up into achievable and measurable steps. Then, he gave me an assignment: Make yourself more visible. He explained that knowing colleagues and having them know me was an essential step to growing professionally in the remote environment. While he could and did make some initial connections for me, he pushed me to determine where my greatest interests lie and seek out knowledgeable coworkers on my own. My director can't just make informal introductions for me in the hallway, so he reinforces the importance of my taking the initiative. Of necessity, my development has become more of a conversation than a series of top-down assignments.

—Caitlin Duke

In today's business climate, common wisdom says that employees must feel empowered to look for their own professional development opportunities. As a manager who wants to encourage good employees to stick around and grow within the company, it's important that you become a partner in your direct reports' development. This is particularly true for the remote workforce.

In a traditional office, your employees have the opportunity to gain incidental visibility. Perhaps the operations team huddles together every Monday morning near your direct report's desk, where they can observe his fantastic project management skills. Or perhaps your employee happens to be standing in the front office and demonstrates top-notch client support skills when an irate customer comes in the door. Both of these examples have two things in common: The first is that they happen organically. The second is that there is no direct analogue in the remote workforce. Your employees can help out other departments and come to the attention of other managers, but this won't happen unless someone deliberately seeks out those opportunities.

This is where you as a manager can step in. Your position gives you access to people and information that your direct report can't reach on her own. You can be her eyes and ears, uncovering new opportunities to keep her engaged or grow in her career. Not all of these opportunities will pan out, of course, but this is not wasted effort; there is nothing quite so engaging as knowing that your boss is your advocate. Your direct report will appreciate what you're doing to help.

Keep in mind that not all growth opportunities mean helping your employee into a new role. Your employee may not be ready for a next step or even know what that next step ought to be. A side project, either within your department or outside of it, could help her build the skills and visibility she may need to grow into a new role in the future. In some companies, where hierarchies are flat and competition for each role is high, side projects are a great way to "interview" for a role that may open at a later date.

Also consider facilitating one-on-one meetings. In a traditional office, your employee can have lunch with someone whom they find interesting. In the remote workforce, the same connections happen over short one-on-one video calls. These meetings can give your employee the opportunity to connect with someone in an interesting department, to complete business with a cross-functional colleague, or simply to grow by comparing notes with others in a similar role.

Securing growth opportunities for your employees will take time, creativity, and perhaps calling in the occasional favor, so it makes sense to be as efficient as possible. You don't want to set up your direct report with a short stint at the call center, for example, only to find out he was really hoping to learn how to manipulate data with the business intelligence team. Talk to your direct report. You may have a good idea of his strengths and weaknesses in his current role, but you can't assume that you know what he wants to learn next or what activities he may want to explore further. Just because someone is great at a particular task doesn't mean they like doing it.

Be direct and explicit in your conversations with your employee. Does your employee want to grow into a different role? What type of role? What types of experiences does your employee need in order to feel confident applying for that role? Not all employees want to move into different roles. You may be in the enviable position of having an employee who is great at her job and wants to stay in her role indefinitely. In this case she may simply need an occasional side project to keep her from feeling stagnant. Or perhaps she would like to further her skills in a particular program that she uses for her job. You won't know unless you ask.

Remember that answers can change. Just as your company can evolve to meet the needs of the current business climate, your employees' desires can evolve over time. Perhaps the company creates a new department or acquires a business that interests your employee. Or perhaps that side project grows into something more long term, and your report wants to devote more of her work life to it. If you build in regular development checkpoints, you will have an up-to-date grasp of your employee's thinking. This will make you a more effective partner in her development. These development conversations don't have to be long or involved, but many managers find that these talks have to be planned in advance and put on the calendar. Otherwise, it is all too easy to let day-to-day crises push these conversations to a future date that never happens.

If your employees are going to discuss their future career goals with you, they need to feel safe in doing so. Some of your employees may have come from companies with unhealthy cultures. It may be that they think talking about career growth implies that they don't like their current role. The best way to demonstrate that they are in a better place is to talk approvingly of people who took on different projects or reached out for new opportunities. Perhaps you could even share your own development experiences as you encourage your employees to do the same. Your actions will speak for themselves.

Acting as a partner in your employees' professional growth takes time and effort, because it requires that you have a current understanding of their desires and that you invest time in seeking out opportunities to help them grow. However, this is time well spent, yielding engaged employees who will benefit the company for years to come.

Knowing How and Whom to Hire

In March of 2015, I began a new position with a daunting objective: develop and launch a nation-wide Ambassador program in five months. I needed my as-yet nonexistent team to get an incredible amount of work done in a short amount of time, and I needed them to do so while working remotely.

This meant being as objective as possible in the interview process and evaluating candidates not only as individuals with different levels of experience, perspective, self-awareness, and capacity for change, but also with the entire group dynamic in mind. To identify the amazing team I needed, I drafted a set of questions that I asked every single candidate in a series of video interviews, meticulously documenting their responses and my observations. I focused on dedication to our mission and vision in addition to the candidates' self-discipline and talents.

In the end, I secured a fantastic team of eight managers and two recruiters who tirelessly worked together toward our common goals. We met via Google Hangouts several times a week, we created group Skype chats for both professional goals and personal bonding, and we were ultimately able to build the trust and relationships we needed. We launched our first training session just four months after I began the hiring process.

—Katie Stanfield

Not everyone thrives in the remote workforce. It's a matter of personality fit, and no onboarding program—no matter how fantastic—can change a candidate's personality. It's important that candidates who have the best chance of succeeding (not just at the job but also as a remote employee) are the ones who make it to the onboarding stage. Don't assume that someone who applied for a remote job will automatically do well as a remote employee. It's up to you as the hiring manager to ask the right questions in the interview. Otherwise, you'll end up with high turnover and need to put additional time into supporting those who stay but struggle.

While an employee doesn't need to be an expert with technology to be successful in the remote workforce, they do need to have a certain level of tech savvy and be comfortable learning how to work online. As a hiring manager, this is something you should take into account when considering candidates for remote roles. If you bring on someone without first confirming their comfort with technology, you run the risk of having to train them not only on their specific job duties but also on the basics of functioning in the remote environment. There are enough challenges with managing people in the remote workplace without the added trouble of hiring someone who can not or will not learn how to operate in it. When evaluating a candidate's technological skills, it's important to note the difference between posting regularly online versus interacting effectively online. A remote employee should be comfortable with managing email effectively, collaborating on shared documents, and troubleshooting technology at a basic level.

That doesn't mean that you should pass on an otherwise great candidate if they don't already use the specific programs the company uses. Check to see how the candidate has handled past gaps in knowledge. If the candidate has a track record of quickly gaining competency in related areas, then this may be enough to let you proceed with confidence. Of course, keep in mind the amount of time you are willing to spend training new employees.

While being tech savvy is an important selection criterion, a bigger consideration is the candidate's ability to self-direct. Your potential future employee will be on his own at home, trying to get acclimated to a new job and, very likely, a new way of working. While there will undoubtedly be opportunities for your new hire to work closely with you, a trainer, or a colleague, for much of his onboarding, he will be on his own and will need to figure out certain tasks himself. An employee who is more accustomed to an open-plan office environment may struggle to accomplish his work alone in his home office. It will be far harder for someone else to notice when he's struggling or heading down the wrong path, so he'll need to be the type of person who is vocal when he realizes that he needs help. He'll also have to be comfortable looking up solutions and processes, rather than solely relying on asking someone else. Due to the nature of the remote environment, it isn't always possible to find someone who is available to help, so it's important for your new hire to be able to figure some things out on his own. Self-sufficiency, therefore, is key.

Along with the ability to self-direct, a remote employee should have polished people skills and high emotional intelligence. Most interactions will take place via some form of written communication. It takes more emotional intelligence, not less, to discern tone and intent when communicating with colleagues in this way.

With all this in mind, it's not really enough to conduct a phone interview. You'll need to get as much information about the candidate as possible in order to identify fit, and it's difficult to do this if you can't see the person. You may have candidates who are familiar with making video calls and others who are not. In those cases, it can be a perfect opportunity to find out how they approach learning new skills and how they react to feedback. Just as it's important to do a video interview, it's also important to consider the candidate's email correspondence. If your potential hire is overly casual in his correspondence with you, that could be a red flag, suggesting that he may not understand a level of formality is required in many situations in the remote environment. This could cause problems down the line when interacting with clients or other stakeholders, negatively impacting the business.

The ability to ask the right questions during a job interview and read the candidate well is an important skill for any hiring manager, but you need to take that ability to the next level when hiring someone for the remote workforce. Through careful analysis of video and email interactions, as well as by asking questions about their technical know-how and how they've demonstrated initiative in the past, you can identify those who have the greatest chance of succeeding in both the specific role and the remote environment in general.

Many people are well suited to remote work. If you apply the hard-won knowledge contained within the pages of this book, you will soon wonder how you and your team managed to work any other way.

Praise for *Reconciliation Blues*

"Ed Gilbreath is one of those prophets who comes out of nowhere with a message from the heart of God. His words make us uncomfortable, but that is the mission of a prophet. . . . Some of what he is saying to us about race and culture is painful to hear, but we must listen."

J. LEE GRADY, editor, *Charisma* magazine

"We've needed a book like this for a long time: strong writing, honest observations and hopeful assessments of a complex but nonnegotiable issue for Christians. By providing both a personal and a social perspective of racial tensions within evangelical contexts, Ed Gilbreath has done us a great service—especially if we pay attention."

JO KADLECEK, author and assistant professor of creative writing, Gordon College

"A fair and balanced, yet frank and honest, assessment of the state of evangelicalism in terms of racism and reconciliation. Gilbreath has lived and worked in the Euro evangelical community for much of his life. He is an appreciative yet frustrated evangelical. . . . Edward Gilbreath writes with knowledge, sensitivity and insight in a way that will benefit both the Afro and the Euro reader."

LOWELL NOBLE, resident professor, John M. Perkins Foundation

"What Gilbreath has done in his well-researched and very personal book is not only to call out the black Christian experience as what it's always been—unique, pain-filled, rich and diverse—but he's given many African American Christians clear validation for not wanting to assimilate into today's version of evangelicalism. Gilbreath has also given people like me—an Asian American Christian who's also felt like the 'token' nonwhite on historically white evangelical boards—more of a basis for our lingering sense of misgiving and even episodes of outrage. I am going to insist not only that my own church staff and leaders read this book; I'm also going to recommend highly that white Christian organizations with the stated goal of racial righteousness study and discuss it. This book clearly stands out among the many other great books on this subject because of the commitment and courage of the author."

KEN FONG, senior pastor, Evergreen Baptist Church of Los Angeles

"This is must reading for anyone committed to racial reconciliation, but especially to white folks like me who have a long way to go in understanding our African American brothers and sisters."

TONY CAMPOLO, Ph.D., Eastern University

"This is a gifted writer's firsthand account of the black evangelical experience in America . . . a beautifully written chronicle of the strange dilemma of being a black evangelical in a predominately white movement. Gilbreath has written a tough account of his experience as a black evangelical, and he wraps the brick in soft velvet. This reads easily, but it is deeply disturbing after all these years. Oh well . . ."

WILLIAM PANNELL, special assistant to the president and senior professor of preaching, Fuller Theological Seminary

"Edward Gilbreath is one of the nation's foremost journalists on Christianity and race. *Reconciliation Blues* is a spellbinding first-person look into his world as he has navigated white evangelicalism. In the process, we are provided with both a powerful teaching tool and an eye-opening journey into what is white about American Christianity. People of all backgrounds will learn much by reading this engaging book."

MICHAEL O. EMERSON, Cline Professor of Sociology, Rice University, and author of *Divided by Faith*

"Edward Gilbreath is a gentle prophet. He forces us to take another look at an issue that many wish would go away, but he does so in a way that encourages us to live up to what we believe. This book both prods us to racial reconciliation and models how to get there."

PHILIP YANCEY, author of *What's So Amazing About Grace?*

"Amazingly authentic! A must-read for anyone who wants insight about blacks who must dance on the evangelical floor of multiculturalism."

DR. DAVID ANDERSON, senior pastor, Bridgeway Community Church, and president, BridgeLeader Network

"Both loving and angry, but always true, Edward Gilbreath's brave exploration of 'white Christianity' takes a daring look at racial disconnection in the evangelical world, then challenges believers to do something redemptive to heal the problem. Bold, topical and urgently on time."

PATRICIA RAYBON, author of *I Told the Mountain to Move* and *My First White Friend*

"This is a fine piece of work. Evangelical Christians need to hear it and take heed. I highly recommend this book."

JOHN PERKINS, founder, John M. Perkins Foundation for Reconciliation and Development, Inc.

RECONCILIATION
BLUES

A Black Evangelical's Inside View
of White Christianity

Edward Gilbreath

IVP Books

An imprint of InterVarsity Press
Downers Grove, Illinois

InterVarsity Press
P.O. Box 1400, Downers Grove, IL 60515-1426
World Wide Web: www.ivpress.com
E-mail: email@ivpress.com

InterVarsity Press® is the book-publishing division of InterVarsity Christian Fellowship/USA®, a student movement active on campus at hundreds of universities, colleges and schools of nursing in the United States of America, and a member movement of the International Fellowship of Evangelical Students. For information about local and regional activities, write Public Relations Dept., InterVarsity Christian Fellowship/USA, 6400 Schroeder Rd., P.O. Box 7895, Madison, WI 53707-7895, or visit the IVCF website at <www.intervarsity.org>.

All Scripture quotations, unless otherwise indicated, are taken from the Holy Bible, New International Version®. NIV®. *Copyright ©1973, 1978, 1984 by International Bible Society. Used by permission of Zondervan Publishing House. All rights reserved.*

Published in association with the Books & Such Literary Agence, Janet Kobobel Grant, 52 Mission Circle, Suite 122, PMB 170, Santa Rosa, CA 95409-5370, www.booksandsuch.biz.

Design: Cindy Kiple

Images: church: Michael Gessinger/Getty Images
*   sign: Loic Bernard/istockphoto.com*

ISBN 978-0-8308-3362-7

Printed in the United States of America ∞

Library of Congress Cataloging-in-Publication Data

Gilbreath, Edward, 1969-
   Reconciliation blues: a Black evangelical's inside view of white
   Christianity/Edward Gilbreath.
      p. cm.
   Includes bibliographical references.
   ISBN-13: 978-0-8308-3367-2 (cloth: alk. paper)
   ISBN-10: 0-8308-3367-6 (cloth: alk. paper)
   1. Race relations—Religious aspects—Christianity. 2.
   Reconciliation—Religious aspects—Christianity. 3.
   Evangelicalism—United States—History. 4. Black theology. 5.
   United States—Race relations. I. Title.
    BT734.2.G523 2006
    277.3'083089—dc22

                                                 2006030081

P	19	18	17	16	15	14	13	12	11	10	9	8	7	6	5	4	3	2	1
Y	24	23	22	21	20	19	18	17	16	15	14	13	12	11	10	09	08			

There is no truth towards Jesus
without truth towards man.
Untruthfulness destroys fellowship,
but truth cuts false fellowship to pieces
and establishes genuine brotherhood.

DIETRICH BONHOEFFER,
THE COST OF DISCIPLESHIP

First go and be reconciled to your brother;
then come and offer your gift.

MATTHEW 5:24

CONTENTS

Prologue

SINGING THE
RECONCILIATION BLUES

The blues are like spirituals, almost sacred. When we sing blues,
we're singing out our hearts, we're singing out our feelings. Maybe we're hurt
and just can't answer back, then we sing or maybe even hum the blues.
When I sing . . . what I'm doing is letting my soul out.

Alberta Hunter

I am sick and tired of racial reconciliation."

That's what a friend of mine e-mailed me recently. We had been talking about Christians and race again, and she was letting off some steam. She's actually a gentle, peace-loving black person, who laughs at cheesy jokes and spends Saturday mornings hunting for Precious Moments figurines at thrift shops. She works at an evangelical Christian company, and white people are generally not afraid of her.

By saying she was sick and tired of racial reconciliation, my friend didn't mean that she was against people of different races coming together in the church. She was simply expressing her fatigue over the running-in-place stagnancy she believed was passing for racial unity among evangelicals.

"I'm roundly discouraged about the possibility of true racial reconciliation in the church," she said. "I honestly don't believe it will ever happen on a large scale—at least not in my lifetime."

At the time of our correspondence, my friend was twenty-six.

Why did she feel this way? Why would any middle-class black American under forty even need to think about race? After all, Jim Crow flew the coop decades ago. And, save for the occasional overzealous cop or overworked server at Denny's, there's very little daily evidence of racially motivated discrimination in America today. Right?

As some of you grumble under your breath at me, allow me to admit that I'm stretching the point a little. Things are by no means all sweet and rosy on the race-relations front. Our nation continues to stumble. But, overall, most people would concede that there's been significant progress. It's almost impossible for people from my thirtysomething generation and below to grasp what racism used to look like. My parents, who adopted me in the early 1970s when they were both well into their fifties, were children of the segregated South—my dad was from Alabama, my mom from Louisiana. For them, "Whites Only" signs were as normal as "No Smoking" signs are for us today. Mom and Dad used to tell me stories about the separate water fountains and the special seating at the back of buses. Yet, like an anthropologist studying a prehistoric civilization, I strained to imagine how it must have felt.

I worked with the evangelist Howard O. Jones on his autobiography a few years ago, and he told me about the backlash he faced when he agreed to become Billy Graham's first African American associate in the late 1950s. Fellow evangelical clergymen shot him dirty looks. A London hotel refused to give him a room. Several of Graham's donors withdrew their support and sent Graham letters with ominous warnings like, "Don't do it, Reverend Graham" and "You're going to ruin your ministry by putting a Negro on your team."

When Howard told me these things, I imagined an uptight white preacher sitting in his church office, turning beet red as he dashed off his angry missive. He probably wrote it right before preparing his Sunday homily on God's unconditional love. And he likely felt he was doing God's will.

Generally speaking, Christians don't do that stuff anymore. We're more enlightened these days. We've read *To Kill a Mockingbird* and analyzed the movie *Crash* over coffee with our friends. We've heard John Perkins speak at our churches and had our feet stepped on by Tony Campolo at our college chapels. We've lit candles at Promise Keepers and volunteered at inner-city churches. We've prayed, apologized and wept. We've broken down walls, stood in the gap and sung Russ Taff's "We Will Stand" a zillion times at our annual combined services. We know there's a racial divide in the church, and we've been throwing our best stuff at it for the last forty years.

In America, and in the church, things have improved—at least on the surface. While few would say racism is completely dead, most suspect it's at least on life support.

Yet my friend's e-mail sticks in my head. Despite all the visible advances in race relations, something is still broken. And *racism* seems like too convenient of a term to slap on it. No, it's now a more subtle and elusive thing. To paraphrase Supreme Court Justice Potter Stewart's famous quote about pornography: "I can't define it, but I know it when I see it."

For many people, "institutional racism" is now the term invoked to describe the unnamable brand of discrimination we experience today. The phrase was first coined by controversial black activist Stokely Carmichael and his coauthor, Charles Hamilton, in their 1967 book *Black Power: The Politics of Liberation*. But sociologist James Jones provided the most concise definition in his book *Prejudice and Racism* when he described it as "those established laws, customs, and practices which systematically reflect and produce racial inequities in American society."

Today's most prevalent examples of institutional racism include the failures of public education in urban communities (why are inner-city schools devoid of proper resources?), imbalances in our nation's criminal justice system (what's with the inordinate number of black males in prison?), and the inability of African Americans and other minorities to keep pace with their white counterparts economically (why do some banks charge higher rates on loans to African Americans and Latinos?).

A popular gimmick on some television newsmagazines bears witness to the reality of institutionalized discrimination. Many will remember the hidden-camera segment on ABC's *Primetime* in which the show sent out two undercover investigators, one white and one black, and recorded how they were treated. There were the employees at the dry cleaner who informed the black person that all jobs in the shop were filled, then moments later told the opposite to the white person. There was the employment agency that was polite to the white but lectured the black. Or who could forget the auto salesman who quoted the black person a higher price and stricter terms than his white counterpart on the same car?

The aftermath of Hurricane Katrina was another gut-wrenching reminder that all is not right. "George Bush don't care about black people!" declared rapper Kanye West, implying that something sinister was afoot. But was the Katrina fiasco a symbol of racism? Middle-class black folk got out of the city early just like middle-class whites, and poor whites were left stranded in the devastated metropolis just like poor blacks. Class, the pundits argue, is the new racism. And there's no question that Katrina magnified the gulf between the haves and the have-nots. Nevertheless, the images of throngs of African Americans trapped in a flooded New Orleans were unsettling. Those are the pictures we remember. If that great meteorological and political catastrophe of 2005 has shown us nothing else, it's that in America, it's virtually impossible to separate class from race.

But institutional racism isn't always the culprit. Periodically, even in this enlightened day and age, racism rears its ugly face in a more blatant, retro fashion—like the Ku Klux Klan marching down Main Street, or a high-profile sports commentator's embarrassing slip of the tongue. Every family seems to have a grandparent or uncle who just can't get past skin color. And I've had white people tell me to my face how much they liked me as a person but would never feel comfortable with someone like me marrying their daughters.

In the summer of 1999, older Americans were reminded of the dark days of commonplace lynchings and other hate crimes when Benjamin Smith, a fanatical white supremacist, went on an evil rampage across Illinois and Indiana. Over the course of four days Smith murdered former Northwestern University basketball coach Ricky Byrdsong, a black man who was walking down a neighborhood street with his kids, and college student Won-Joon Yoon, who was standing outside his Korean Methodist church. Smith also wounded an African American minister and six Orthodox Jews before taking his own life.

During Smith's shooting spree, I remember how hard it was to wrap my mind around the fact that this guy was targeting people because of their race and ethnicity. Though the pattern was clear, I couldn't comprehend it. I had to actually think twice before going outside to retrieve the morning paper.

But Aren't Things Better?

Thankfully, heinous, racially motivated crimes no longer happen with the frequency they once did in our nation. Killing sprees and natural disasters notwithstanding, things have improved. A 2004 Gallup-AARP survey of two thousand people revealed that 55 percent of Americans think the state of race relations is good. And four years earlier, a *New York Times* poll of a thousand African Americans found that only 7 percent thought racism was the most important problem for the next generation of Americans to solve.

These findings tend to jibe with our everyday experiences too. Though many blacks inevitably have a story or two of being watched closely by a store clerk or having to suffer through a racially insensitive joke, for the most part we no longer worry about the possibility of being lynched when we leave for work in the morning.

We can see the change in local churches as well. Eleven o'clock Sunday morning may still be "the most segregated hour in America"—what book about religion and race would be complete without that line?—but these days there are more exciting examples of multiracial churches than ever before.

Pentecostal and charismatic-style churches, with their long history of racial diversity, represent some of the most vibrant multiracial congregations. But even among less-expressive evangelicals, it's no longer unusual to see a variety of races and ethnicities worshiping in the same sanctuary. Consider Faith Community Church in West Covina, California, a megachurch with a technicolor blend of whites, Latinos, Asians and blacks, or the Little Rock, Arkansas, congregation Mosaic, whose black, white and Latino members meet in a former Wal-Mart. Then there's Judson Baptist in Oak Park, Illinois, an eighty-five-year-old church just across the western Chicago border that has evolved with its community over the years to become a solidly multicultural congregation.

The boldest examples of racially blended congregations are usually the result of an intentional focus on ethnic diversity. But a lot of this new diversity also has to do with the changing face of the middle class.

In my daily commute through overwhelmingly white DuPage County, in Chicago's western suburbs, I pass at least three large churches that one might classify as multiracial—or at least they're not exclusively white. American suburbs, once the enclave of white families running away from the cities, are becoming increasingly multiethnic as more African Americans, Latinos and a variety of immigrants stake their claim to a piece of the American dream.

When I began working at the magazine publisher Christianity Today International in 1992, for the longest time I was the only African American on a staff of more than a hundred people. When I did see the occasional black person—who was usually visiting the offices for a business appointment—I gawked in awe. I didn't know whether to be excited or embarrassed. Were they proud to see a brother working at a prominent Christian publisher? Or were they wondering, *What in the world is this guy doing hiding out in this lily-white company?*

In time, a few other African Americans joined the staff and relieved me of my awkward predicament. Today there are nine African Americans at Christianity Today out of about a hundred and fifty. That falls way below the national percentage of African Americans in the United States (13 percent), but it's a heck of a lot better than where we were. Our company's conservative business philosophy has always been "crawl, walk, run." As far as diversity goes, we're not quite to the toddler stage. But the progress is undeniable.

And Christianity Today is not alone. Once upon a time, finding people of color at any major evangelical organization was as rare as a short-winded preacher. Integration seemed an afterthought. Now, I'm regularly delighted to hear word of a new black or Latino or Asian staff member at a Christian ministry or publisher or college. We've come a long way in a decade. But is it far enough?

THESE FOLKS ARE NOT ALARMISTS

My friend's e-mail reminded me that, even though things are looking up quantitatively, privately many of my fellow evangelical integrators harbor doubts and frustrations. If we've made such progress in race relations, why are many of us so glum about the subject?

In preparation for this book, I sent out an informal survey to more than fifty African American evangelicals—male and female, young and old, clergy and laypersons. One of the questions I asked was, "Do you think racism is still a problem in the American church?" Here are a few of the comments I received:

> "If today's brand of racism is financial oppression and blocking access to positions of power and authority, then the American church is guilty."

> "White evangelicals do not on a consistent basis examine or acknowledge the role their racial identity plays in the formation of their faith practice. Just look at the curriculum at

most evangelical seminaries—it's driven by a Eurocentric perspective."

"Two words: white privilege."

"I have had many experiences with the 'institutional racism' that many churches practice. The vast majority of these churches are not ill-intentioned; I am convinced that the major issue is ignorance."

"About ten years ago, I was involved in a sports program at a white church run in part by the youth pastor. When I expressed that softball was not a favorite sport of mine, he made an off-the-cuff comment that he thought 'my people' were good at all kinds of sports. While I knew this man of God meant no harm or malice, it was a statement born out of the ignorance of institutionalized racism. I was young and a new Christian at the time and did not have the eloquence to express how taken aback I was by his statement, considering he was a pastor and I was a baby Christian."

"I've experienced whites who were clearly afraid of me, I believe, because of the stereotypes of how 'black women are forceful and strong-willed.'"

"I recently served on the board of a white evangelical Bible college. I was there to 'integrate' the board. But I found out quickly that integration really meant assimilation."

I wasn't shocked by these comments, but I was challenged to ponder their underlying meaning. This wasn't just standard-issue African American griping.

In his much-discussed book *Losing the Race: Self-Sabotage in Black America,* black scholar John McWhorter explores the self-defeatist attitude he believes is rampant among African Americans. He coined the phrase "the cult of victimology" to describe the mindset that leads blacks to blame all of their problems on racism. I've seen this phenomenon in action, maybe I've even participated. But I knew that the common refrain I was hearing from my respondents and friends was not about playing the race card.

The men and women I surveyed were not angry black activists or impetuous loose cannons. They were born-again, Bible-believing, deeply committed Christians who have devoted their lives to serving Christ and humanity. All of them, like me, work closely with whites on a daily basis and have a number of tight interracial friendships. Several of them have white spouses. They are servants and kingdom-builders, pragmatists who would rather pray through a conflict to find understanding than complain for the sake of stirring the pot. I knew their protests and concerns were coming out of a desire for healing, not destruction.

So what's going on here? To paraphrase Louis Armstrong, "What did these evangelicals do . . . to be so black and blue?"

WHY WE'RE SO BLUE

Some people are born into the faith that they will wear, with varying degrees of comfort, for the rest of their lives. Others pick it up as they go, trying on different sizes and styles before realizing what they really are.

I contemplated the various schools of Protestant Christianity for years, flirting with different varieties of devotion, before I realized that there was a name for the way I believed in God and the manner in which I practiced my faith. I was—and am—an evangelical.

Over the last forty years, a growing number of African American Christians have consciously made their beds in the evangelical wing of the American church. In earlier decades, many black churches subscribed to a biblically conservative but socially progressive theology that would have qualified them, however loosely, as evangelicals—if they had cared about such labels. But they didn't. Identifying themselves with a white-dominated theological movement was not a priority.

Unlike their predecessors, today's post–civil rights generation of black evangelicals is well aware of the theological nomenclature. And consequently, they're grappling with what it means to live with this strange, DuBoisian dichotomy—a "double-consciousness" that often requires them to see their faith through a white cultural lens.

They are people like Dwight Perry, a high-ranking leader of the Baptist General Conference and a former professor at the Moody Bible Institute. Dwight became a Christian as a young adult in the 1970s through an evangelical parachurch ministry. "As a result," he writes in his book *Breaking Down Barriers*, "my perception of my culture was altered, and my theology was filtered through a grid that reinforced middle-class white values. In looking back, I realize that this early influence was beneficial to my spiritual development, but it hindered my ability to connect with my own community."

They are people like Brenda Salter McNeil, a consultant on diversity issues and a popular conference speaker. For years, Brenda was a director for InterVarsity Christian Fellowship before launching her own ministry. She relates to Dwight's experience. "In many of our evangelical organizations," says Brenda, "people of color either leave to preserve their racial identity or become so 'white' that they feel alienated in their home community."

What really troubles some black evangelicals, and you might have picked this up from the earlier comments, is that their white counterparts don't even realize how much their "whiteness" affects their faith. After confessing that she was "sick and tired of racial reconciliation," my young friend who wrote me that e-mail added: "The white Christians I encounter often display a shocking provincialism—a real naiveté about the world around them. Frankly, it's as if they are stunned to find out that their cultural, political, and religious frame of reference is not the only one."

Others share similar observations about feeling disconnected, patronized, marginalized, misunderstood. Yet, like me, they know that the evangelical world is where they belong. For better or worse, this is where

God has called us to serve him. This is home.

And that, in essence, is what this book is about—the loneliness of being "the only black," the frustration of being expected to represent your race but being stifled when you try, the hidden pain of being invited to the table but shut out from meaningful decisions about that table's future. These "reconciliation blues" are about the despair of knowing that it's still business as usual, even in the friendly context of Christian fellowship and ministry.

As a journalist, I've had the privilege of interviewing all sorts of people on a wide range of topics. But the subject I tend to come back to again and again is this matter of race relations in the church. In the pages that follow, you will meet some of the individuals I've encountered during my quest to better understand this issue. They are men and women whose faith in God has brought them to serve, work, worship and live within the borders of American evangelicalism. Through their stories and mine, I hope to give you a glimpse of what it means to be black and evangelical. My hope is that this inside perspective on what I regretfully call "white Christianity" can help both blacks and whites get a better sense of the condition of our racial reconciliation and the distance we need to travel to make it something more authentic and true. If you're looking for "three easy steps" or "ten principles," this is probably not the book for you. Instead, my aim here is to share with you voices, opinions and personal stories that can lead us all to a fresh and more honest conversation across racial lines.

The last thing I want to do is add my voice to the monotonous chorus of black folk crying racism. This book is not meant as an indictment of white Christians. Racism most certainly persists, but my concern is something deeper. Ellis Cose observes in *The Rage of a Privileged Class*, "People do not have to be racist—or have any malicious intent—in order to make decisions that unfairly harm members of another race. They simply have to do what comes naturally." I think this is true for people of all races. Whether it's the sin of racism, greed, pride or indifference, doing what comes naturally is what always gets us in trouble. Better to

channel our thoughts, actions and desires through the purifying filter of
God's Spirit and his Word.

NOT JUST BLACK AND WHITE

Though this book deals primarily with the black-white relationship,
since that is my personal experience, this is by no means just a black-
white issue. Not anymore.

Native Americans, our nation's first occupants, are a people whose
voices are typically forgotten or ignored in our discussions of racial justice. In 2002 the Latino population, boosted by high immigration rates,
surpassed African Americans to become the largest minority group in the
United States. The Asian American populations are also growing at
record paces. Already, in states like California, Texas and Hawaii, whites
are no longer the majority race.

Evangelical believers from these ethnic communities know how it
feels to live on the margins of the movement. In chapter ten, you'll hear
some of their stories as well.

THE CHURCH'S OPPORTUNITY

Julius Lester, an award-winning children's author, explains in *The Blues
Singers* that the blues "are like having the flu in your feelings. But instead
of your nose being stuffed up, it's your heart that needs blowing."

When it comes to race relations among evangelical Christians, our
hearts, heads and souls need frequent blowing. For years, evangelicals
were on the wrong side of the issue—the conservative, status-quo-
maintaining, wait-and-see, please-be-long-suffering, don't-rock-the-
boat side. And while things have clearly improved, there remain shad-
ows of distrust, misunderstanding and inequity. To put it gently, we
ain't there yet.

That's why the reconciliation blues isn't just a sob story; it's a call to
action.

The good news is that, despite our frequent missteps, the church is the one institution that's best equipped to overcome the racial divide. In the late nineteenth century, the anti-slavery movement was forged in the Christian church. Despite secularist attempts to marginalize its religious roots, the civil rights movement of the twentieth century was at heart a church-birthed affair. In both of these cases, the faithful response of a few daring believers gave way to powerful demonstrations of God's deliverance, justice and grace. After a long human struggle, God broke through.

That's why the reconciliation blues can also be a harbinger of hope. To paraphrase the psalmist, "The blues may endure for a night, but joy comes in the morning" (Psalm 30:5).

LIVING IN TWO WORLDS

When you travel, remember that a foreign country is not designed
to make you comfortable. It is designed to make its own people comfortable.

Clifton Fadiman

One Sunday morning in 1977, a school bus from a white Baptist church rolled into my black neighborhood. I don't know how they got my name or when the negotiations with my parents took place, but the folks in the Memorial Baptist Sunday school department targeted me during one of their annual church-growth campaigns, and the next thing I knew, I was sitting in a partitioned room watching flannelgraph Bible stories, mentally salivating over the promise of doughnuts after class.

My parents, who were not regular churchgoers at the time, saw Sunday school as a useful way to get me some additional moral instruction. My mother especially was diligent about keeping me on a positive course. The boys who had nothing to do but hang out on the streets were usually up to no good, she'd often say. She was right.

The bus was the first thing I liked about the white Baptists. Their Bible songs, large gymnasium, and sweet pastries were fine. But it was the bus that initially won my eight-year-old affection. It was different from the one I boarded each weekday morning for my cross-town trek to grade school. This school bus wasn't caution-sign yellow but brown and white, like a petting zoo pony. It had rounded edges, not the boxy angles of the yellow bus. Colorful pictures of smiling children were taped to its interior walls, and the seat cushions didn't numb your cheeks. And get this: The bus actually pulled up in front of my house and a nice white man came to my front door and knocked each Sunday morning. In contrast, the stop for the yellow bus was a half-mile hike down the road.

Buses played a pivotal role in my life back then. Far more than transportation, they became a strange symbol for who I was, where I could go, and what I could and couldn't do.

Shortly before I entered kindergarten, the Rockford, Illinois, school district began requiring a number of students of my racial and social complexion to ride buses across the Rock River to the other side of the city, passing numerous other grade schools, so we could attend Bloom Elementary. The seven-mile ride took about an hour, once you factored in the half-dozen additional pick-ups along the way.

There were days, sitting precariously on the edge of an aisle seat, that I wondered to myself why the students on my overcrowded bus couldn't go to McIntosh or Ellis or William Dennis. Were those schools not good enough for us? And if they weren't, why were most kids from our neighborhoods forced to go to them? Why had a random slice of us been chosen to get up earlier, travel farther and get home later?

I didn't understand anything then about school desegregation or *Brown* vs. *the Board of Education* or the Civil Rights Act of 1964. I didn't perceive myself as being a piece of a larger social experiment, a supporting player in a nation's court-ordered mission to undo two hundred years of systemic injustice. For me, it was just an inconvenient bus ride.

Of course, there were also times when I felt special about my privileged status as a "bus kid." After all, I got to leave the "poor" side of town each day to spend time in the "rich" section. The neighborhoods were cleaner, the white girls seemed friendlier, and I was usually better at kickball than any of the little white boys. (There were some perks to being one of the only black kids at your school.)

Still, for me and dozens of other kids from my side of town, our sense of worth was tied to those yellow buses. Each day the bus took us to a brighter, more hopeful life, only to bring us back home seven hours later.

In mundane ways, the school bus defined who we were. The rich kids walked home or were picked up by their parents; the bus kids had to load up at 3:15 p.m. or risk being left behind. The rich kids could stay after school for sports or Cub Scout meetings; the bus kids didn't have the luxury of extracurricular activities, nor did we get home in time to watch reruns of *The Brady Bunch* or *Batman*. (Shameful confession: some days I would feign illness so I could stay home to watch Adam West in gray tights.) Each school day offered real-life lessons in what it meant to be, in the truest sense of the phrase, from the other side of the tracks.

Most American cities have an unspoken dividing line that splits black communities from white, poor from middle class, urban from suburban. It might be a highway, a park or a literal railroad track. Whatever its form, it provides a physical landmark for the social separation that, by fate or choice, we all practice.

In Rockford, the dividing line is the Rock River, a gorgeous body of water that cuts through the tree-draped town of 150,000 like chalk across the center of a soccer field. To live on the east side of the Rock means nicer houses, bigger yards and easier access to shopping and other services. To live on the far west side (where I am from) means public housing, weed-infested concrete and empty storefronts.

Even as a child, I recognized the difference. I understood that there were essentially two Rockfords.

I don't mean to sound ungrateful. Growing up on the west side wasn't bad, relatively speaking. My childhood was full of lovely memories. I lived in a two-parent home, unlike a lot of my friends who resided a few blocks away in the government-subsidized Concord Commons apartments (a.k.a. "the projects"). I had a yard to play in and a hyperactive mutt named Sherwood. As a young kid, I was content with my life—that is, until I got on the school bus and was confronted with how the other Rockford lived.

The west side was my reality. But the school bus was my entrée to the larger world. It was no small thing, then, that my introduction to white Christianity should come via a bus.

Jesus in White Skin

Like Oreo crumbs in a glass of milk, there was just a sprinkling of black kids in the Memorial Baptist Sunday school program, and I was the only black child in my class. I knew I was different, but at that time I didn't know how much race mattered in America—and especially in American churches.

The first thing I learned in Sunday school was that black is the color of our hearts without Jesus, red is the color of Jesus' redeeming blood, and white is the color of our cleansed hearts after we accept Jesus as our "Lord and Savior." There were even visual aids, construction-paper cutouts that demonstrated the red blood washing away the black sin to reveal a brand-new white heart.

Racial subtext notwithstanding (I was a few years away from making those kinds of hypersensitive inferences), this was riveting stuff for an eight-year-old. Though he didn't wear a cape, this Jesus was a heroic character.

Actually, I was somewhat familiar with Jesus already. My parents periodically took me to a black church around the corner from our house, and he was regularly invoked there: "Praise your name, Jesus!" "Give Jesus the glory!" "Help us, Lord Jesus." But most of the time, I could never figure out what the sweat-drenched preacher was saying beneath his gravelly wails and singsong declarations. In years to come, I would grow to love the unique power and expression of the traditional African American church. But as a young lad, sadly, I didn't get it.

Jesus also hung prominently on our living room wall, where he gazed out ethereally from a bronze-plated wire frame. That the man in the painting looked more like the lead guitarist of a British rock band than a Jewish Messiah didn't bother me much back then. This was the bearded white Savior who was mightier than Santa Claus, Superman and Muhammad Ali all rolled into one.

There were prayers to God in my house. My parents made sure of that. They were usually over dinner or during bedtime. The prayers were short, reliable utterances like "The Lord is my shepherd" and "Jesus wept" and "Now I lay me down to sleep." Though simple, they kept me cognizant of an invisible God who, for whatever reason, had a special interest in our lives.

The God-Jesus thing was a bit more nebulous. My parents taught me that Jesus was good and that somehow he was God. But I didn't really get the full story until I sat in that Sunday school class at Memorial Baptist Church.

"Jesus is God's Son, and he wants to come into your heart," the Sunday school teachers told us each week. "We all are sinners, and we need Jesus to save us."

We learned that it wasn't something you could earn or work for. Jesus' salvation was a free gift. And so I accepted Jesus into my heart about every other week. To recast an old Chicago saying, I was saved early and often. Salvation was free, so I wanted to get as much of it as I could.

We sang bouncy songs like "Jesus Loves the Little Children" and "Roll Away," which had us gesturing wildly like NFL refs as we sang, "Roll away, roll away, roll away. Every burden of my heart, roll away."

There also were those flannelgraph Bible stories and obligatory lessons on obeying our parents and telling the truth. But the main attraction, week after week, was always the "personal relationship with Jesus" message.

Though I went through a variety of teachers during my three-year tenure at Memorial Baptist, the one I remember best is Mr. Kaiser. A tall, heavy-set man with a tight buzz cut and dark-rimmed glasses, Mr. Kaiser would have probably looked more fashionable in the *Leave It to Beaver* era than the disco and *Star Wars* vibe of the late seventies. But he fit the fundamentalist mold to a T.

I remember Mr. Kaiser because he gave me my first Bible. It was a shiny black, hardcover King James Version with color relief maps of the Holy Land printed across its inside covers. I loved the smell of its crisp new pages. It was my unexpected prize for winning the "invite a friend" contest during one of the church's many attendance campaigns. With the tantalizing report of doughnuts and fruit juice after class, I was able to lure the next-door neighbor kids and my buddies from Concord Commons to Sunday school. Four Sundays in a row, I out-invited all the other kids in my class to take the contest crown. Mr. Kaiser signed the front leaf of my new Bible, thanking me for my efforts.

I still have that prize Bible on my bookshelf, though it's no longer shiny and the pages now smell like musty newspapers. What I value more now is the memory of Mr. Kaiser. He was an average, working-class man who answered a call to teach young people about God. Looking back, the image of this thick, redneckish white man teaching a little nappy-haired black kid about Jesus couldn't seem any weirder.

What my head tells me today is that, for many people, the stereotype of a white man who looks like Mr. Kaiser is one of a warm-blooded bigot, the kind you see in black-and-white video clips badmouthing Dr. King or aiming fire hoses at helpless marchers. But what my personal history tells me is different.

LIFE AFTER INTEGRATION

As a post–civil rights baby, the majority of my life has been spent integrating institutions—public schools, white churches, Christian colleges, evangelical ministries. Like many African American professionals from my generation, most of my days take place in settings where I am the only person of color in the room.

I am not lamenting the situation, nor am I blind to how I got here. My faith, family and career have been indelibly shaped by my experience as a child of integration. It has meant the chance for education in better schools. It has meant opportunities to knock on professional doors that, given a different set of circumstances, would have been off limits to someone from my neighborhood. It has meant becoming a part of a Christian tradition that, when true to form, brings God's love and truth to bear on every aspect of life.

But it also has meant living within a religious movement that takes for granted its cultural superiority. It has meant disregarding the occasional stray epithet or ignoring shortsighted comments that beg for a retort. You've heard them, perhaps said them: "I don't even think of you as black," or "Why do black people need to have their own beauty pageants and magazines and colleges? If whites did that, we'd be called racists."

I've never thought of myself as "the token black," but I have enjoyed the privileges of being the only African American in the house. For a long time, I lived in blissful denial of the inadequacy of this arrangement. While certainly conscious of race, I didn't consider it something that would affect people's perceptions of me, nor did I allow it to influence my view of others. I wore color-blinders.

I was the approachable black guy, the white community's friendly interpreter of all things African American. And hey, it was great! I admit it. At moments, I prided myself on being the only black person some white people would ever know personally. When another black person would come into the picture from time to time, I'd feel threatened—like they were trying to intrude on my territory. "These are *my* white people!" I'd think.

The problem, of course, is that no single person can legitimately represent an entire race. Though I lived with that delusion throughout much of my young adulthood, I got a rude awakening once I began to ascend the professional ranks at white evangelical institutions. After a period of racial hibernation, I awoke to the reality of my otherness. I realized once and for all that, as an African American evangelical, I am a black Christian in a white Christian's world.

This fact smacked me upside the head in a variety of ways—the acceptable worship songs at church, the photos used to illustrate magazine articles and ministry ads, the feeling of always having to reeducate my white friends and colleagues. Sometimes it was as blatant as an offhand comment from a white superior at work: "If we publish too many articles on the black church, our audience (i.e., white men) might feel alienated."

Other times, it was in the form of an innocent oversight that had embarrassing consequences: In 2005, several members of our staff at Christianity Today International headed up the planning committee for the annual Evangelical Press Association convention, which was held in Chicago that year. When the brochure for the event came out, I noticed that the entire lineup of plenary speakers and entertainers were white. Odd, I thought, for a convention that purported to echo the vibe of its host city. When I mentioned this to the chairman of the committee, he was apologetic. He assured me it wasn't an intentional dis. The omission might have been avoided, I suggested, had a person of color been included on the planning committee. He agreed.

I hate it when stuff like that happens. I hate having to play the race cop, persistently notifying whites of their lapses in cultural sensitivity. I don't like making my white brothers and sisters feel guilty or ashamed. On the other hand, if I didn't say anything . . .

Many days the weight of it all leaves me exasperated. Sometimes in the silent thumping of my heart, I am haunted by the thought that I will always carry the mantle alone—terrified by the realization that, on a daily basis, if I do not speak up to voice a nonwhite perspective, it will go unheard, like a tree falling in a deserted forest.

I am often confronted, once again, with the same dilemma that beset me when the school bus transported me to the other side of town. I am in the white world but not of it. I have been granted limited access to a place that will never fully be mine. I am a tourist with an expiring visa.

Call of the Wild

By now you might be thinking, *If it's such torture, why does he stay? Why doesn't he just pack his bags and get his black behind out of those white set-*

tings? Find a black church. Find a job at a black organization or in a secular context, where diversity is less of a struggle. Drop the racial angst and just live life.

I know people who have done that—left their white evangelical churches, colleges or jobs to find a place where diversity (or the lack of it) wasn't as much of a daily drain. And many of them became happier souls.

For some of us, though, it's not that simple.

My friend Clarence Shuler, a diversity consultant based in Colorado, was the first African American to play basketball for Moody Bible Institute in the early 1970s and the team's first African American captain. He graduated from Southwestern Baptist Seminary in Texas in the early eighties and was the first African American to work at the Southern Baptist State Convention in Illinois. In 1995, he was offered a job at a major evangelical ministry in Colorado. The group wanted to expand its outreach to African American pastors, and they wanted Clarence to spearhead the effort.

"I took my whole family out there to visit, and they offered me the position on the spot, which is never a good thing," Clarence recalls. At first, he was reluctant to accept. Having been one of the first blacks in evangelical ministries before, he knew how challenging it would be. But then he prayed. (Ah, that dangerous thing called prayer!)

Clarence couldn't sleep for the next two nights. But finally he sensed God speaking to him. "He told me to trust him," Clarence says. "So I took the job."

Chanel Graham, who's in her early twenties, grew up in a mostly white suburb in Orange County, California. It was an established, upper-middle-class community that was filled with million-dollar homes long before everything else in California cost a million dollars. Chanel and her family lived in an apartment complex—"but it was right across the street from the million-dollar homes," she laughs. She became accustomed to being one of the only African Americans in her social circles.

"In school, I was one of the first black people that my friends knew who could 'speak their language,'" Chanel says. "I grew up around whites. I know how they think, and I didn't see much of a racial distinction between people. When they met me, it was like, 'Wow, she's really nice. She's not angry about race or anything.'"

In high school, Chanel attended Saddleback Community Church, pastored by *Purpose-Driven Life* author Rick Warren. Though she grew up going to black churches, Saddleback is where she eventually settled. A graduate of Biola University, an evangelical college near Los Angeles, she now works for a real estate company and is a member of a cutting-edge, but mostly white, evangelical church in Hollywood.

"The worship is mainly David Crowder Band and Matt Redman," she says, lamenting that there isn't a more culturally diverse approach. "I'd love to sing some Fred Hammond songs sometime." Still, Chanel attends this church because it's the place where she feels naturally drawn.

"I am quite comfortable being the only African American in my church," she says. "However, I do have moments when I feel slightly isolated from the rest of the congregation because of my pastor's illustrations or anecdotes. Also, I sometimes miss worshiping with people who may have similar families or cultural practices." Despite these occasional feelings of incongruity, Chanel believes she's where God wants her.

Most Christians are acquainted with the biblical notion of having "a call." We've read the classic passages of Scripture where God calls Moses, David, Isaiah. We've seen Jesus calling out his disciples one by one. We've witnessed Christ's Spirit, in a blinding flash of light, knocking Saul on his butt and spinning his reality a hundred and eighty degrees.

What's more, we've heard this call ourselves. Sure, many of our days are spent listening to heaven's silence, wondering if God is even there. But then, without warning, the Spirit moves. Our senses are sharpened, our thinking transformed. And we know deep in our gut that God is calling.

Sell your car and go to Africa.

Ask her to marry you.

Move to the city and teach at-risk kids.

For some of us, the call is less explosive and more of a slow boil. We've always known we would be preachers or writers or zookeepers. Throughout our spiritual highs and lows, we've never lost that awareness.

That's how it is being a black evangelical, I think. It's God's call. A slow-boiling conviction that, despite our loneliness, frustration or flat-out rage, this is where we're supposed to be. This is where we belong.

"EVANGELICAL"—THERE'S JUST SOMETHING ABOUT THAT NAME

One of the jokes that evangelicals like to tell is that
you know you're an evangelical if liberals think you're
a fundamentalist and if fundamentalists think you're a liberal.
There is something of that middle-ground character to evangelicalism.

Alan Jacobs, professor of English at Wheaton College

Some of the moments I've felt most keenly aware of my "otherness" have had nothing to do with race. They are the times I've been prejudged or condescended to because of my faith.

In October 1997, I went to Washington, D.C., to cover Stand in the Gap, the historic gathering of Christian men that became Promise Keepers' answer to the Million Man March. There, in the shadow of the Washington Monument, more than seven hundred thousand guys turned out. It was not a terribly hot day, but the overwhelming mass of hairy bodies on the National Mall created a sort of greenhouse effect that left the air heavy and, let's just say, less than fragrant.

My main assignment was to interview some of the men who attended the event, but I also wanted to capture a slice of the politically charged atmosphere in which Stand in the Gap was taking place. Across the street from the National Mall was a small army of anti-PK protesters. Ever the thrill-seeker (or perhaps just a glutton for punishment), I decided to grab our photographer and check it out.

There was a religious zeal of a different sort over there. The protesters, made up of members of the National Organization for Women and a variety of gay, lesbian and secular humanist groups, were clearly ticked off. But it felt like a prefab rage, the kind you dutifully summon on command when you need to rail on the opposition. By this time, it had become a sport for secular groups to beat up on the "men only" focus of Promise Keepers. The protesters' gallery of placards listed the usual grievances against the controversial men's ministry—claims of sexism, racism, homophobia. A small but vocal band of atheists raised poster boards declaring, "Keep religion out of government." I tried to interview some of the demonstrators, but once they discovered I worked for a Christian magazine, they didn't want anything to do with me.

Naive me; I fancied myself a neutral, objective journalist, and I expected others to view me that way too. Didn't they know I read the *New York Times* and listened to NPR? For all they knew, I could have voted for Bill Clinton. But the adjective *Christian* immediately sent up red flags in the minds of the protesters. Any joy they seemed to be taking in standing up for their cause quickly froze over when I tried to engage them. To them I was as much the enemy as those sweaty men across the street.

"I suppose you think I'm going to hell because of who I am?" an older gay man said to me. "I just don't want you guys shoving your religion in our faces," added a young atheist man.

The NOW protesters were the most standoffish. But one woman, an attractive twenty-five-year-old Arab American with sunglasses stuck in her silky black hair, agreed to chat with me. I asked her why she felt so strongly about opposing the Promise Keepers assembly.

"I'm here to challenge any ideology that suppresses women," she told me. "Fulfilling your roles as husbands and fathers doesn't give you the right to put down women and block their opportunities."

The young woman's eyes seemed more weary than defiant, but she was clearly ready to rumble if necessary. Part of me wanted to tell her that not all Christian men were out to oppress women, that Promise

Keepers was one Christian organization that genuinely seemed to have an agenda free of right-wing grandstanding. But then the journalist part of me kicked in again, and I thought better of it. At that moment, it was not my role to defend the merits of PK or be an apologist for evangelicalism. I was there simply to report the story. Besides, I could tell nothing I said to her on the fly was going to crack her tough shell. I just wanted her to understand that not all evangelical men were jerks. I thanked her for her time and smiled. But she refused to let down her guard and shot me a cold, cynical stare as she walked away.

CLOSE ENCOUNTERS

As someone who went to a Christian college, dated and married a pastor's daughter, and now works at a Christian company, there aren't many times of the day when I'm outside the warm, protective bubble of the evangelical community. I work in here, live in here, eat in here. But every now and then, I get the chance to wander outside the bubble and experience some real-life friction with those who don't buy into the whole evangelical thing. And though it's a little jarring at first, it feels strangely refreshing. It's refreshing because the hostility aimed at me has nothing to do with the color of my skin.

It's humbling to be reminded that everyone does not automatically accept my evangelical faith. Some people don't believe this stuff. In fact, some people, like those protesters in D.C., think I'm a crazy bigot. Yet God calls me to be patient and compassionate in the face of their anger and unbelief.

More unnerving are the encounters I've had with some conservative Christians who are suspicious of the term *evangelical*. For them it's code for someone who's just a bit too loosey-goosey with the Bible.

A couple of summers ago, I was playing with my kids at a park when I began chatting with another dad who, like me, had been assigned park duty by his wife. My family had just moved to this suburb a few months earlier, so it was nice to connect with other people. This man, with his thinning hair and wire-rimmed glasses, was like a Caucasian version of me. My white twin! We had a nice conversation about the community (he lived just a few streets away from us), and I discovered that he, too, commuted to his job, which was in banking.

Things were going along swimmingly until we started talking about churches. I told him that my family had been on a church hunt for a few months but that we'd recently settled at a local Evangelical Free congregation. He didn't seem impressed.

"You should visit our church," he said matter-of-factly. "We attend Heritage Baptist."

I had driven by the church many times and had even contemplated visiting. But in the phone book it was listed under the subheading of "Fundamentalist Baptist," which, I admit, set off my denominational alarm. If a church is serious enough to intentionally identify itself as fundamentalist, then it must *really* be fundamentalist, which could imply all sorts of things, good and bad. For me, it simply meant my family wouldn't feel comfortable there. (Which, I admit, is based on my own preconceived notions of fundamentalists.) I didn't want to get into any of this with my new friend, but I began to sense that he was on a mission.

"We preach the Word of God at my church," he said, making me wonder what he thought they were preaching over at the Evangelical Free church. "I'd love to have you and your family visit us and then come to my house for a barbecue."

Whoa there, player! Slow your roll. I wasn't ready for that kind of commitment. Our fledgling friendship was moving a little too fast for my taste. "Well, we're really starting to get involved at our current church, and . . ."

I managed to weasel my way out of giving a solid answer. It's hard to negotiate conversations with fellow believers who want to proselytize you into their particular branch of the church. In those moments, I get the same queasy feeling in my gut that I did when Jehovah's Witnesses just happened to show up on my doorstep—for the third time in a month—on a Sunday morning as my family was leaving for church. (Can you say "ambush"?) While the label evangelical may be positive or neutral for some believers, for others it's an invitation to set you straight.

WHAT'S IN A NAME?

What is it with that word? In the New Testament, "evangelical" comes from a Greek term—*evangelion*—which relates to the declaration of the gospel, or "good news," of Jesus Christ. Historically, the term has been used to identify the brand of Christ-centered theology that grew out of the Protestant Reformation in the sixteenth century and was rejuvenated through the various "spiritual awakening" movements in eighteenth-century England and North America. More recently, it has been loosely applied to any Christian who might describe himself or herself as "born-again."

Unfortunately, *evangelical* has lost its luster in our day and age. In fact, many outside the church view it as a derogatory term.

Author Philip Yancey, whose travels have taken him around the globe, devised an informal survey to break the ice with the people sitting next to him on airplanes. "What do you think of 'evangelical Christianity'?" he'd ask them. His seatmates' responses were typically negative. They associated the term with things like hypocrisy, political extremism and intolerance. Never once, says Yancey, did people talk about grace or forgiveness or the love of God.

It's sad but true. For the world, *evangelical* has become interchangeable with terms like "Christian right" and "right-wing conservatives." These names say a lot about morality, politics and maybe even religion, but very little about Jesus' good news.

Place the modifier *black* in front of *evangelical*, and you stir up even more commotion.

In surveying African American Christians about the meaning of the word, I quickly found that, while some were happy to wear it in its classic sense, many rejected the term because of its current connotations.

Some random responses:

> "I am an evangelical because I align myself with other conservative Christians who display traditional values and spread the gospel message of Christ."

> "I consider myself an evangelical, but I resist being defined or labeled by terms that automatically put you into categories or alliances that suggest certain social or political values."

> "Though I am often called an evangelical, I consider myself primarily a Pentecostal."

> "I reject the evangelical label; I am a Christian. Although I understand the term to refer to people who share their Christian faith, I have never used it to identify myself because of its cultural and political overtones (i.e., white Christian conservatism)."

These are the comments of men and women who attend evangelical churches, went to evangelical schools, work at evangelical organizations and run in evangelical circles. That many of them have trouble embracing the evangelical name is both compelling and disturbing. It's compelling because, for each of them, there's a heartfelt story behind why they resist the term. It's disturbing, at least to me, because I still like the name and think it's a shame that it has become so repulsive to a group of Christians whose sweat, prayers and godly examples actually bring honor to the term.

James McGee, a former InterVarsity Christian Fellowship director in Atlanta, is a tall and handsome man with quietly graying hair. He's also a remarkably deep thinker who has spent a lot of time pondering the realities of race in the church. (It's unclear whether that has anything to do with the gray hair.) Though obviously evangelical in his beliefs and affiliations, James prefers not to refer to himself as such.

"The belief system I inherited from my parents and my black church was similar to evangelicalism and fundamentalism," he told me. "But as I get older, I have found those terms have become pejorative and lack meaningfulness to my experience as an African American Christian who also embraces his ethnic and cultural identity."

James worked with InterVarsity for sixteen years, ministering to students at Atlanta's historically black colleges and leading the organization's Pilgrimage for Reconciliation, which took students and staffers on life-changing journeys to deepen their understanding of civil rights history. In 2005 he launched his own consulting firm to help churches, ministries and other institutions with diversity issues, strategic planning and spiritual formation. After corresponding via e-mail, I finally met him at a racial reconciliation event in Indianapolis.

"Man, you are an evangelical if I've ever known one," I told him. "Why the phobia of the term?" I wanted to know why he and so many others got bent out of shape by the term. Why let others hijack a perfectly good word?

He smiled. "If the definition is restricted to its view of God, Scripture and Jesus, then I resonate with it," he said. "Unfortunately, the term carries too much freight that distracts from its true meaning. I'd rather refer to myself as simply a believer and follower of Jesus."

I know what some of you are thinking: *Get over it, Ed! It's just a name.*

Does it really matter what we call ourselves? The early church members were certainly not attached to labels. Indeed, "Christians" was what others called them, not something they created for themselves (Acts 11:23-26). Still, names do matter. So much of our identity and sense of self are tied up in our names and the way others perceive them—or the way we suspect others perceive them. When we can, we like to control that transmission. For many black Christians in evangelicalism, where the default setting always seems to take you back to a "white" view of the world, this is especially the case.

A FAITH IN TENSION

I'm not ashamed to identify myself as an evangelical because, to my mind, the word encompasses much of what I believe as a Christian. If you're an evangelical, it's more or less understood that you've had a born-again experience, that Jesus Christ plays a central role in your life, and that your spirituality may be personal but it's definitely not private.

An evangelical has an active faith—one that is curious, compassionate and engages both the spirit and the mind. An evangelical takes the Bible seriously, is committed to the tenets of orthodox Christianity (the virgin birth, the Trinity, salvation by faith in Christ alone, the bodily return of Christ and so on), but realizes that God's truth is not just about "being good" or escaping hellfire; it's about transforming our world here and now and becoming living representatives of God's love and grace.

C. S. Lewis, that great patron saint of evangelicalism, wrote, "Our business is to present that which is timeless (the same yesterday, today, and tomorrow) in the particular language of our own age." For very practical reasons, the Great Commission calls us to be conversant with the wider culture. I don't want to be closed off from the world; I want to engage it. I want my faith to be one that is nurtured, strengthened and stretched by the Psalms, the Gospels and the Epistles, as well as Bono, MLK and *The Matrix*.

But most of all, I want Jesus.

Do you see the rub? From the first-century believers to the Protestant Reformation to the civil rights movement, the church's role has been defined by tension and paradox—to be wise as serpents and gentle as doves, to lose your life to find it, to be in the world but not of it. The Christian life is a precarious balance between heaven and earth, Christ and culture, spirit and flesh. And evangelicalism was born out of that tension.

Throw race into the mix and things get even trickier.

For people outside the church (and many in it), the term *evangelical* especially means "white." Recent studies by sociologists and political scientists estimate the number of evangelicals in the United States at 25 to 30 percent of the population, or between seventy and eighty million people. However, these estimates usually separate out nearly all of the nation's African American Protestant population (roughly 8 or 9 percent of the U.S. population), which, as I've pointed out, is typically pretty evangelical in theology and orientation. Indeed, 61 percent of blacks—the highest of any racial group, by far—described themselves as "born-again" in a 2001 Gallup poll. As hard as it might be for some secular researchers to believe, there is such a thing as a black evangelical. And we're so diverse that even we don't agree on the name.

"WHY DO ALL THE BLACK STUDENTS SIT TOGETHER?"

Education is not preparation for life; education is life itself.

John Dewey

When the student is ready, the master appears.

Buddhist proverb

From 1988 to 1992, I was a student at Judson College, a Christian school about forty-five minutes east of Rockford. Before Judson, terms like *evangelical*, *conservative*, *liberal* and *fundamentalist* meant almost nothing to me. In the milieu of a Christian college, however, those labels (and their dogmatic application) began to come into focus. This was the place where I first began to think of myself as an evangelical.

Of all the things that a college education bequeaths to us, self-discovery is probably the most dangerous. I got mine at Judson, or at least a significant chunk of it. I've heard the stories of many others who arrived at that startling moment of clarity while in college—that call to ministry, medicine, marriage. For me, it was a call to become a bridge-builder, someone who could bring together people from different races and life experiences and help them find common ground. In a way, it's what I had been practicing my entire life. At Judson I had the opportunity to share a dorm room with three guys—one Mexican, one Laotian and one Caucasian—who would become some of my closest friends in life. Around the campus, Uriel, Neng, Matt and Ed became known as the Rainbow Boys because of our multiracial composition (not that other thing you're thinking). We learned a lot from each other that year.

I also saw myself developing an insatiable hunger for education, which was a far cry from who I was in high school. Though I had worn glasses and looked rather bookish—okay, nerdy—since middle school, I was not genuinely curious about learning until I got to college. Once there, though, I began going beyond my class reading lists, ingesting whatever I could get my hands on—world history, philosophy, theology, literature. The Scottish writer Thomas Carlyle said, "What we become depends on what we read after all of the professors have finished with us," and I can vouch for that.

Sometimes, though, self-discovery leads to more traumatic mental milestones, such as bouts of doubt or even flat-out renunciation of stuff we've unthinkingly believed all our lives, like religious faith. I witnessed at least a few students at Judson who, because of intellectual wrestling or theological questions that wouldn't resolve, decided to take a break from their faith—at least the clear-cut one they'd been practicing since children's church.

I was able to hang on to my faith, but not without it undergoing some major adjustments.

INHERITING A NEW CULTURE

I first visited Judson College upon the suggestion of my high school guidance counselor, Mr. Underhill, who happened to be a devout Methodist. Knowing my interest in writing and Christian ministry, he thought Judson would be a good option for me to explore.

Sitting on the winding banks of the Fox River in the far-west Chicago suburb of Elgin, Judson comprised some six hundred undergraduate students. After a weekend tour of the picturesque campus, I decided to sign on the dotted line. The school's liberal arts emphasis, small class size and short commute from my hometown were all selling points. But the deal-sealer was the generous financial aid offer. The prospect of adding my brown skin to the 98-percent white student body probably played a role in my recruiters' enthusiasm, but I never thought of myself as a beneficiary of any sort of affirmative action. It's hard to see yourself as a piece of the larger social puzzle when you're still trying to figure out how to be an adult.

Judson was founded in 1963 by the American Baptist Convention (ABC). Famous today for being the segment of Baptists who sided with the Northern abolitionists during the Civil War, the ABC's members continue to wear a "progressive" tag that, among other things, distinguishes them from their more "conservative" kin in the Southern Baptist Convention.

The ABC named the school after Adoniram Judson, a pioneering American missionary to Burma (now Myanmar). Judson, who lived the bulk of his life in the early nineteenth century, had one of those unfathomably tragic personal histories that defined his legacy as an evangelical hero. Driven nearly mad by an unjust prison sentence and the deaths of his first wife and their three young children, he labored on for more than thirty years, overcoming sorrow, loneliness and extreme hardship to translate the Bible into the Burmese language. During his lifetime, he led only a handful of Burmese people to the Lord, but the ripple effect has been profound. Today more than one million Burmese Christians trace their roots to Adoniram Judson. It was stories like his that helped me understand the extraordinary heritage that I was a part of as an evangelical believer.

There were more banal inheritances as well. At Judson College, I began to hear and eventually embrace the distinct lingo of Bible-believing Christians. Handy phrases like "If God's willing" and "I'll pray about it" and shorthand terminology such as "quiet time" and "spiritual walk" became rooted in my vocabulary.

And although I tried, I could not escape the ubiquitous rhythms of evangelical pop music. My fellow students raved about stars like Amy Grant and Michael W. Smith with the intensity I had previously seen reserved for Madonna and Duran Duran.

I slowly realized that resistance was futile. At an evangelical Christian college, you either adopt the idioms and conventions of the wider culture or you go someplace else. In fact, many of my fellow African American students did. By my sophomore year, there was almost a complete turnover in minority students. Most of us who did stay the entire four years already had experience being minorities in white settings.

For a guy like me, Judson's lopsided white-to-black ratio was nothing out of the ordinary. In fact, I was invigorated by my round-the-clock exposure to this living, breathing, worshiping thing called the evangelical subculture. I thrived on its social and spiritual energy.

That's not to say I was totally disconnected from my reality as one of the school's handful of minority students. I received periodic reminders of my skin color from random words and situations. Occasionally a white student would innocently crack a joke with racial overtones, forgetting that I was in the room. I usually took it as a sign that I was "just one of the guys," despite my hue.

One day a white friend asked me why most of Judson's black students all sat at the same table during mealtimes. We were still a few years away from the publication of Beverly Daniel Tatum's seminal book—*"Why Are All the Black Kids Sitting Together in the Cafeteria?"*—so I was not able to offer a particularly cogent or insightful response. I think I said something like, "Why do all the *white* students sit together?" and tried to laugh it off. In my gut, though, I knew there was an important answer to that question. I just didn't know how to get at it. Not yet.

SHAKEN IN THE CHAPEL

In February 1991, during my junior year, I served as the student chapel coordinator. Working with a faculty member, I scheduled speakers, planned the week's three services and made sure the P.A. system was fired up come 10 a.m. As a result, I got to introduce guest speakers and rub shoulders with the occasional Christian celebrity who dropped by our campus. Gary Chapman, the now well-known author and marriage counselor, was about a year away from releasing his perennial bestseller, *The Five Love Languages*, when he came to share at chapel. Looking back I realize he was test-driving some of his book's sage advice on our student body. Singer Michael W. Smith, who was mentored by one of Judson's Bible professors, put on a private concert for our campus. Back then, his ballad "Friends" was the one song guaranteed to make Christian girls cry and was therefore a favorite of Christian guys hoping to get their dates in the mood.

We rarely had African Americans or other people of color speak at our chapels. When we did, it was usually an international speaker for Missions Week or a black preacher for Black History Month, which brings us back to that February morning in '91.

I was not familiar with the Reverend Russell Knight, but it was my job to introduce him to the chapel audience. His credentials seemed safe enough: a Moody Bible grad with more than twenty years with Youth for Christ. The one entry on his résumé that should have given me a clue was his role as president of the Chicago Urban Reconciliation Enterprise (CURE), but the fact that it was a branch of Youth for Christ kept me off the scent. Because it was Black History Month, I figured he'd give us a good "black preacher" sermon, the kind that gets white audiences charged up with its emotional zing. But Knight was not a histrionic orator. A compact man with streaks of gray brushed across his Afro, he possessed a deceptively low-key manner. This was not a preacher who demanded a lot of "amens" or "hallelujahs" from his listeners. Instead, he quietly but deliberately laid out his thesis: America is a racist nation by nature, and the American church is complicit in this sin if it continues to remain silent.

What's going on here? I thought to myself, nervously looking around to check the comfort level of the mostly white congregation. *Is it okay to say stuff like that . . . here?*

"Who will speak for justice and risk his own life?" Knight asked us, sounding both literal and rhetorical. "Will you speak for brotherhood if there's a chance that you may lose your own popularity? Will you speak for equality if suffering is in sight? Will you speak for liberation if all other voices are silent?"

Those words—*justice, brotherhood, equality, liberation*—seemed strangely out of place at our chapel service. Not that they were profane or heretical. They just seemed so—foreign. The majority of the messages delivered from our chapel pulpit were about keeping your heart pure before the Lord or going out into the world—usually overseas—to evangelize. Everybody I knew agreed with that stuff already; there was no risk of ruffling feathers. What Knight was talking about, however, felt more provocative, and potentially explosive.

"One of the blights on American history will be that we the church, those of us who call ourselves by God's name, did not lead in the struggle for racial reconciliation, that we did not provide a model, that we were not the ones showing the way."

Of all the things that divide people in the church, Knight said, isn't it odd that it should be something as flimsy and uncontrollable as race and the color of our skin? That's like telling God, "You made a mistake. You shouldn't have made some of us one shade and some of us another." He quoted the apostle Paul: "So from now on we regard no one from a worldly point of view. Though we once regarded Christ in this way, we do so no longer. Therefore, if anyone is in Christ, he is a new creation; the old has gone, the new has come! All this is from God, who reconciled us to himself through Christ and gave us the ministry of reconciliation: that God was reconciling the world to himself in Christ, not counting men's sins against them. And he has committed to us the message of reconciliation" (2 Corinthians 5:16-19).

The key word for Knight was *reconciliation.* I had read that passage of

Scripture many times, but the word never stood out to me before. Not like it did that morning. Suddenly, it became not just a clumsy theological term for our new life in Christ but an urgent announcement of our job description as believers. Just as Christ reconciled himself to us, we have a call to be reconcilers—bringing people to God but also healing the divisions between people.

"Right here on this campus, we can be divided many ways," Knight continued. "But God's purpose is that we should be reconciled. The world awaits a different statement from the Christian community about race. Racial reconciliation has been a very difficult thing for the American church to pursue. We've gone all over the world to win souls, but we haven't dealt very well with racial reconciliation right here in America."

Racial reconciliation. I had never heard the expression before, yet it felt so familiar and true. That combination of words provided an official phrase for what I had been grappling with all my Christian life. As an African American who was usually alone in my Christian surroundings, I knew something wasn't quite right in the church when it came to race. But I was slow to question it. Besides, it seemed like too messy a subject to drag into the bright and tidy world of contemporary Christianity. It hadn't occurred to me that the church was exactly the place where the subject needed to be broached. Knight didn't turn on the light bulb for me as much as he cranked the dimmer switch to full shine.

"To be born white in America makes it almost impossible to escape being a racist." Knight's words were loaded like an automatic weapon, and I could feel an inaudible gasp throughout the chapel. My muscles stiffened as I imagined what all the white people in the room would do with that one. I feared that Knight might have taken it too far. Then he circled back. "I draw a difference between racism and prejudice. Anyone can be prejudiced against another person because of color or class or culture. Racism has to do with one person being prejudiced against the other but also having the power of the system to effect harm or hurt on those who are powerless."

By Knight's definition, minorities in America could be prejudiced but not racist. Only those with the institutional power behind them (i.e., the white man) could fit that bill.

He went on. "You might say, 'I am not racist. I have not done anything to anyone personally.' But the problem with racism is that we have to be careful that we do not enjoy the benefits of it. When we silently enjoy the benefits of racism; when we do not protest injustice to those who are poor, powerless and oppressed; when we decide it's not our problem and go on enjoying the fruits of a racist system, then we too are racist."

I spied a few visibly irritated students and faculty members in the crowd, but several folks actually nodded their assent. Everyone displayed a polite, if not enthusiastic, demeanor.

To be honest, Knight's message probably was more jarring to me than to any of my white friends because it woke me up from a lazy malaise. It gave me permission to think publicly about racial matters and their implications for the church. It challenged me to wonder whether God was calling me to be more than just a silent integrator. Perhaps he was calling me to be a voice for racial reconciliation as well.

Knight concluded his message with a return to the text: "We are therefore Christ's ambassadors, as though God were making his appeal through us. We implore you on Christ's behalf: Be reconciled to God" (2 Corinthians 5:20).

Closing his Bible, he paused for what felt like a brief eternity, then tried to ease the tension with a gentle but serious smile. "My issue is not really with society; my issue is with the church—those of us who say we are followers of Christ. How do we differ from those in our society who are racist?

"We are all ambassadors for Christ," he concluded. "It is not a question of whether or not we are; it's more a question of, what kind of ambassadors will we be? Are we people of reconciliation?"

And just like that, my college journey took a sharp turn.

EDUCATION AND EXASPERATION

In 2000, as part of my job with *Christianity Today* magazine, I attended a conference at Boston University sponsored by the Council for Christian Colleges and Universities. The event, titled "Beyond the Impossible: Strengthening the Bond Between Urban Churches and Christian Universities," brought together about one hundred pastors, students and educational leaders in an attempt to explore the cultural challenges minority students face at white Christian colleges and the practical challenges those schools face in recruiting (and then keeping) nonwhite students. A large part of the weekend involved talking about our experiences as students and graduates of Christian colleges. In one workshop, I listened as person after person recounted the loneliness and isolation of being a minority student at a mostly white school. For some, the struggles were as mundane as not being able to find a suitable barber or beauty salon for black hair (since many Christian colleges are located in out-of-the-way areas where ethnic specialty shops are as common as cheap tuition). Others shared their painful memories of being excluded from cliques, of not connecting with the worship at chapel, of always feeling like an outsider.

I recently was reminded of those stories when I spoke to Chris Williamson, who pastors Strong Tower Bible Church, a multiracial congregation near Nashville. A Baltimore native and the grandson of a Baptist preacher, Chris was passionate about football and rap music in the mid-1980s, so a fundamentalist college in the Virginia boondocks was the last thing on his to-do list. But his church had a relationship with Jerry Falwell's Liberty University, and a visit to the campus opened his eyes to a whole new world.

"I liked the environment," he says. "It was so peaceful and quiet, nothing like Baltimore." Though he felt the Lord compelling him to go there, he also struggled with the temptations of street culture.

"I was still a rather carnal Christian at that point," he explains. "But my dad was the one who said to me, 'I'm not going to tell you what to do, but you need to go to Liberty.'" Chris got the message.

He broke his leg during summer football practice and could not play for Liberty's team like he'd hoped, but he was able to sense a divine plan. "God began to move football and even hip-hop out of my sight as things I had been worshiping more than him. I began to read my Bible and learn how to pray."

He also found a mentor in a man named Michael Faulkner, who at the time was Liberty's only African American vice president. "Michael took me under his wing and discipled me," Chris says. "He challenged me to write raps about God and took me out with him when he would minister around the country. I'd do my little raps, and he'd preach, and folks would come to Christ."

After Faulkner left Liberty to pastor a church in New York, Chris began to feel the frustration of being one of the few minorities on campus. "It was hard, because there was nothing at the school that showed they were even interested in ministering to the African Americans there," he says. "It's like staying at somebody's house and all they fix is macaroni and cheese every night. I'm cool with macaroni and cheese, but how about a little variety? You got some folk here who want to eat other stuff, too!"

He laughs at the oddly appropriate feel of his metaphor. "That's how I felt it was at Liberty. They would keep the macaroni and cheese coming. Very seldom would they have any kind of soul food."

As he looks back today, Chris sees his Liberty experience as a decidedly mixed bag. On the one hand, he grew spiritually and developed his heart for ministry. On the other, he was immersed in a white fundamentalist culture that, he now realizes, limited his perspective on God and life.

"Don't get me wrong. I'm grateful for Jerry Falwell because he gave me a scholarship and I was able to go to school," Chris says. "But I also feel shortchanged because it took me awhile to shake the white off I got there—the stiffness, the narrow theological perspectives. I didn't hear anything about the black church or about Martin Luther King. I didn't have any African American professors. I was taught theology and church growth by conservative white men, as if the only people I was going to minister to were conservative whites. It was difficult."

Chris's story is not unusual. But it's not the only black experience at an evangelical college. David Anderson also pastors a multiracial church, this one in the Baltimore area. David, who grew up in a racially mixed suburb of Washington, D.C., started attending white schools in the fifth grade. Once he was saved at eighteen, he knew the Lord wanted him to be a minister, so he applied to the Moody Bible Institute in Chicago. It was the early 1980s, and the school was still predominantly white despite its urban setting. But that didn't bother David.

"Most African Americans who live in an integrated environment learn to become sociologically ambidextrous," he says. "I was accustomed to living in both worlds."

At Moody, David jumped right in, getting involved in public ministry and student government. The only culture shock he experienced, if you want to call it that, was the white community's reaction to him. "They viewed me as exceptional," he recalls. "I'd never been seen as exceptional before. I had grown up in a two-parent household in a middle-class neighborhood, so I had that kind of stability. I wasn't your poor child from a single-parent home who lived in the projects. But in the eyes of many white people, that's exactly what they saw. They translated it to, 'Oh, David is such an exceptional African American with wonderful skills.'"

It was an ignorant reaction at best; at worst, a racist one.

David acknowledges there were times when he felt alienated or singled out because of race. He laughs now about having to be "the voice of all black people in the world." In many instances careless or ignorant words were directed his way, but he chose not to dwell on those occasions.

"At that point, I had a real vision for multicultural ministry," he says. "I knew that was what God was calling me to, so I turned those negatives into teaching moments. Instead of getting angry and being a recluse, I turned it into energy. For example, I was elected student body president at Moody. I was the first African American to win that office, so it was a big deal! Then I ran my presidency on a theme of unity—I preached on it in chapels, spoke and wrote on it, and used it as a platform to minister."

Because he did not get bogged down in the angst of being a black student on a mostly white campus—real though it was—David was able to change hearts and open minds. On more than one occasion, a white student would come to him and say, "Man, I'm really glad I met you. You're the first black person that I've ever met in person." David wasn't offended by such comments. Again, he focused on the positive. "I'd say to myself, 'Great, I'm glad it was me he met first and not a gangbanger or someone who could have tainted his whole view of African Americans.' If I was the first, and I was his campus leader and a positive experience for him, then praise the Lord! I'll take that."

A MIRACLE AT BIOLA

While doing research for this book, I ran into numerous stories like David's and Chris's. Some individuals took the frustrations as opportunities to enlighten while others felt lost or cheated. My point isn't to judge either response but simply to show that the complexities of race and religion present minority students with unique challenges on Christian college campuses.

Throughout American history, race and higher education have had an uneasy alliance as discrimination and inequities in the system have created an uneven playing field for people of color. Sadly, this has proven to be the case in the evangelical world as well. For many, the account of a young Martin Luther King Jr.'s failure to gain entrance into an evangelical seminary in the early 1950s because of his race is emblematic of the opportunities squandered by evangelicals because of racism. King, of course, went on to receive his training at a more theologically liberal school (and, ironically, many conservative Christians have held that against him ever since). Years later, when evangelical schools began admitting people of color, the transition was not always smooth. For instance, at Columbia Bible College and Seminary in South Carolina, three board members resigned when the decision was made to admit black students in 1963.

Thankfully, evangelicals have progressed since those shameful times. Even so, we're periodically faced with moments of reckoning that grant us an opportunity to measure our progress—events like the L.A. riots, the O.J. trial and the aftermath of Hurricane Katrina, for instance.

In 2005 Biola University was the scene for a moment of reckoning that, according to those present, was a major step forward in improving race relations on the suburban Los Angeles campus.

When Karisa Prescott, a white senior, began noticing how some of her white peers where treating blacks on campus, it disturbed her. Then, after attending a campus event and discovering there were more African American students at Biola than she'd assumed, she suddenly realized how socially segregated her school was. So she set out to change it. Karisa began intentionally meeting nonwhite students, and she wrote an article for the campus newspaper titled "We Are Not All Equal." Sympathizing with her black friends, she hoped to bring some of the racial issues to the attention of white students who seemed oblivious to them.

The paper refused to print the article, citing it as inflammatory, so Karisa posted it online via the campus intranet system, causing a whirlwind of discussion on race. A forum was scheduled to be held in a small classroom, where only a few students were expected to show. The room filled with more than two hundred students, some spilling out into the hallway where they strained to hear the comments of their classmates.

"We all shared stories of our own sinfulness and blindness on the race issue," says Chanel Graham, a senior at the time. "And students admitted to past racist behavior."

It became a powerful and constructive moment in the life of Biola on which the school continues to build. But it wouldn't have happened without the soul-searching of one brave student.

STIRRING MY SOUL

We didn't have a Karisa Prescott at Judson back in '91, but I'm glad Russell Knight blew onto our campus that fateful day to stir our school toward its own moment of reckoning. The crashing waves of Knight's brazen assertions about racial injustice and our obligation to confront it kept things rocking in campus conversations for weeks to come.

Not one to hit and run, Knight remained on campus that day through lunchtime to interact with students and faculty. I was among the handful of people who dined with him. And I'm glad I did. I was able to see that, though he spoke hard truths, he wasn't a rabble-rouser—even if some of the whites on campus had written him off as one. It was refreshing to hear someone speak to a part of my soul that had been waiting for exhortation.

During our meeting, Knight referenced an evangelist named Tom Skinner, a black intellectual who had started questioning the value system of the evangelical church some two decades earlier. Skinner was making waves during a time when Christians were far more ensconced in the racist customs of the day. I jotted down his name, along with the title of his 1968 autobiography—*Black and Free*.

A PROPHET OUT OF HARLEM

The Legacy of Tom Skinner

Understand that for those of us who live in the black community, it was not the
evangelical who came and taught us our worth and dignity as black men.
It was not the Bible-believing fundamentalist who stood up and told us
that black was beautiful. It was not the evangelical who preached to us that we
should stand on our two feet and be men, that God could work his life out
through our redeemed blackness. Rather, it took Malcolm X,
Stokely Carmichael, Rap Brown and the Brothers to declare to us our dignity.
God will not be without a witness.

Tom Skinner, Urbana Missions Convention, 1970

When I said that self-discovery is the most dangerous thing we receive
from a college education, I was thinking of the world of issues and ideas
that was opened to me when I tracked down a library copy of *Black and
Free* and read Skinner's story. In Skinner I saw a reflection of my own
questions and struggles. Though we came from different eras and widely
different circumstances, he and I shared a common sense of evangelical
identity and a common frustration with the way the American church
handled racial matters.

I read the book in one sitting. By the time I closed its yellowed
pages, I knew I would never be able to sidestep race again. God seemed
to be summoning me to get serious about the reality of my African
American heritage and the precarious condition of race relations in the
evangelical movement.

In the years to come, as I more extensively researched Skinner's life and ministry, I discovered that my youthful restlessness was nothing new. God had used Skinner (and leaders like Russell Knight) to rouse college students before. In fact, at the zenith of his groundbreaking career, Skinner inspired a mini-movement of young and precocious black evangelicals to get serious about both the spiritual and social implications of their faith.

Unconcerned about winning popularity contests, Skinner offered a persistent critique of the majority culture, including white evangelicals, challenging his listeners to address issues of racial and social injustice. His closest associates say he was not comfortable in either the white or the black Christian communities. Still, they also say no one has done more to build bridges between black and white evangelicals.

A DOUBLE LIFE

Thomas Skinner was born a Baptist preacher's son in 1942 amid the urban rush of New York City's Harlem. A gifted child, he was aware of his intellect at an early age. "By the time I was 14 I could tell you the difference between existentialism and rationalism; between Freudian psychology and behavioristic psychology," he writes in his autobiography.

Although religion was a part of Skinner's life from the beginning, growing up in inner-city New York gave it little credibility in his estimation. "As a teenager I looked around and I asked my father where God was in all this," he writes. "I couldn't for the life of me see how God, if He cared for humanity at all, could allow the conditions that existed in Harlem."

Despite his father's role as a minister, Skinner came to believe that Christianity was the religion of the American white man. "All the pictures of Christ I saw were the pictures of an Anglo-Saxon, middle-class, Protestant Republican," he often remarked to audiences. "And I said, 'There is no way that I can relate to that kind of Christ. . . . He doesn't look like he could survive in my neighborhood.'"

During his teen years, Skinner began leading a double life. By day he was president of his high-school student body, a member of the basketball team, president of the Shakespearean Club and an active member of his church's youth department. But come nightfall, Skinner could be found among the Harlem Lords, one of New York's most notorious street gangs. Under Skinner's leadership, the Lords rioted, looted, robbed and assaulted other gangs for turf and respect.

He kept up this double existence for several years without his parents' knowledge. But the young man's tortured duality came to a head on the eve of what Skinner expected would be the largest and most significant gang fight ever in New York City. "It would have involved five gangs," Skinner writes in his 1974 book *If Christ Is the Answer.* "If I were to succeed in leading the fellows to victory . . . I would emerge as . . . the most powerful leader in the area."

But as Skinner prepared for the brawl, God—and a rock-'n'-roll radio station—intervened.

At 9 p.m., Skinner expected to hear his favorite deejay's radio show. However, on this particular night, "an unscheduled program came on and a man began to speak from 2 Corinthians 5:17. . . . 'Therefore, if anyone is in Christ, he is a new creation; the old has gone, the new has come!'" The man sounded rough and unpolished, the kind of preacher Skinner found distasteful. But he could not stop listening. "He went on to tell me that Jesus Christ was the only person who ever lived who was both the truth about God and the truth about man. . . . I could never be what God intended me to be without inviting this Christ—who died on the cross because He was capable of forgiving me of my sins, and who rose again from the dead—to live in me. Apart from Him I could never become a new person."

Years of anger, deceit and violence had turned the seventeen-year-old Skinner into a disillusioned young man with no regard for the consequences of his actions. But the Word of God, delivered by an undistinguished radio preacher, broke through his shell of bitterness. Skinner bowed his head and challenged Jesus Christ to turn his life around.

Leaving a street gang was tricky. Few had voluntarily left the Harlem Lords without losing their lives. So when Skinner went to his 129 fellow gang members to announce he was quitting, he knew he would probably not leave the room alive.

Terrified, he informed his gangbanging comrades that he had become a Christian and could no longer be a member of the Harlem Lords. Not one sound came from the bewildered gang. He slowly turned to leave the room. Still no response.

To his astonishment, Skinner left the room in one piece. Later, the gang member who had been Skinner's second-in-command told him that he had felt a duty to kill him that night but that a strange force prevented him. Skinner went on to lead that young man and several other members of the Harlem Lords to faith in Christ. That marked the end of the agnostic gang leader and the beginning of the Harlem evangelist.

Like a street-smart apostle Paul, Skinner preached on the streets of Harlem to a ready-made congregation of prostitutes, drug dealers and homeless people. He also ministered to the youth of Harlem, particularly its gang members. He spoke at neighborhood churches and became a respected figure in the community. Soon Skinner teamed with a group of twelve young church and community leaders in Harlem to form the Harlem Evangelistic Association.

With Skinner as its chief evangelist, the Harlem Evangelistic Association scheduled its first major crusade for the summer of 1962 at the famous Apollo Theater. The group took a crash course in crusade planning and was able to gather the people and resources needed to make the event happen. In the process, however, Skinner began to sense the dilemma of being a black evangelical in America. When his organization approached white evangelicals in New York whom they knew had experience in crusade development, they were met with "cold shoulders." Skinner writes in *Black and Free:*

> I then became aware of how so many white evangelicals are
> willing to say that the Negro community needs Christ and
> needs the preaching of the Gospel, but when it comes to ac-
> tion, they are not willing to join forces with brave and uncom-
> promising Negro evangelicals who make the Gospel of Christ
> relevant in such a community.

It was not only from the white evangelical community that Skinner
and his coworkers felt resistance. Blacks were likewise suspicious of this
young contingent of black men. Skinner continues:

> [We] began to approach Negro evangelical leaders of estab-
> lished reputations in New York City. And again, from many
> of them, we met polite coldness. They said, "It's a wonderful
> thing you're doing. We're behind you . . . we'll pray for you
> . . . but we really can't get involved." Minor doctrinal dis-
> agreements kept Negro evangelicals from joining together in
> a cooperative venture such as the one we proposed.

Nevertheless, Skinner and the Harlem Evangelistic Association perse-
vered. During the eight nights of the crusade, thousands of people from
both Harlem and the greater New York area gathered to hear Skinner's
messages, breaking attendance records for any single event at the Apollo.
Skinner tailored his messages to pique the curiosity of his audience and
to address social and economic concerns of African Americans. Those
expecting a "black Billy Graham," as many had tagged him, were jolted
by Skinner's unconventional sermons with titles like "The White Man
Did It" and "A White Man's Religion."

"At several of the rallies I deliberately chose controversial subjects to
attract the crowds and challenge them with the claims of Jesus Christ in
my own life," Skinner notes. "I knew the implications, and yet I felt that
God was deliberately calling me to go right into the middle of the controversy and make Jesus Christ known."

By the Apollo crusade's end, more than twenty-two hundred people had responded to his presentation of the gospel, and the twenty-year-old evangelist was hailed as a preaching phenomenon.

Skinner's reach quickly extended beyond the Harlem community. A radio ministry took his preaching to listeners throughout the country. Soon, the Harlem Evangelistic Association was relaunched as Tom Skinner Associates, and the evangelist began speaking at urban arenas and on college campuses throughout the United States.

BACKGROUND CHECKS

As an assistant editor with *Christianity Today* in the early 1990s, I attended a variety of conferences and Christian meetings on issues concerning crosscultural ministry, social justice and race relations in the church. Over time, I began to notice a pattern as I spoke to the various evangelical leaders who frequented those events: They all had some connection to Tom Skinner. Prominent megachurch pastors, theologians, business executives and even a few politicians all numbered themselves proudly among Skinner's disciples.

I finally met Skinner himself in the pressroom during a 1993 Promise Keepers conference in Boulder, Colorado. Though I didn't get to speak to him at length, it was an honor to shake the hand of the man who had molded a generation of black Christians—and ruffled more than a few evangelical feathers. A year later, at fifty-two, Skinner was dead of leukemia.

In 1996, to commemorate the fortieth anniversary of *Christianity Today* magazine, the editors commissioned a series of articles on the evangelical movement's "movers and shapers" from the previous four decades. As part of the package, I snagged the assignment to write about Tom Skinner's legacy.

As I spoke to his friends and former associates around the country, the key moment from Skinner's career that kept coming up again and again was a speech that he delivered at the 1970 Urbana Missions Convention, sponsored by the InterVarsity Christian Fellowship college ministry. More than any other moment, that speech defined his reputation as the voice of a generation and laid out the agenda for the thousands of future evangelical leaders who listened to his passionate charge that day.

THE VOICE OF A GENERATION

There had been a buzz in the air at Urbana 70, even before Tom Skinner took the stage in front of some ten thousand people at the famous student missions convention. College students from all over the United States had descended on the campus of the University of Illinois in Urbana-Champaign during the last five days of 1970 to study their Bibles, sing hymns and hear noted evangelical preachers like John Stott and Leighton Ford talk about discipleship and world evangelization. However, on the second evening of the convention, with Skinner at the helm, the event was about to take a whiplash-inducing turn from its typical program.

By its ninth triennial convention, Urbana had become an influential and highly anticipated occasion where countless young adults made decisions to enter full-time Christian service. InterVarsity Christian Fellowship was known as one of the evangelical movement's premier campus ministries. And the Urbana convention was its prime laboratory for mobilization and renewal.

But controversy had also surrounded the event. Three years earlier at Urbana 67, about sixty African American students, all InterVarsity members, had come to the conference with idealistic notions of finding a connecting point for their black evangelical sentiments. What they found instead was a "white" event, not only in terms of attendance but also in terms of vision. To the black attendees, there seemed to be a shocking disregard for the presence and needs of students from non-Anglo cultures.

"I went there bright-eyed and naive," remembers Carl Ellis, then a sophomore at the historically black Hampton Institute (now Hampton University) in Virginia. "But it didn't take long for me to realize something wasn't right. I didn't see anybody from my neighborhood there. I didn't see anyone talking about missions to the cities or about the concerns of the black population. And I said to myself, 'I hope these people aren't deliberately doing this.'"

Ellis and other African American students who had the same misgivings tempered their frustration with a firm commitment to the biblical ideals of evangelicalism. But if they could not find fellowship and encouragement through organizations such as InterVarsity, where were they to go?

The students gathered for an impromptu prayer meeting that went on for hours. "We weren't planning on staying up all night," Ellis continues, "but it was an evening of absolute, fervent prayer that God would raise up an army of African Americans who would be able to minister to our community, our people."

After Urbana 67, Carl Ellis and others recruited and campaigned to ensure the next Urbana convention would not be without a notable black presence. Ellis, Hampton Institute's InterVarsity president, was named to the national advisory committee for Urbana 70. He convinced InterVarsity that a twenty-eight-year-old African American evangelist named Tom Skinner should be added to the list of plenary speakers.

As the winter of 1970 approached and Skinner officially signed on to speak, there arose a confidence among young black evangelicals across the nation that a new day was imminent: Urbana 70 was going to be different. And Skinner was the reason.

"Tom was the most visible black evangelical we had at that time who was willing to tell the truth," Johnnie Skinner, the late evangelist's younger brother, told me. Now a Baptist minister in Knoxville, Tennessee, Johnnie also was influenced by his big brother's ministry. "It was extremely difficult for any black leader in that type of position to tell the hard truth all the time, but he was trying."

Evangelical activist John Perkins agrees. "Tom Skinner had the clearest understanding of the gospel of anyone that I've ever heard, and he was able to articulate it," Perkins says. "He understood the importance of 'on earth as it is in heaven,' and that was the heart of his message—living out the kingdom of God. He was a prophet without honor because he was hitting at themes of reconciliation that were too radical for blacks and whites alike."

Perkins, who is himself revered as arguably the most important champion of racial reconciliation among evangelicals, places his own name on the long list of those influenced by Skinner's work, even though Perkins was more than a decade older than the late evangelist. He told *Christianity Today* in 1994, "Those of us who were brought up in the South, in a more oppressive society, were not able to say some things that needed to be said. Tom was different. He felt freer to express himself, to confront white people, because he had a strong sense of personal dignity.

"After he confronted an audience, people would be glad when someone like me came along, because I seemed moderate in comparison."

In 1970, the U.S. Civil Rights Act was six years old, both Martin Luther King Jr. and Malcolm X were dead, and urban race riots were a common feature of the nightly news. The nonviolent resistance of the King era had given way to the militancy exemplified by Stokely Carmichael and the Black Panthers. A sense of dashed hopes had seized the civil rights movement. Despite key advances, American race relations appeared stalled. And in the estimation of many blacks, they were in fact edging backward.

Not coincidentally, just as Skinner's ministry was attracting more attention from whites, his outspoken views on issues of social injustice facing the black community intensified (a fact that would lead many Christian radio stations to drop his program due to its "political" content).

In countless speeches and in books such as *How Black Is the Gospel?* and 1970's *Words of Revolution*, Skinner declared Christ a radical revolutionary, not unlike Barabbas or, by extension, the Black Power revolutionaries of his own day. No-holds-barred presentations of Scripture marked Skinner's style. In *How Black Is the Gospel?* Skinner portrays Barabbas as a violent Jewish insurrectionist who, with his band of angry "guerrillas," hurls Molotov cocktails into the homes of the "honky" Romans to usurp the corrupt Roman Empire. And Christ is a revolutionary who agrees with Barabbas about the oppressiveness of the Roman occupation but who advocates a different kind of insurrection. Skinner writes, "Jesus would have . . . said, 'Barabbas, when you burn the Roman system down, when you have driven the Roman out . . . what are you going to replace the system with?'" The solution did not lie in the violent overthrow of "the Man," Skinner said, but rather in a spiritual revolution within men's and women's minds and hearts.

His freewheeling interpretation of the Scriptures was intended to grab his audience's attention and shock them into a new understanding of Christ. So it was no surprise to Skinner that whites found his assertions harsh and at times irreverent. But if the evangelist's shock tactics lost him audiences among whites, Skinner's fan base among African American students on college campuses boomed.

Many young black evangelicals, while committed to Christ, had been captivated by the Black Power rhetoric of the late sixties. The Black Panthers and the Nation of Islam challenged black students to abandon any hopes of seeing racial progress within the parameters of white power structures. And the pressure was even greater for young black evangelicals, who were often ridiculed and mocked for adhering to "the white man's religion." For them, Tom Skinner's radical approach to Christianity provided the firepower needed to defend their faith against Black Power assaults.

Ron Potter, a theologian and minister based in Jackson, Mississippi, first met Skinner while a student at Wheaton College in the late sixties. According to Potter, the group of African Americans at Wheaton during his era represented the first significant black student presence there. In 1969, Potter's group rallied to have Skinner speak on the Wheaton campus. "Few black evangelicals in the late sixties were able to take on the charismatic evangelists of the secular Black Power movement," says Potter. "But Tom was able to help us address the attacks made upon us."

He adds that Skinner also assisted Wheaton's African American students in responding to racial injustices at their school. "We were experiencing a lot of subtle forms of racism at the time, but we could not describe what it was," Potter recalls. "Tom was able to articulate for us what we had been feeling. He helped us to differentiate between biblical Christianity and the Christ of the white evangelical culture."

Kay Coles James, a former presidential appointee under George W. Bush, and a noted conservative speaker, was a student at Hampton Institute in the late sixties when Skinner made several visits to that campus. "We were trying to figure out what it meant to be black and Christian in the culture of that day, and we realized we were not going to find all the answers through groups like InterVarsity," she says. "What we found in Tom Skinner was a towering figure of a man, straight off the streets of Harlem, who had a real connection with our unique needs. He gave us hope and empowered us as Christ's ambassadors to those blacks on our campus who were skeptical toward Christianity."

And, to the delight of Potter, James and hundreds of other young black evangelicals across the nation, this was the Tom Skinner who arrived at the Urbana 70 missions conference ready to stir ten thousand students to a higher understanding of the gospel message.

As a result, in 1970 more than five hundred black students and Christian leaders flocked to the Urbana convention. The black evangelical renaissance that the students had prayed about three years earlier actually felt within reach.

"THE LIBERATOR HAS COME"

Soul Liberation didn't look like any other music group that had ever performed on the Urbana stage. Their Afros and multicolored attire made them seem more like a sanctified Sly and the Family Stone than an evangelical praise and worship ensemble. And the predominantly white Urbana crowd was not entirely prepared for their style of ministry. The group regularly accompanied Skinner to college campuses and evangelistic rallies, but as they took the stage to do a song prior to Skinner's key-note address, the band members knew they were heading into un-charted territory.

After a day and a half of singing familiar hymns and choruses, the Urbana crowd was startled when Soul Liberation began playing the group's gospel anthem, "Power to the People," whose lyrics borrowed liberally from Black Power idioms. "It was such a radical departure and so different that people gasped when we began," says Henry Greenidge, the group's leader. "Our clothes, the drums, the bass; it was too much for them."

After the initial shock, however, the audience jumped to its feet to sing along as it picked up on the Christ-centered focus of Soul Libera-tion's song. For the white students, it was an instant lesson in contem-porary black culture.

Greenidge, who is now senior pastor of Irvington Covenant Church in Portland, Oregon, remembers that second night of Urbana 70 as being "very electric." "It felt like something historic was happening," he says. "Tom was our spokesperson, and we knew as soon as we finished he would be giving a major address. I think Tom's speech and our music had a hand-in-glove effect."

When Tom Skinner finally stepped to the podium, the crowd was al-ready charged for what they anticipated would be a revolutionary ad-dress. The majority of the black students sat together in front of the plat-form, awaiting sage words from the man who, for at least that evening, would be their Moses.

Skinner began his Urbana address, officially titled "The U.S. Racial Crisis and World Evangelism," with a friendly, humorous warm-up that offered a brief history lesson on the plight of the "Negro" in Amer-ica. Drawing from secular and biblical sources, the young evangelist dramatically uncovered the sad state of race relations in the United States and the American church's failure to address the problem. One by one, Skinner picked apart the issues that held evangelicalism captive to white prejudice and indifference.

On U.S. nationalism: "As a black Christian I have to renounce Americanism. I have to renounce any attempt to wed Jesus Christ off to the American system. I disassociate myself from any argument that says a vote for America is a vote for God. I disassociate myself from any argument which says God sends troops to Asia, that God is a capitalist, that God is a militarist, that God is the worker behind our system."

On white fears of miscegenation: "I don't know where white people get the idea that they are so utterly attractive that black people are just dying to marry them."

On white evangelicals who ignored the plight of the inner city: "If you . . . told him about the social ills of Harlem, he would say, 'Christ is the answer!' Yes, Christ is the answer. But Christ has always been the answer through somebody. It has always been the will of God to saturate the common clay of man's humanity and then send that man in open display to a hostile world as a living testimony that it is possible for the invisible God to make himself visible in a man."

After some twenty minutes of provocative preaching, Skinner brought it home with a proclamation of a revolutionary Savior who had come to "infiltrate" and "overthrow" the existing world order to establish his Father's kingdom.

At the end, Skinner's voice scraping its upper registers, he reached for one last oratorical blast: "You will never be a radical," he said to the students, "until you become a part of [Christ's] new order, and then go into a world that is enslaved; a world that is filled with hunger and poverty and racism and all those things that are the work of the devil. Proclaim liberation to the captives . . . go into the world and tell men who are bound mentally, spiritually and physically, 'The Liberator has come!'"

A thunderous and seemingly endless standing ovation, from black and white alike, shook the University of Illinois assembly hall. The Liberator had come.

"It was incredible," remembers Ron Potter. "It was like heaven on earth."

"Tom was absolutely prophetic that night," says Carl Ellis, now president of Project Joseph, a church renewal ministry in Chattanooga, Tennessee. "I knew several people who were there who just didn't give a hoot about Christianity, but they were shaken to their foundations that night."

"That speech was a pinnacle of visionary and prophetic expression," says Albert G. Miller, a professor of religion at Oberlin College in Ohio. "It gave both African Americans and whites a vision of what being a black evangelical Christian could be. That they could actually impact not only a community, but a world."

Pete Hammond is a white InterVarsity executive who was instrumental in planning Urbana 70 to include more African Americans. Through the years, he has worked hard in the areas of urban ministry and theology, taking to heart the message of leaders like Tom Skinner. But that evening at Urbana, after Skinner's speech, Hammond felt a rush of conflicting feelings. "For me [back then], it was a mixture of fear and joy," he told me. "I was fearful that we were going to polarize white evangelicals who had never engaged the subject of race so directly. But I was joyful over seeing young black leaders together in a national position to worship, to celebrate and to find affirmation and a platform to bring their brilliance to the church."

William Pannell, a professor emeritus at Fuller Seminary in Pasadena, California, and the onetime vice president of Tom Skinner Associates, remembers sitting behind Skinner on the platform as he delivered his address. "It was the most powerful moment that I've ever experienced at the conclusion of a sermon," he says. "For perhaps the first time in the history of the Urbana conventions, not only was a black evangelical a keynote speaker, but he was able to cast the Christian mission in the context of a world that was falling apart. Tom was not just talking about going into the world to evangelize; he was talking about linking hands with the Savior who came to take over."

A HUMAN LEGACY

By the 1980s Skinner had discovered a new direction. Having survived a divorce, years of rejection from many in evangelical circles and bouts of depression, his ministry turned away from an evangelistic emphasis and focused more on Christian leadership training. In addition, Skinner's role as chaplain of the Washington Redskins football team expanded his influence in mainstream celebrity circles.

In 1981 Skinner married Barbara Williams, an attorney and secretary for the Congressional Black Caucus in Washington, D.C. With marriage to Barbara came new happiness, and through her connections his ministry made inroads into the black political elite and traditional black church leadership that Skinner had once disparaged. Powerful figures in the black community such as Jesse Jackson became his close confidants.

But even while reaching a more mainstream audience, Skinner's central motif of the "kingdom of God" never shifted. "The stories might have changed, but his main theme remained the same," says Barbara Williams-Skinner, who now directs the Skinner Farm Leadership Institute in Tracy's Landing, Maryland. "He was constantly looking for that body of believers who were the life expression of God's kingdom."

Patrick Morley, a white Orlando, Florida, business executive and Christian author, was deeply affected by Skinner in the latter half of the evangelist's life. After Skinner delivered seminars to Morley's company, the two became fast friends. "Tom poured hundreds of hours into discipling me around our dinner table, after tennis or in a car going somewhere," Morley told *Urban Family* magazine. "He never would give up on anyone; [he saw] the potential in everyone, even when others would write you off."

Skinner and Morley joined together in 1993 to launch Mission Mississippi, a racial-reconciliation ministry based in Jackson. The pair also traveled to Israel together in January 1994, just four months before Skinner's death. "Tom made some blacks and some whites angry," says Morley, "but he deeply influenced an entire generation of people to think more deeply about their lives."

Skinner's untimely death came as a shock to many. At his funeral, an unusual collection of individuals from all corridors of American society came to pay their respects. The diverse lineup included Jesse Jackson, poet Maya Angelou, Malcolm X's widow, Betty Shabazz, and Nation of Islam leader Louis Farrakhan—not to mention the countless evangelical men and women who had followed and worked with Skinner during his heyday in the late sixties and early seventies.

"He was a true reconciler," says Johnnie Skinner about his brother. "Even in his death, he was bringing different people together."

Today, more than thirty-five years after Skinner's landmark speech at Urbana 70, there is still a fresh sense of hope and purpose among those young black evangelicals who were inspired by Skinner's memorable words.

"The real meaning of it is becoming increasingly apparent to me as I continually encounter men and women who have made the choice for ministry in part because of what happened there," says Henry Greenidge. "Back then, we wanted to see white evangelicalism make wholesale changes, but it wasn't happening. However, out of that movement came people like Tony Evans, Crawford Loritts and many other black leaders who are making a huge impact in today's church."

Adds Ron Potter, "When Tom died, an era came to an end. But that means those of us who were mentored by Tom now have a responsibility to carry on that vision. We sometimes complain that 'the Liberator' he preached about is late. Well, he may be late because he's waiting on us."

STILL TALKING

Before joining Tom Skinner's team, William Pannell was a popular itinerant evangelist and worship leader on the Youth for Christ circuit. In 1968, at age thirty-nine, he stirred up the evangelical community with his provocatively titled book *My Friend, the Enemy*, which offered a black evangelical's frank (and sometimes blistering) critique of white evangelicalism. In a positive review, *Christianity Today* called it a "stinging and slashing attack on white complacency, hypocrisy, paternalism, and smugness." The controversial tome became required reading for anyone who cared about the church's response to America's racial crisis in the late sixties.

When I interviewed Dr. Pannell for this book, we chuckled at the similarities between the premise of my project and his thirty-seven-year-old book. "It's funny," he told me. "I was speaking to a friend of mine recently, a white woman, who was rereading *My Friend, the Enemy.* She was struck by how current the book feels. She said, 'Change a few names and words here and there, and it reads pretty much as if it were written today.' It was a sobering observation."

Tom Skinner's books, especially *Black and Free,* possess a similar timeless quality. In today's church, many of the same race issues remain on the table—even though our nation's civil rights situation has improved markedly.

Skinner's message is still relevant. That people my age and younger have now stepped onto the trail left by the iconoclastic evangelist and his associates signals both good and bad news.

The good news: Brand-new generations of black evangelicals are being challenged and empowered by a latter-day prophet who put his finger on the pulse of the evangelical church's dysfunctions on race and social justice when most people were afraid to talk about it.

The bad news: We still need to talk about it forty years later.

5

THE FIRST SHALL BE LAST
On Being the "First Black"

Whenever you take a step forward, you are bound to disturb something.
You disturb the air as you go forward, you disturb the dust, the ground.
You trample upon things. When a whole society moves forward,
this trampling is on a much bigger scale; and each thing that you disturb,
each vested interest which you want to remove, stands as an obstacle.

Indira Gandhi

When Brooklyn Dodgers general manager Branch Rickey decided to add a black baseball player to his team's roster in 1947, people thought he was nuts. Segregation was the order of the day and meddling with it was like playing percussion on a hornet's nest. After World War II, some voices did insist the practice should end: "Black soldiers defended our nation's freedom in the war, yet they can't eat in the same restaurants with us?" But the separation of the races was so ingrained in our national psyche that it would take a Herculean effort to expunge it, something bigger than just taking down the Jim Crow signs. It would take a grand act of the imagination, something almost mythic. And what better venue for it to happen than in major league baseball, that most allegorical and American of sports?

Branch Rickey was devoutly religious and a huge fan of Abraham Lincoln, but his main motivation for wanting to integrate baseball was not altruistic; he wanted to beat the Yankees. The Negro Leagues were full of superstar talent, and he wanted the Dodgers to be the first to tap into it. All the initial headaches of crashing the segregation party would be worth it if he could field a team that would bring a championship to Brooklyn, he reasoned.

The famous account of Rickey's first meeting with Jackie Robinson has been told so many times that fact and legend are probably indistinguishable. But we do know Rickey spared no candor in prepping Robinson for the venomous resistance he would face while integrating America's national pastime.

It wouldn't be easy, Rickey told him. Robinson was guaranteed to be on the receiving end of racial slurs and physical taunts from opposing teams, the crowds in the stadium and possibly his own teammates. Rickey tested him by playing the role of a foul-mouthed bigot. He got uncomfortably close up into Robinson's face and spewed a sampling of the vile epithets the man would likely hear. He piled insult upon ugly insult until he could see the contempt burning in the ballplayer's eyes. Then, as the story goes, he stepped back and took a swing at Robinson's head.

He missed, but his point didn't. "You're going to have to put up with a lot of this kind of stuff," he told Robinson.

The tall, athletic Robinson was visibly rankled by this white man's role-playing. *Was he looking for some passive fool?*

"Mr. Rickey," he said, "do you want a player who doesn't have the guts to fight back?"

And that's when Rickey delivered his most memorable sound bite. "Jackie, I want a ballplayer with the guts *not* to fight back."

Rickey pulled out a copy of Giovanni Papini's classic novel *Life of Christ* and presented it to Robinson. The lesson was clear: No matter what, turn the other cheek.

And thus began baseball's "great experiment."

As Rickey had predicted, there were wild balls aimed at Robinson's head from the pitcher's mound—along with rocks, watermelon slices and Sambo dolls raining down from the stands. There were vicious epithets. There were even death threats.

Through it all, Robinson's task was to turn the other cheek. And because he did, he opened the door for other black athletes to integrate professional sports in America. But more than that, his example provided a model of hope that transcended sports and inspired a generation to have the guts to confront segregated strongholds in every part of our society.

Today, Jackie Robinson's name is synonymous with the idea of being "the first" African American to integrate a particular institution or participate in some venue formerly reserved for white Americans alone. Hence my friend Howard Jones was hailed by *Christianity Today* as "the Jackie Robinson of evangelism" for his achievements as Billy Graham's first African American team member. Invoking this baseball legend's name signals both a conferring of honor and a remembering of how far we've come.

It's an ultimately bittersweet tribute.

WHO'S ON FIRST?

Because of our nation's sad history of bigotry and injustice, identifying and documenting "the first black" has become a popular pastime in the African American community. There are shelves and shelves of books devoted to the stories of "first blacks" from every amateur and professional rank in American life.

As a child, I remember the wonder and pride on my parents' faces whenever they'd encounter a black doctor or lawyer or even a black contestant on a TV game show. "Stella, come here," my dad would shout. "Come see this colored woman on *The Price Is Right*." Among blacks (and I'm sure other minorities in America), it's a big deal when we're able to see tangible evidence of our emergence into the mainstream and our ascent up the rungs of achievement.

One would think that, by now, we'd have moved beyond the need for "first black" excitement. But it's still news when Colin Powell becomes the first black secretary of state or Halle Berry becomes the first black woman to win a best lead actress Oscar. Today's first blacks are far less controversial. They don't get death threats anymore. And one clear sign of our nation's racial progress may be the groundswell of popular support for the idea of someone like Colin Powell or Condoleezza Rice or Barack Obama running for president. As *Chicago Tribune* columnist Clarence Page said, "It's great that we have advanced so quickly from a time when black skin was an indisputable liability for a presidential candidate to it becoming a measurable asset."

Once again, however, it's easier to point to racial breakthroughs in secular culture than in the evangelical world. While one can now find African Americans at the helm of mega-corporations like Time Warner or Ivy League schools like Brown University, good luck finding them at a major evangelical publisher or college.

Some people will argue that there simply aren't enough "qualified candidates" out there. But if that excuse were ever true, it certainly isn't any longer. These days, at conferences and other events, I regularly meet incredibly gifted current and future Christian leaders from the African American community who would make fine additions to any evangelical organization's staff or board. The question is, how serious are we about finding these "qualified candidates"?

Rodney L. Cooper, a professor of leadership and discipleship at Gordon-Conwell Theological Seminary, laments the dearth of African American professors at major evangelical seminaries. He wonders if evangelical institutions spend too much time reacting to change rather than leading it.

"Most of the roles I've filled in evangelical organizations have been more accidental than intentional," he told me from his office in Charlotte, North Carolina. "I'm the only African American on a faculty of thirty-three people, and Gordon-Conwell [whose main campus is near Boston] is the third largest seminary in the country. Even at Dallas Theological Seminary, which has had more than three hundred black graduates, I don't think they have any full-time African American professors. Something's wrong with that picture."

On the positive side, Cooper said his seminary's last major hires included himself, a woman and a Korean-American man. So he knows change is possible. But first, he added, change needs to happen at the uppermost levels of evangelical organizations—on the boards and in the presidents' offices—before any real progress will be made.

"I know that a part of the reason I'm here at Gordon-Conwell is because we have several African Americans on our board, as well as several whites who are committed to intentionally integrating the faculty," he said, adding that the greatest resistance to this focus on diversity has come from the older white faculty members. "They feel endangered. I tell them what they're feeling is what we, as African Americans, have been feeling for a long time—the possibility that you may not be selected, that you won't get a chance. That's a new feeling for many of my white colleagues, and it's threatening. There's still a cadre that wants to protect and make sure they take care of their own."

This isn't just a matter of affirmative action or politically correct integration, especially for the Christian community. (Truth is, we now have plenty of minority professionals who are doing just fine on their own. There's a whole subculture of successful, middle-class African Americans who frankly have no need or desire for white approval or interaction.) But in our efforts to advance the gospel, shouldn't we want our institutions to reflect the diversity of God's kingdom? Wouldn't each of us benefit professionally and personally from being exposed to those whose cultural backgrounds and experiences are different from ours?

A recent Stanford University study revealed that when white college students are placed in discussion groups with black students—or with students who hold opinions in the minority—they display higher levels of complex thought. The report goes on to suggest that racial diversity has positive effects on education and intellectual growth. Though the study was done in a college context, it's easy to imagine its implications for the church and Christian workplace as well. Pursuing diversity is not just for the benefit of minority groups; we all stand to gain from it. But without a sustained, intentional effort to make changes, it's easy for evangelical institutions to fall right back into their "white" default mode.

I don't mean to sound jaded or cynical. I understand that a big reason for this lack of a sustained, intentional effort is the natural human tendency to gravitate toward that with which we're most comfortable. But I'm also guessing that much of it has to do with appeasing donors and constituencies. Money and economic control go to the systemic root of a lot of our race problems in the evangelical church—but I don't want to dwell there. Suffice it to say, it's risky for a nonprofit to upset its funding base. Whether it's a matter of donors, subscribers or even church members, it's a lot easier—and cheaper—to keep an existing patron than to find a new one. When Jesus said, "You cannot serve both God and Money" (Matthew 6:24), he was foreshadowing one of the fundamental complications of running a Christian organization today. Ask any pastor or ministry leader; it's a crazy balancing act. Yet it speaks to the heart of where our priorities are, and who we are as people of God.

WAIT UNTIL THEY'RE DEAD?

During my interview with Pastor Chris Williamson, he recalled a discussion he had with one of the old pioneers at Jerry Falwell's Thomas Road Baptist Church.

"We were talking about diversity in Christian organizations, because he knew that my church was interracial," Chris said. "But this older man said something to me that was very revealing. He said that things won't change in the American church until his generation dies off, that that's just the way it is. He wasn't proud of it. In fact, he was rather embarrassed, and I appreciated his honesty. But I later thought to myself, *Wait a minute, evangelicals never just accept things the way they are. They're going to step out and try to change situations as it pertains to same-sex marriage or*

abortion or evolution in schools. But when it comes to social justice and insti-
tutional racism, then all of a sudden they just accept it the way it is until a gen-
eration dies off? Come on! The idea of that really sickened me."

Is it good enough to just wait on the older generation to pass before
addressing the core issues that hold us back from real racial progress? I
think most God-fearing evangelicals would reject that kind of defeatist
thinking.

Many books and articles have noted that the younger generations of
evangelicals have already mounted a formidable challenge against the
tired status quos of our various institutions. Some predict that, as
younger evangelicals rise into greater leadership roles, things will indeed
change for the better. I don't completely dismiss that theory. But what's
more likely to happen is that, once given power, those younger generations will settle into the habits of their predecessors. It's only natural.
Like daytime soap operas, the actors may change but the storylines endure. Despite their innovative new churches and progressive approaches
to ministry, the next wave of evangelicals will invariably follow the same
script as their elders—unless the pattern is broken here and now.

Crawford Loritts, who spent nearly three decades as one of Campus
Crusade for Christ's top speakers, is now the senior pastor of Fellowship
Bible Church, a predominantly white congregation that draws more than
two thousand people each Sunday in Roswell, Georgia. In the welcome
video on the church's website, Loritts tells viewers, "We are a people that
love other people . . . and we're a people that love God." Neither he nor
the church seem to play it up, but it's hard to overlook the fact that
Loritts, an African American, is leading a dynamic, majority-white
church in a former Confederate state. For many people, the true sign of
racial progress in the evangelical world will be indicated by the willingness of whites to be led by people of color. "When that becomes a common thing," one black leader told me, "then you'll have proof that our
'racial reconciliation' is real."

In a prescient moment back in 1989, Loritts shared one reason he believes it's crucial for evangelicals to pursue racial unity:

> By the year 2010 this country is going to be majority minor-
> ity. White evangelicals, whether they like it or not, they need
> us. It's not a question of whether it would be a nice thing to
> team up and do something with one another. We are indis-
> pensable commodities of one another's existence. In this
> world, with all the mess that's out there, the only solutions
> are going to be from joint partnership—and unity.

Racial unity is not just a matter of being nice to each other (though that's helpful) or feeling good about our annual choir exchanges (those things can be both inspiring and brutal). No, unity in the body of Christ is an essential part of our mission as ambassadors of the gospel. Without unity, we will never shine as brightly as God intends.

GETTING UNSTUCK

I know many of my white friends and colleagues, both past and present, have at times grown irritated by the black community's incessant blab-bering about race and racism and racial reconciliation. They don't un-derstand what's left for them to do or say. "We have African Americans and other people of color on our staff. We listen to Tony Evans's broad-cast every day. We even send our youth group into the city to do urban ministry. Can we get on with it already? Haven't we done enough?"

I can empathize. I know for a fact that black people are tired of all the blabbering as well. I would love to move on. Somehow, though, on our way to racial resolution, we've gotten stuck in the mush of familiar pat-terns. These patterns lead us to believe we've accomplished something simply by, for example, hiring a person of color or speaking to a person of another race at church or hugging someone we don't know at a conference three hundred miles away from home. Again, I don't want to trivialize peo-ple's intentions. These types of gestures are good and necessary. But we should not let symbolism displace the purpose of the acts themselves.

White Christian, you have people of color on your staff, but are you seeking their ideas and perspectives? Does your corporate culture reflect sensitivity to the feelings and concerns of nonwhite individuals? You've spoken to the black people who attend your church, but have you had them over to watch the game after service? Have you invited them to join your small group?

Black Christian, have you been keeping at an arm's distance those white acquaintances who have attempted to get to know you better? Have you written off some whites as racist because of a silly comment they didn't realize was offensive? Have you taken the time to educate them about your culture, answering all of their probing questions about your hair care or your opinion of some black celebrity?

White Christian, you hugged and apologized to that nameless black person at an out-of-town conference, but have you made any new friends across racial lines since you've returned home? Are you now more attuned to the subtle ways society treats whites differently from blacks?

Black Christian, are you hanging on to unresolved bitterness against whites? Are you harboring bigotry of your own? Have you been ignoring God's command to extend grace? Are you resisting his call to become a bridge between the races because you realize that bridges, by definition, must be stepped on?

CHALLENGING THE STATUS QUO

As Christians, it's possible for us to do wonderfully holy things crossculturally without ever experiencing a fundamental change in our thinking about crosscultural matters.

Just think about the vexing predicament of the apostle Peter. Urban missions expert Ray Bakke calls Peter's radical transformation in Acts 10 the apostle's "second conversion," but it did not come without a struggle. At the time Peter was the premier evangelist of the early church, the leading voice of the movement. It was a pivotal period in the life of the young church, and decisions had to be made. Would the church remain a primarily Jewish outfit, or would it allow itself to be shaped by the growing presence of Gentile believers? Despite his profound love for Christ and all of his success in ministry, Peter was a man torn by prejudice. Says Bakke, "Deep down he still cared deeply about his own culture. He did not relish becoming a minority in his own church. He hadn't resolved completely his own ethnic and cultural identity."

Peter does eventually come to terms with his bigotry, thanks to a dramatic vision and a divinely arranged meeting with a Roman believer named Cornelius. Peter's amazing turnaround sets the stage for a multicultural church where all of its members stand on equal footing. At Cornelius's house, Peter humbly declares, "I now realize how true it is that God does not show favoritism but accepts men from every nation who fear him and do what is right" (Acts 10:34-35).

Reflecting on Peter's transformation, Bakke (who is white) confesses to seeing shades of his own experience in the great apostle's struggle. He remarks:

> Peter reminds me of myself and others who know the gospel
> and preach orthodoxy in the traditionally approved manner
> in our churches. . . . Many souls, perhaps hundreds or even
> thousands, have turned to Christ as a result of our ministries.
> But deep down, like Peter, we really wish the new converts
> would learn to sing our songs and do ministry our way. Peter
> had been with Jesus and made many adjustments in word
> and deed over the years, but still had become the epitome of
> the cultural status quo.

To break out of the white cultural status quo of today's evangelical movement, we must confront hard truths about ourselves and about the things that truly drive our institutions. If we don't, we'll never find ourselves in that place of total freedom and faith and unity that allows us to be used by God in radical ways. As evangelical leaders, are we trusting in God to use us to build his kingdom—in all its glorious diversity—or are we too busy trying, in his name, to preserve our own?

If we expect to see God move us toward a place of true and lasting unity, we cannot do business as usual. Nor can we wait for an older generation to pass away.

6

WHEN BLACKS QUIT
EVANGELICAL INSTITUTIONS

We smile, but, O great Christ, our cries
To thee from tortured souls arise.

Paul Laurence Dunbar, "We Wear the Mask"

I used to take a certain amount of pride in being the first African American on staff at *Christianity Today* magazine. But I was routinely humbled when I realized that being the first isn't all it's cracked up to be. When you're the only one, there's always a sense that you're in an extremely unstable position, as if one healthy gust of wind could topple you—and with you, the hopes of other people with your skin color. I often found myself having to voice the "black Christian perspective," as if I could somehow represent an entire community's views. Sometimes I had to remind myself to "be black," to make sure the rest of the editors weren't overlooking some important point or advancing something that might be insensitive to nonwhites. After a while, this became far too exhausting. On the one hand, I wanted to be a good race man and represent "my people" well. But on the other, I hated all that responsibility. I just wanted to do good journalism and be an excellent editor.

Washington Post sports columnist Michael Wilbon echoed the opinion of many African Americans when, in a column about golfer Tiger Woods, he wrote, "There's a social responsibility that comes with being black in America, regardless of the profession, and that obligation increases exponentially with stature. There are rules adopted out of necessity, even desperation, by the subculture we as black folks inhabit. . . . One of the rules is you speak up, even if it means taking some lumps."

I did my best to speak up when it seemed necessary, and at times I caught grief for it. Other times I decided it would be best to act like Jesus before Herod and simply say nothing. It gets old, you know—this taking-your-lumps business.

I like the way Jackie Robinson framed it as he boldly began the mission of integrating baseball: "I know that I have a certain responsibility to my race, but I've got to try not to feel that way about it because it would be too much of a strain." He added, "I also know that I've got to hit."

Robinson understood that no amount of racial protest or rhetoric would make any difference unless he backed up the symbolism of a black player integrating the majors with tangible results. At the end of the day, he still had to hit the ball.

I want to hit the ball. I want to let my talent, sweat and integrity do the talking. Often that's the only way to get your message across to a majority culture that, after ages of doing things their way, sometimes has difficulty seeing or hearing you, even though you're standing right in front of them.

"People sometimes ignore you," says Bruce Fields, a professor of systematic theology at Trinity Evangelical Divinity School in Deerfield, Illinois. "Or, if there is attention directed toward you, it is subtly communicated that you are not to be taken as seriously as a white person of similar status, experience and credentials."

Fields was the first full-time African American professor on Trinity's staff, and in July 2005, he became the first to be tenured. Yet being one of the few blacks at the institution, he continues to harbor doubts about his presence there. "I think about being a minority here all the time," he confesses. "There is rarely a time when I am not thinking about it. I am thankful for who God has made me, and I am grateful for his call on my life—but not all the time. I find myself being distant, untrusting and often angry that I have internalized a certain sense that I am not good enough. I know this is wrong, and I've been working with a support network to overcome it. But it's difficult."

From a young age, many of us have been told that it isn't good enough just to be good. As a black person, you had to be better than whites in order to make it. I think this notion was probably even more true in past years, but there will always be some whites (and even blacks) whose opinions of African Americans are so low that they're just waiting for them to slip up. Oftentimes, whites don't even realize they think this way. It's a reflexive response.

When I was in college, I was invited to speak to a youth group that one of my friends led at a local suburban church. They were on an overnight ski trip to Wisconsin, and I was to share some devotional thoughts with the kids around the fireplace during an evening session—a fireside sermon, if you will. My friend wanted me to "give my testimony" and encourage the kids in their relationship with God. Simple enough. But on the trip up, I started freaking out. Though I was a good six or seven years older than most of the teens, I was worried about my coolness factor. Would they find me hip and fun enough? What's more, I was the only black person in the group. I was used to being the Solo Negro, but being at a predominantly white ski resort—a hundred miles away from familiar turf—*and* having to deliver words that were both funny and engaging before a demanding teen audience left me petrified. As it turns out, it wasn't the teenagers I should have been concerned about.

When it was time for me to talk, my adrenaline surged. I was ready. My spiritual lesson included a mixture of Scripture, corny jokes and C. S. Lewis quotes, and it was going well—until one of the parent chaperones started chiming in during my talk. She was trying, I suppose, to legitimize my message for the kids. Now, I'm not against an engaged audience, but it became clear that this parent was interjecting because, for her, my words didn't carry enough credibility. I couldn't imagine her doing that to a white speaker. I doubt she even understood what she was doing.

I felt the perspiration beading on my forehead and on my chest beneath my sweater. It was hard enough speaking to a mercurial pack of teens; I didn't need a patronizing white woman "clarifying" everything I said. I felt angry, humiliated and demoralized all at the same time. But I couldn't let anyone see that.

So I put on my mask.

BEHIND THE MASK

When I talk about "wearing a mask," I'm making reference to a famous poem by Paul Laurence Dunbar, an African American poet from the late nineteenth and early twentieth centuries. I discovered Dunbar in high school and, as an aspiring writer, was immediately drawn to him. His eloquence and boldness with words and ideas inspired me to pursue my dream of a career in the communication arts.

Dunbar, who was the son of former slaves and a classmate of Wilbur and Orville Wright at his all-white high school in Dayton, Ohio, worked as an elevator operator until he could establish himself nationally as a writer. The industrious young man even sold copies of his first self-published book for a dollar to his elevator passengers. A prolific author, he wrote short stories, novels and a play. But poetry was his primary claim to fame. He died in 1906 at age thirty-three.

In his day, Dunbar was torn between the expectations of white audiences and his own sense of identity as an artist. Some literary critics marveled at the fact that his lineage was of pure African descent, with no Caucasian ancestors. Whites loved his colorful dialect poems (the hip-hop of that era, perhaps), which portrayed nineteenth-century plantation life. The poet, however, also wanted to be respected for his less-popular "pure" English works. "We Wear the Mask" and countless other poems express the struggle and internal ache of living as a black person stifled by the stereotypes and meanings projected on him by a white world. "We wear the mask that grins and lies, / It hides our cheeks and shades our eyes," begins Dunbar's classic verses. When I first read them, my soul trembled.

I love Paul Laurence Dunbar not only for his inspiring collection of writings but also for his courage and insight as a human being—his willingness to tell the truth, as best he could, in an age when black artists were embraced and marginalized at the same time.

CRYING OUT

Metaphors such as masks and invisibility are common throughout the history of African American literature and art. In 1952's *Invisible Man,* Ralph Ellison uses stunning surrealism to expose the realities of a twentieth-century America that not only divided blacks from whites but from each other—and, ultimately, from their own sense of self. After the novel's nameless protagonist bungles an assignment to chauffeur a white trustee of his black college, he returns to the school to face the wrath of the college president, Dr. Bledsoe. The protagonist tries desperately to explain that it was the white man who insisted he take a detour into an unsavory part of town, that he was just trying to please him. Bledsoe explodes, "*Please* him? . . . Why, the dumbest black . . . in the cotton patch knows that the only way to please a white man is to tell him a lie!"

For many, Ellison's biting cynicism still resonates as a salient commentary about the unspoken social contract between blacks and whites.

Through the years, African Americans have found freedom and power in cloaking their protest and brokenness in the colors and rhythms of their creative passion. And like the psalmists of Israel, whose recurring cries of rage and despair jolt the pages of the Old Testament, some black artists, such as Dunbar at times, have found renewal and liberation in directing their shouts to God.

I suggested earlier that I do not want to engage in a pity party for black evangelicals crying racism. This is not about McWhorter's "cult of victimology." Rather, I'm trying to address a family matter. When so many otherwise successful African American Christians still express frustration and disappointment over the state of race relations in the church, as my research indicates, something is not right. We need to listen and learn. As members of the body of Christ, we should be determined to hear and understand the concerns of our brothers and sisters. If one part of the body is hurting, we should respond. But first we need to understand the reasons why. Why do so many successful black evangelicals feel compelled to wear their masks? Worse, why are some giving up on the idea of racial unity in the church altogether?

SHENENEH HAS A HAIRBALL

Anita Morgan (not her real name) is in her early thirties. Before moving to California to attend graduate school and work for a secular firm, Anita was employed by an influential Christian group in Washington, D.C. When she arrived at the organization as its only African American staffer at the time, she was fresh out of college and eager to grow. But her four years there were marked by ongoing problems with two coworkers who, Anita says, "had entrenched racist attitudes."

"One of them was a twentysomething white woman whom I'll call 'Mary,'" Anita says. "She was originally from the Southeast and literally tried to force me into a friendship with her. I quickly picked up that it had something to do with white guilt. She invited me to lunch during my first few weeks on the job, and in a rush of emotion blurted out, 'I don't know many black people. I want to learn from you, Anita.' In my mind I thought, *Are you joking?* But I also detected a fierce insistence that lay underneath her seemingly humble words. I realized she thought she could control my friendship."

New to the organization and to full-time professional life, Anita felt trapped. "I knew that I didn't owe friendship to anyone," she says, "but my instincts told me if I ignored Mary's 'offer of friendship,' she could make life very unpleasant for me because she held an important position in the corporate structure."

Moreover, Mary was one of four members of the strongest social clique in the office.

"I needed her friendship in order to socialize and gain credibility with the other women who were also lower-level administrators. As a result, I attended book clubs at Mary's house, spent Friday evenings at her dinner parties, and allowed myself to be introduced as her good friend. I made all of these compromises because I wanted to be successful in my job."

Anita didn't necessarily dislike Mary, she just felt smothered and preyed upon, like she hadn't been given a say about the terms of the relationship. Sometimes well-meaning whites can, in the name of racial reconciliation, come on too strong. In their desire to have a crosscultural friendship, they unknowingly perpetuate the classic dynamic that gives the white person the upper hand.

Anita continues, "The second person I had difficulty with was 'Liz,' a fortysomething white woman who replaced Mary after she left her position. Liz had a different approach to crosscultural relationships. She felt that she was an expert in black-white relations because she had grown up as a missionary kid in Latin America."

Liz had also dated and then been engaged to an African American man for eight years, during which time she played the role of "auntie" to his little nieces. Even though their engagement dissolved, Liz believed she had a special connection to the black community. In fact, much to Anita's dismay, she had named her black-and-white cat "Sheneneh" after the stereotypically "ghetto" character from the television sitcom *Martin*. "For some reason, I found the cat's name extremely offensive," says Anita. "The first time I heard her nonchalantly mention it, I almost started hyperventilating."

When she first met Liz, Anita wore her hair in a short, natural hairstyle. A few months later she started having it straightened and curled. "One Friday evening I stayed overnight at Liz's home after a late-night social outing with the women from the office," Anita says. "While we settled in for the evening, she complimented me on my new hairstyle. I said, 'Thank you' and was ready to move on to the next topic. However, she raved for over five minutes about how the new style was such an improvement for me."

The implication, of course, was that Anita's hair looked better straight—i.e., "white." She felt hurt and insulted.

"I thought Liz's obsession with my appearance showed her slightly superficial nature," she says, "but more than that, I got this sinking feeling in the pit of my stomach that she also had some major racial issues to work through."

Anita verbally walked Liz through the process of uncovering the prejudicial beliefs that made her think only white people's fashion sense could be used to measure beauty. Liz gasped audibly as she began to realize her racially insensitive behavior. Tearfully, she began recalling other experiences from the previous eight years. That evening Liz experienced a series of revelations about the dysfunctional way she had related to her black fiancé. Says Anita, "During our two-hour conversation she grew very cold and vindictive with me. I believe my presence became a sort of mirror that revealed her past mistakes."

In the two years that followed, Anita avoided Liz in work and social situations. "I did not feel the need to indulge her in the same way I had with Mary, because by then I had two years' worth of credibility within the company," she says. "Plus I had moved to a department that was not closely tied to hers."

Anita defines racial reconciliation as "creating a climate where people deal honestly with racial and cultural issues. It should put an emphasis on action, so that leaders make changes based on feedback learned through dialogue (both formal and informal)."

She adds, "To me, the proof of racial reconciliation is when the culture of an organization allows for different styles of leadership and self-expression so that people from all cultural backgrounds can be considered competent without hiding their cultural distinctives from others."

As a whole, Anita says, the church has done a poor job of creating the climate she describes. However, it was through a local church that she met two white friends who, she says, "demonstrate true racial reconciliation to me at this point in my life."

She says both of these friends have given her genuine, no-strings-attached friendship and even introduced her to their families. "Both of them focus on the academic and social interests that we share rather than our cultural differences. Both of them take a very humble approach to our relationship, and neither would describe our actions as 'racial reconciliation.' We simply deal honestly when we interact with one another."

BLACK FLIGHT

How many times does something need to occur before it qualifies as a trend or a phenomenon? Anita Morgan's experience is not an isolated one. Over the years, I've noticed a pattern of African Americans joining evangelical organizations, often as the first black, only to leave two, three or four years later—usually in frustration.

Remember my friend Clarence Shuler from chapter one, the one who after much prayer and deliberation finally accepted a position at a big ministry in Colorado? He left after three years. He doesn't regret his decision to work there. He launched a new department for the ministry that is still active today, and it was a time of spiritual growth for both him and the organization. "I had a bad attitude at times," he admits, "because I was working in an organization designed without people of color in mind. We were tolerated but not embraced as equals. That kind of thing eventually wears you down."

As the first black manager at the organization, Clarence didn't feel like a "golden boy" the way he had before, even with a bigger salary and new house. He simply obeyed God's call to work there. He says, "God used my struggles to humble me, and for that I'm grateful. I eventually learned to follow God again, instead of telling him what to do."

But the problems Clarence experienced didn't stem simply from his pride. There were legitimate issues with certain leaders in the company that left Clarence flustered and questioning their commitment to true biblical diversity. "It honestly was a battle all the way," he says, "but my interactions did help some of those very conservative people adopt a more biblical view of God's perspective on diversity, and that was worth some of the pain."

Five years after leaving, Clarence met with the ministry's president to discuss his ordeal at the organization. That emotional meeting concluded with the president apologizing to Clarence for the unchristian attitudes he had encountered while employed by the company. And Clarence, in turn, apologized for not always responding to the adversity in a Christlike manner. He finally experienced closure.

But not all endings are as . . . tidy.

"Listen. You could not pay me to be the head, or even on the board, of another evangelical organization."

That's Darrell Davis (not his real name; some identifying details have also been changed). Before moving to the East Coast to become senior pastor of a large African American church, he was a youth pastor and ministry leader in California and then, most notably, the director of a large parachurch ministry in the Dallas-Fort Worth area, a position he took in the early nineties. Darrell stayed at that organization four years before bolting. He says, "The fact of the matter is that African American males usually last four years or less in management or upper-management positions at evangelical organizations. That's about as long as it goes."

But why? Saying that it's because of racism is too easy. Everybody says that. What concrete, identifiable problems lead to black flight from high-level jobs at evangelical institutions—especially when it takes so long to get African Americans into those positions in the first place?

Darrell, a firm yet soft-spoken preacher, talked to me a few years ago for an article I was writing on African American leadership. He told me he hadn't been looking for a job when that large parachurch ministry called. "They had interviewed over a hundred people, but more than one person had told them about me. I fit all their descriptions." After Darrell interviewed for the position, "the Lord spoke to my heart, and said, 'This is going to be your job.' And as my wife was praying, she got the same message."

So when they offered him the position, he accepted. For a while, things were fine—"I was the flavor of the month," he said with a smile. But over time, Darrell began to sense tension between himself and his colleagues as he tried to implement new ideas. "I wasn't trying to make trouble," he told me. "I was just there to do my job. But people will read into what you do out of their own fears and insecurities."

I asked him if he could elaborate for the record; he politely declined. But after a brief pause, he said, "Let me tell you a story." So I listened.

> It was my third year with the ministry. By that time I was very well known in the local community because of the level of management I was at, running the ministry for the entire country. I knew everybody and they knew me—not just locally, but from all over the country and around the world. So I got a call from a prominent white Christian leader, and he asked to go to lunch with me. I met him and his vice president at a Chili's. And as we're sitting down eating, all of a sudden this guy starts crying, and I'm sitting there wondering what's going on. Then he told me this emotional story about how he hadn't been able to sleep. He explained that God had blessed him, his children were healthy, he was known throughout the country. But, he said, "I've had a hard time sleeping throughout the night." And I was thinking to myself, *Why is he telling me this? I'm not a therapist.*
>
> "I just came back from an annual conference on the other side of the country," the man told me. "Normally after this conference, a group of leaders meet and deal with other issues. A bunch of us got together to discuss reconciliation and cross-

cultural ministry. Normally, I can deal with the things going on in the back room."

Then he admitted to me, "Usually, when your leaders come into the meeting, we make them feel right at home and let them be part of the decision-making process. But to be honest with you, Darrell, the decisions are made before your leaders ever get in there. I'm used to hearing the jokes and the use of the n-word. But this time when the jokes were going on and people were saying things, it didn't sound right to me."

He paused to wipe the tears from his face.

"I've been home two or three nights," he continued, "and I can't sleep. It's bothering me."

That's when the other guy starts crying. And this leader said, "How can I get over this? How can we be friends?" Then he began going through this whole sort of Promise Keepers spiel.

I looked at him and said, "That's what this is about?"

"Yes, brother," he answered.

I was silent for a moment, then I asked him, "Do you like football?" He seemed a little puzzled, but he said yes. "I do, too," I told him. "I used to coach high school and college ball, and I have a lot of friends who play pro. I love a good game, and I love to cook out. So, here's what we do: I need to get to know you, and you need to get to know me. Why don't you come over to my house?"—I was the only black in my suburban neighborhood at the time. I said, "Bring your wife and meet my wife, and we'll just sit and talk and get to know each other. I'll barbecue some steaks, and let's start there."

He was taken aback. He said, "You want me to come to your house?"

"Yes," I told him. Then I said, "If you want me to sit here and clear your conscience for all the crap you did, I can't do that. Friendship is not cheap. It takes time and commitment." I gave him my home phone number and told him to give me a call, that I'd be looking to hear from him.

I never heard from him again.

Many months later, Darrell opened up a little more about why things had soured for him at the parachurch ministry. Through his many church contacts, Darrell had connections with civil rights matriarch Rosa Parks. In the middle of his tenure as director, when Darrell was in search of a speaker for a major fundraising event, he got the idea to invite Mrs. Parks. To his delight, she agreed.

At first everyone at the organization seemed thrilled. A spectacular banquet was planned, and North Central Texas was brimming with excitement. A living legend was set to headline the fundraiser, and the buzz couldn't have been greater. All signs pointed to a successful event. Then, without warning, Darrell received a call from his organization's top leadership. They were pulling the plug on the banquet.

"They were concerned that Mrs. Parks might be viewed as too liberal for some of their supporters," he recalls. "They were worried that she didn't seem to come from an evangelical background."

That fiasco, says Darrell, was the beginning of the end. When he left the organization, people accused him of being angry and bitter. "Listen," he told me, "when I was gone, I was gone. I wasn't bitter. I love God. I don't have time for bitterness."

These days, Darrell stays busy with his church responsibilities and national speaking engagements, as well as faith-based community development projects near his church's inner-city neighborhood. Though he insists that he harbors no resentment toward white evangelicals, he does say, "There are some of us who have worked with our white brothers on the other side who probably will never do it again. And it's not that we don't love them; it's that we don't have the time. We don't have the heartbeats available. After that frustration kicks in, time after time, you get tired.

"Besides," he adds, "there's a lot we can do over here [in the black church]. There's a lot going on right now that can actually bless all of our evangelical brethren and help teach them."

I could sense Darrell's sadness as I spoke to him. I could tell he'd been wounded by his experience. I believed him when he said he wasn't bitter—but I also believed him when he said he'd never work at a white evangelical organization again.

A PROVIDENTIAL PARTING

Perhaps one of the most famous and important "first black" defections was that of African American publishing giant Melvin Banks. In 1970 Banks left a comfortable position at Scripture Press in Wheaton, Illinois, to start Urban Ministries Inc. in his basement. Nearly forty years later, UMI is the largest independent publisher of Christian educational materials for African American churches.

In the late 1950s, Banks was one of the only black students at Moody Bible Institute and later at Wheaton College, where he earned a bachelor's degree in biblical archeology and a master's degree in New Testament. In 1960 he was hired by Scripture Press, which had been challenged by black pastors to extend its outreach to their churches. Banks's assignment was to network with black churches and turn them on to Scripture Press's materials. But there was one problem—the materials themselves. Black pastors were not eager to sign up for Sunday school curriculum targeted to a white, middle-class market.

"One of the first things that occurred to me was that we needed to include some black faces," Banks told me in a 1999 interview.

Upon his urging, Scripture Press began including some nonwhite faces in its curriculum, "but not nearly enough." When some of the publishing company's white clientele voiced concern about the inclusion of too many black faces, Banks began to wonder if diversifying the existing materials was a bad idea.

In 1966 he presented a proposal to start a line of black-oriented products, but the idea was rejected. Two years later, James Lemon arrived as the new vice president of marketing; he was fascinated with the proposal and over the next two years helped Banks launch *Inteen*, a magazine-like Sunday school curriculum for African American youths. By this time, Banks was convinced that the product would never survive and thrive as part of the Scripture Press line. So, with Lemon's blessings, he started his own publishing company. *Inteen* became the first publication of Urban Ministries Inc.

For its first twelve years, UMI operated out of the basement of Banks's home on the South Side of Chicago. To its credit, Scripture Press paid his salary during UMI's first year and provided design and printing help for the premiere issue of *Inteen*. "They were very gracious," Banks said.

Today, Banks is founder and chairman of a fifteen-million-dollar company that serves more than 100,000 Sunday school, vacation Bible school and Christian adult education programs across the nation. In addition, a nonprofit wing of the company funds conferences and outreach ministries, including the Circle Y Ranch in Michigan, which hosts more than six hundred inner-city children each summer. In the world of evangelical publishing, Banks is regarded as a pioneer and a legend.

"Looking back, I can see that God wanted to make sure UMI was his organization, not mine," Banks told me. "The route that he took me through to get here makes it mandatory that I must always give him the credit."

IF AIN'T BROKE . . .

So what to make of this "black flight" phenomenon? Honestly, I don't know. Perhaps it's not for us to figure out or fix. Sometimes I wonder if anything is even broken.

For one thing, I'm thinking like a black evangelical who has always swam in the white evangelical pool. To my mind, racial unity means fellowshiping and serving in the same churches and the same ministries—and, especially on the business end, that typically means blacks and other minorities going over to the white side to mix things up. But the journeys of Melvin Banks, Darrell Davis and others force me to reexamine my assumptions. The onus need not always be on nonwhites to cross over. The bridge should go both ways, right? And fruitful partnerships can result even when we're not joined at the hip.

Sometimes, I suppose, "separate but equal" isn't necessarily a bad thing. But is it the *best* thing?

WAKING UP TO THE DREAM
Evangelicals and Martin Luther King Jr.

Injustice anywhere is a threat to justice everywhere.
We are caught in an inescapable network of mutuality,
tied in a single garment of destiny.
Whatever affects one directly, affects all indirectly.

Martin Luther King Jr., "Letter from the Birmingham Jail"

As one of only two blacks attending Los Angeles Baptist College (now known as The Master's College), Dolphus Weary was having the time of his life experiencing a new world of white faces and middle-class culture. Born and raised in rural Mississippi, Dolphus had assumed he would spend the rest of his life there—until a recruiting team offered him and a friend a chance to attend a Christian liberal arts college in Southern California. Other Christian schools he had been interested in refused admission to black students. But through the urging of a bold admissions director and an ambitious basketball coach, this thirty-year-old ultraconservative institution agreed to make Dolphus and his friend its first "Negro" students.

Dolphus earned above-average grades (knowing anything less would be unacceptable) and helped lead the school's basketball team to a nineteen-and-five record. Things were good. The poverty and provincialism of black life in southern Mississippi were out of sight, out of mind. He was glad to have escaped it—that is, until the day's big news made its way across campus.

As Dolphus left the library on April 4, 1968, a white student approached him and said, "Did you hear? Martin Luther King got shot."

"I remember running to my room, flipping on the radio and listening to the news report," he recalls. A rifle bullet had ripped into King's neck as he stood on a motel balcony in Memphis, Tennessee. The civil rights leader was rushed to a hospital in serious condition. "I was devastated," Dolphus says.

As he sat on his bed holding back the tears, he could hear voices down the hall: white students talking about King's shooting. But Dolphus quickly realized that they were not just talking; they were laughing.

"I couldn't understand what I was hearing," he says. "These Christian kids were glad that Dr. King—my hero—had been shot. I wanted to run out there and confront them." Instead, he steeled his nerves and lay prostrate on his bed. Finally, as the newscaster delivered the awful update—"Martin Luther King has died in a Memphis hospital"—Dolphus could hear the white voices down the hall let out a cheer.

Today Dolphus Weary is a national speaker and the executive director of Mission Mississippi, the Jackson-based community-development ministry started by Tom Skinner and Patrick Morley. In a state Dr. King once described as "sweltering with the heat of oppression," Mission Mississippi has drawn together black and white Christians under the common purpose of justice and reconciliation.

After hearing the white students cheer on that terrible spring day in 1968, reconciliation was the last thing on Dolphus's mind. "I had to ask God how to respond," he told me for an interview for *Christianity Today.* "It was around the time that H. Rap Brown, Stokely Carmichael and other young militant leaders were starting the Black Power movement, and I was tempted to join them. Laughing at Dr. King's death was just like laughing at me—or at the millions of other blacks for whom King labored."

Deep inside, Dolphus wanted to hate white people, to distance himself from their prejudice. "But then I remembered the heart of Dr. King—

responding to hate with love. The Lord brought to my mind that those students were only playing back the tapes that had been recorded in their heads, and I needed to help change the tape."

Dolphus, who was also a student disciple of racial-reconciliation activist John Perkins, resolved to "take every opportunity on that campus to help those young minds think differently." He engaged students and professors in discussions about race. He welcomed them to ask him questions about the Negro experience in the South. He rechanneled his anger into building genuine relationships with his white peers.

"I think that is the way Dr. King would have approached it," he says. "King's heart was to look at the broader picture. The small picture is to be angry. The broader, more prophetic picture is to devote yourself to changing the system and changing minds. That was King's great work: He brought the race issue to the table and put it on the minds of the American people. It was not on our agenda before that. But he came along and told us that we're all created in God's image, and that we ought to start looking at each other as brothers and sisters, especially those of us in the Christian church."

Nearly four decades after the death of Martin Luther King Jr., the race issue is still very much on our minds. Across the nation the news is regularly filled with stories of racial tension and economic disparity between different groups of Americans. No Child Left Behind. Hurricane Katrina. Overcrowded prisons. Welfare reform. Immigration laws. Police profiling. Affirmative action. Heck, even the viewers' voting patterns for *American Idol*. All of these things ultimately bring us back to discussions about the racial divide in the United States.

Against the backdrop of our enduring dysfunction with race, Martin Luther King's name has entered the national lexicon, evoking idealistic notions of integration, unity and brotherhood—or, as King used to say, "the beloved community." For many, King *is* black history; his memory is emblematic of both our ugly past and the better society that we can one day become. For others, depending on their generation, King might be viewed as either a communist sympathizer or a warm-and-fuzzy folk hero, one step removed from John Henry.

For the church, King's legacy is as multifarious as the nation he sought to reconcile. While some revere him as a hero and a martyred prophet of peace, others look on him with disdain, an attitude that was magnified by revelations of King's sexual improprieties, male chauvinism and lapses in ethical judgment regarding some of his seminary papers. Nonetheless, the enduring importance of King's life and achievements has led many evangelicals who once dismissed him as a liberal rabble-rouser now to acknowledge the spiritual validity of his social mission.

KING IN THE MAKING

Though I was born in April 1969, a year after the assassination of Dr. King, nobody had to give me a history lesson on who he was. From the beginning, it seemed he was always there: in books on our family bookshelf, in stories shared around the dinner table, on the living room wall hanging near the portrait of Jesus. For me, King was a man of superheroic proportions. In fact, he was often the only black hero to be given a paragraph in our school textbooks.

As a child adopted by older parents, I had a unique view of the past. I heard the tales of a bygone era, remembrances of a different America. Unlike the tendency among some today to invoke the race card at the first sign of adversity—whether justified or not—my parents witnessed racial injustice firsthand. The prejudice they saw was real. The seating at the back of the bus and near the restaurant kitchen (if they were even allowed to enter) was real. The separate water fountains and movie theaters and schools. The hurling of derogatory names, the mysterious lynchings—these things were real.

To my folks, it was all quite normal. They never thought of things as changing or getting better. Nothing in their experience gave them reason to expect an upgrade to first class. That is until December 1, 1955, in Montgomery, Alabama, when an unassuming seamstress named Rosa

Parks, who just happened to be the secretary of the local chapter of the NAACP, decided not to surrender her seat on the public bus. Montgomery's segregation laws required blacks to yield their seats to white passengers when necessary. Parks, it turned out, had had enough. And thus began the revolution.

Martin Luther King Jr., a twenty-six-year-old Montgomery minister, was chosen to be the public voice for a boycott of the city's public transportation. King and his wife, Coretta, were still adjusting to their first pastorate at Dexter Avenue Baptist Church when he accepted the call to lead the protest. (He was drafted to direct the campaign partly because of his charismatic leadership skills, but also because of his newness to the community—he hadn't made any enemies yet.) The eventual success of the Montgomery boycott would ignite a national movement.

The young preacher from Atlanta did not, of course, come to the movement with his ideas fully formed. He had to learn to be Martin Luther King. As one of his contemporaries said, "The movement made Martin rather than Martin making the movement."

Emerging from a long line of Atlanta clergymen, King's call to lead the civil rights struggle afforded him the opportunity to put into practice his Christ-inspired convictions about servant leadership and his Gandhi-inspired notions about nonviolent protest. He wrote in 1963, "Through nonviolent resistance we shall be able to oppose the unjust system and at the same time love the perpetrators of the system."

This spiritual vision was at the heart of King's moral and political strategy.

KING'S AMERICA

King's intellectual curiosity and desire to understand the very unchristian race situation in the South (combined with his education at liberal northern seminaries) compelled him to ask questions that would stretch his theology far beyond the fundamentalism of his Baptist youth. Nevertheless, on a practical level, King's Baptist heritage always shone through.

"In the quiet recesses of my heart," he often said, "I am fundamentally a clergyman, a Baptist preacher."

In August 1963, King's movement organized its massive March on Washington, the event that begat the legendary "I Have a Dream" speech and represented the pinnacle of his fame. A Nobel Peace Prize came in 1964. And there were rousing legislative victories as well, such as the Civil Rights Act of 1964 and the Voting Rights Act of 1965.

King's political efforts received criticism from white religious leaders from both conservative and liberal circles. His famous "Letter from the Birmingham Jail"—a sort of civil rights era epistle—was actually an impassioned response to eight "moderate" clergymen in Alabama who saw King's continued use of nonviolent resistance as "unwise" and encouraged him to let the fight for integration continue in the local and federal courts. Unlike those clergymen, King could not fathom a separation between his faith and politics. He wrote:

> In the midst of a mighty struggle to rid our nation of racial and economic injustice, I have heard so many ministers say, "Those are social issues with which the gospel has no real concern," and I have watched so many churches commit themselves to a completely otherworldly religion which made a strange distinction between body and soul, the sacred and the secular.

As the tumultuous decade of the sixties raged on, King's unyielding commitment to nonviolence would eventually make him a target of black critics as well. Although the movement had made strides against racism and Jim Crow in the South, issues like poverty, unemployment and racial discrimination were raging out of control in the North. As a result, younger members of the broader civil rights community grew impatient, and the movement began to splinter. Leaders of groups such as the Student Nonviolent Coordinating Committee (SNCC) and the Congress of Racial Equality (CORE) tossed aside King's "ineffective" nonviolent strategies in favor of more radical Black Power tactics.

Malcolm X had been killed in 1965, but the Black Muslim movement continued to win converts in the inner cities. In 1966, SNCC leader Stokely Carmichael vowed never again to "take a beating without hitting back." King, though troubled, understood what drove the militant factions. "The Black Power slogan did not spring full grown from the head of some philosophical Zeus," he said. "It was born from the wounds of despair and disappointment."

Nevertheless, Black Power did not understand King. He was branded an "Uncle Tom" and marginalized by those who, ironically, had found their voice as a result of his trailblazing leadership. Soon race riots were breaking out on a regular basis in cities throughout the nation. King's dream appeared to be morphing into a nightmare.

DYING DAYS

James Earl Massey, a renowned evangelical preacher and theologian, was the senior pastor of Detroit's Metropolitan Church of God in the late sixties. On a steamy July evening in 1967, his plane touched down at the Detroit airport. Massey had been attending a clergy convention when one of the worst urban riots in U.S. history erupted in the Motor City. Incessant gunfire filled the evenings, rocks and bricks bashed downtown windows, storefronts were looted of their goods, flames consumed entire city blocks. When it was over, forty-three lives and fifty million dollars in property damage had been the cost.

To get home, Massey had to drive through the riot zone. He made it safely, but the biggest challenge still lay ahead for him and the other leading Detroit ministers who began working to restore peace to their tortured city.

In 1998 I interviewed Massey and other black evangelical leaders for a *Christianity Today* article commemorating the thirtieth anniversary of Martin Luther King's death. With his neatly trimmed mustache and stately demeanor, Massey has sometimes been said to resemble his friend

King. He often spent time with King during King's trips to Detroit and was aware of his distress and self-doubt over the fragmenting movement he had helped propel. Massey told me that, although King remained committed to methods of nonviolence, he was making a clear shift in his rhetoric. "He had moved on to speaking out strongly against poverty and America's participation in the Vietnam War," he said. "He was, in fact, sounding quite radical."

In what would be his last book, King wrote, "Whites, it must frankly be said, are not putting in a mass effort to re-educate themselves out of their racial ignorance. . . . It is an aspect of their sense of superiority that the white people of America believe they have so little to learn."

FBI director J. Edgar Hoover (and others) labeled him a communist, and for many white Americans, Martin Luther King and urban unrest became synonymous. The anger and hostility he had been encountering at different events, particularly in the large cities, began to visibly erode King's spirit. "In the pictures of him marching in Memphis [just days before his murder], you can see the grimmest look on his face," Massey told me. "He was very tense. And the speech he gave the night before his death reveals how much he was expecting hostility to rise against him."

Despite struggles with exhaustion and disillusionment, he continued to speak prophetically to the issues of the day. In the spring of 1968, King was working to organize a massive Poor People's Campaign in Washington for both blacks and whites. But he would not live to see it. On April 4, while in Memphis to support a Negro sanitation workers' strike, King was killed. He was thirty-nine.

Massey recalls being at a Detroit television studio that night with his church choir to record a local broadcast for the following Sunday. "While we were preparing to tape, the studio announcer called me aside and told me the news. My heart sank. I didn't tell the choir until after the taping, because I knew they'd be too upset to sing. After King's death, something in me just died."

Something died within the black community as well. King's assassination sparked riots in 125 cities, which led to 21,270 arrests and forty-six deaths.

NOT JUST A BEAUTIFUL DREAMER

Looking back, it seems clear that most white evangelicals were out to lunch during the civil rights movement—or, worse, on the wrong side of the struggle. According to Don Argue, former head of the National Association of Evangelicals and the current president of Northwest University in Kirkland, Washington, "When African Americans had their Moses in the person of Martin Luther King, we were either indifferent or, in some cases, critical and hostile toward what was happening. We missed our golden opportunity the first time."

Today, it's not unusual to hear white evangelicals speak unashamedly of the positive contributions of the slain civil rights leader. However, in King's day, his nonviolent resistance and liberal theology were considered suspect. Even evangelist Billy Graham, who since 1953 had worked to desegregate his crusades and invited King to pray at his 1957 event in New York, was hesitant to cast his wholehearted support to King's movement. "Some extreme Negro leaders are going too far and too fast," Graham said in the early sixties. "Only the supernatural love of God through changed men can solve this burning question."

But King saw his "social gospel" as a natural outworking of God's supernatural love. He explained in 1965, "The essence of the Epistles of Paul is that Christians should rejoice at being deemed worthy to suffer for what they believe. The projection of a social gospel, in my opinion, is the true witness of a Christian life. . . . The church once changed society. It was then a thermostat of society. But today I feel that too much of the church is merely a thermometer, which measures rather than molds popular opinion."

What looked like a radical social gospel in the sixties now doesn't seem that different from the activism employed by evangelicals who protest abortion or same-sex marriage—at least in principle. Political engagement is no longer taboo for conservative believers.

For Dolphus Weary, Martin Luther King's activism was precisely what was needed in southern churches during that time. "I used to see many preachers being exploitative of the black community," he says. "They would say stuff like, 'It's okay that you're going into the back door of restaurants. It's okay that you're going to second-class schools. It's okay that you're the last hired and the first fired. Because one day you're going to heaven, and everything will be all right.' But then King came along and said, 'No! You're not a second-class citizen. God is concerned about you right now. Go vote. Go stand up for your rights.' It was what we needed to hear."

But what of King's legacy among evangelicals today? Though he now has a national holiday and "I Have a Dream" is memorized and recited by schoolchildren of all races, do we truly grasp and appreciate the impact of this man who was driven by a "right now" understanding of the gospel?

Many of the scholars I've spoken to about King believe we've missed the heart of the man, that the King many evangelicals now embrace is only a shadow, a mythologized symbol of the real man.

Oberlin College's Albert G. Miller believes the church has a watered-down understanding of King's vision. "I think we are stuck in our image of King at the 1963 March on Washington," he told me. "The 'I Have a Dream' King was a kinder, gentler King. There was a more complicated man that evolved after that point who was very frustrated with what he saw with the limited progress of blacks. In his latter days, King was not just protesting for blacks to eat at the lunch counter, but for blacks to have employment at the lunch counter and to own it."

Cheryl Sanders, professor of Christian ethics at Howard University and senior pastor of Washington's Third Street Church of God, concurs. "The problem with the 'Dream' language is that it draws attention away from the reality of what King was speaking about throughout his life. There's a danger of only seeing him as a dreamer, and if we only see him as a dreamer, we too easily let ourselves off the hook from dealing with the realities that he was dealing with."

A WILLING SERVANT

Because of King's work, many people today—and in years to come—will be challenged to rethink the right-now relevancy of their faith in God. And for some that will mean giving more than politically correct lip service to issues of racial equality and social justice. King was not a perfect man, but he was a man who put his life on the line for what was right. He once remarked, "If a man has not discovered something he is willing to die for, he is not fit to live." King took seriously Jesus' declaration in Matthew 16:24-25: "If anyone would come after me, he must deny himself and take up his cross and follow me. For whoever wants to save his life will lose it, but whoever loses his life for my sake will find it."

In *Dreamer,* a fictional take on King's life, novelist Charles Johnson re-creates a real sermon preached by the civil rights leader just after the march into the Marquette Park neighborhood of Chicago in the summer of 1966. It was a particularly violent event. The marchers were assaulted by a mob of angry whites, and King had been struck in the head with a large rock. But during the climax of his sermon, according to Johnson, King said:

> Every night when I get down on my knees to pray or close my eyes in quiet meditation I'm holding a funeral for the self. I'm digging a little grave for the ego. I'm saying, like the lovely Catholic nun I read about who works with the poor in Calcutta, that I will despoil myself of all that is not God; I will strip my heart of every created thing; I will live in poverty and detachment; I will renounce my will, my inclinations, my whims and fancies, and make myself a willing servant of the will of God.

King's example teaches us, in profound fashion, how to take up our cross for the sake of justice and truth. He demonstrated how we must put feet to our prayers. He showed us that perseverance and committed relationships are essential if we hope to get anywhere. Real reconciliation will require time and sweat. And possibly blood.

IS JESSE JACKSON AN EVANGELICAL?

My constituency is the desperate, the damned, the disinherited,
the disrespected, and the despised.

Jesse Jackson

He's one of the most racist, divisive people on the earth.
His only interest is in promoting himself.
He is a very bad man, and is not a "man of God."

post on a Christian message board

In the early 1960s, long before he became the pastor of a Chicago mega-church, James Meeks presided over the funerals of his family pets. "I would wear a long towel as my clerical robe and put on a service before I'd bury them," he recalls. Meeks grew up in the Baptist church, was baptized at age six, and a year later settled on his life's vocation. God had spoken, and it was clear. While other seven-year-olds fantasized about being firefighters, ballplayers or boxers, Meeks wanted to be a minister.

Like everyone, Meeks followed the exploits of Martin Luther King Jr. The civil rights movement, as it unfolded in American cities and on family television screens, represented heady times for aspiring black preachers. The nation's conscience was being operated on, and black church leaders were the surgeons.

Martin Luther King was assassinated when Meeks was eleven. A few years later, however, Meeks found another hero. He was a brash young preacher with South Carolina roots who had been a member of King's team of activist clergymen. His Chicago-based ministry, Operation PUSH (People United to Serve Humanity), was located near Meeks's own south side neighborhood. More than a decade before the Sugar Hill Gang or Grandmaster Flash popularized rap, this preacher spoke to audiences in effortless rhymes, intoning mantras such as "Keep hope alive!" and "It's not the bark you wear but the fruit you bear." He exhorted crowds of black youths to "stay in school, stay off drugs," and "Repeat after me: I am . . . somebody! I am . . . somebody!" When not rallying students in gymnasiums, he confronted corporate America—Coca-Cola, Burger King and Ford Motors all faced the calculated fury of his protests. He showed how boycotts and demonstrations could be used not only to desegregate buses and schools, but also to open up jobs and economic opportunities for minorities.

The young preacher, of course, was Jesse Jackson. And by age fifteen, Meeks was smitten. "I was a fan of his to the point that every photograph of him that I found in *Ebony, Jet* or the newspaper, I cut out and put on a board in my room—I had over seventy-five pictures," he says. "Reverend Jackson's influence helped me understand that ministers are leaders who could help people both in and outside the church."

Today, James Meeks is the senior pastor of Salem Baptist Church, a seventeen thousand-member congregation on Chicago's far south side. Meeks is renowned locally for setting audacious goals—and then meeting them. In seminary, he read books by white evangelical preachers John MacArthur and Charles Swindoll and decided he wanted to grow a church as large as theirs. He did. When he founded Salem in 1985, Meeks set the goal of having the largest Sunday school program in Chicago. It started with fifty students; today there are two thousand. In early 1999, Salem launched an ambitious evangelism campaign to bring twenty-five thousand people to Christ; by year's end they had recorded twenty-seven thousand "confessions of faith"—and three thousand of those people joined the church. In 2005 Salem opened The House of

Hope, a fifty million-dollar, ten thousand-seat, state-of-the-art worship center, which the church rents out for sports and civic events when it's not holding its services there. Salem's list of ministries reads like a city directory: a daycare center, a five hundred-student grade school, Chicago's largest Christian bookstore, a soup kitchen, a counseling program for substance abusers.

Meeks's sermons are unabashedly Christ-centered. He is a frequent speaker at Moody Bible Institute's annual conferences. One of his close friends and prayer partners is Charles Lyons, a white Southern Baptist pastor from Chicago's Northwest Side. In 2001, Meeks completed a campaign to deliver cassette tapes of the New Testament to each of the 38,170 prison inmates in Illinois. He is, by all accounts, a passionate evangelical Christian.

But there's just one thing. Meeks is the executive vice president of Jesse Jackson's Rainbow/PUSH Coalition. For many onlookers, this is a glaring stain on an otherwise gleaming résumé. "I love Reverend Meeks's ministry," says one black Chicago woman who watches the weekly TV broadcasts of Salem Baptist's services, "but, for the life of me, I cannot understand why he associates himself with that Jesse Jackson."

She's not alone. Many people wonder how a person as evangelical as Meeks can be aligned with someone so famously unevangelical as Jackson. In fact, many speculate that Meeks is compromising his ministry—and message—for the national prestige and influence that come through his relationship with Jackson.

Further attesting to Jackson's impact on his life, in 2002 Meeks ran for an Illinois State Senate seat as an Independent candidate and won. And so, it would seem, the facsimile is complete—minister, activist, politician. Like Jesse, like James; the protégé also rises.

How can this be? How can a real evangelical—a true-blue Bible-believing preacher—find such an easy alliance with one of our country's leading exemplars of liberal theology and moral compromise?

The truth is, Meeks is not the only theologically "conservative" Christian with whom Jackson associates. As it turns out, a surprising number of black evangelicals have been inspired and shaped by the work of Jackson. And many of them are card-carrying members of Rainbow/PUSH. They are theology professors, parachurch leaders and senior pastors; politically, they are both Democrat and Republican. There are no hard figures on the exact number of evangelicals directly influenced by Jackson, but the anecdotal evidence points to a wide trend.

"Jesse Jackson is the premier civil rights leader and social activist of our time," says Baptist General Conference leader Dwight Perry. "Jackson teaches us the importance of not dichotomizing the gospel, that the essence of the gospel is how I am relating to my neighbor, regardless of his race or social condition."

Jerald January, who pastors the Vernon Park Church of God on Chicago's South Side, believes evangelicals can learn a lot from Jackson. "What I find missing in a lot of evangelical Christianity is a focus on the importance of social justice. We understand the evangelistic part, but there is still a need for someone to cry out for justice. Jesse fills that void for a lot of us."

Many things can and will be said about Jackson's public and personal foibles, but the untold story on the Reverend Jackson is this: His true heirs will not be radical activists like Al Sharpton or others identified more by their politics than their faith. No, his successors will be honest-to-goodness Christian churchmen who, like Meeks, have a call to ministry both in and outside the church.

"GOD IS OLDER THAN GENESIS"

"I take Luke 4:18 seriously," Jesse Jackson tells me as we sit in his Chicago office. "To preach good news to the poor, to bind up the wounds of the brokenhearted, to proclaim freedom to the captives. If I preach the gospel of truth and reconciliation, I can touch hard hearts and make things happen. That's my calling."

I am interviewing Jackson for a profile in *Christianity Today*, a profile that I had to scratch and claw through at least two levels of upper management to get into the magazine. Sitting behind a large desk cluttered with books, papers and framed photographs of his family, Jackson is gracious and personable but utterly serious about this business of being Jesse Jackson. He rarely smiles and handles my questions with the no-nonsense determination of a weary graduate student defending his dissertation.

In the interest of full disclosure, I should tell you that I like Jesse Jackson. I grew up liking him. In the 1970s and '80s, he was one of the few living African American heroes, outside the realms of sports and entertainment, that a young black boy could look up to. Jackson could always be counted on to rattle the status quo. Sometimes he triumphed, as during his presidential campaigns in 1984 and 1988 (though he lost the nominations, he brought a whole new constituency of voters into the political mainstream) or his rescue of American hostages from Syria, Iraq and Yugoslavia. Other times he stumbled, like his insensitive "hymie" remarks about Jews or his ill-advised defense of delinquent students in Decatur, Illinois. Still, overall, Jackson's good accomplishments seemed to outweigh the bad. When I met with Jackson in late 2001, I had to remind myself that I was there as a journalist, not a fan.

The rap against Jackson for many evangelicals is that he is a Christian minister who does not have a credible "spiritual witness." He craves the media spotlight and imposes the "race issue" on all his dealings, whether legitimate or not. He seems stuck in a black victimization mindset that deters some African Americans from taking personal responsibility for their conditions. What's more, his political positions on issues like abortion and homosexual rights run counter to that of most people who interpret the Bible as God's inspired Word.

Then there was the announcement in 2001 that Jackson had fathered a daughter outside of his marriage. For many of his disparagers this confirmed what they had suspected all along—that Jackson was a spiritual phony, a shyster, a playa. The man who for decades had preached sexual purity and male responsibility had besmirched everything for which he stood. Worse, his supporters seemed to turn a blind eye to the issue and shamelessly welcomed Jackson back into public life after a laughably short time away from the spotlight. This was the lowest point of a career that has had no shortage of dramatic highs and lows.

When I told many of my white friends and colleagues that I was working on an article about Jesse Jackson, I could see the contempt spread across their faces. There was an almost visceral distaste for the man. And this was from progressive evangelical types who had made racial reconciliation and social justice priorities in their churches and personal missions. Dislike of Jackson is not just a white thing either. A significant number of blacks are rubbed the wrong way by the Reverend's rhetoric and tactics.

Eugene Rivers, the Boston activist and Pentecostal pastor, has become a prolific critic of Jackson and the "civil rights industry," as he calls it. "We in the black community have to move beyond the gratuitous use of the race card to retard the debate and move forward towards a focus on measurable outcomes," he once told CNN in reference to Jackson.

"Reverend Jackson's approach is to look for technical answers to spiritual questions," says Star Parker, president of the Coalition on Urban Renewal and Education in Los Angeles. A conservative and former welfare mother who turned her life around after becoming a Christian, Parker has debated Jackson and others on CNN and ABC's late-great *Politically Incorrect*. She adds, "His approach misleads people to depend on him instead of the Lord."

By now Jackson is used to criticism. But he still seems irked by the notion that people question the veracity of his faith. To him, it's similar to the adversity faced by two of his heroes: Jesus and Martin Luther King. They too were misunderstood by the religious communities of their day. Jackson regularly—some might say presumptuously—invokes their examples in relation to his own experience.

"Jesus was brought under a death warrant and killed by a conspiracy between the religious order and the government in the same night," Jackson says. "Evangelicals had a negative view of Dr. King, too. That's why the 'Letter from the Birmingham Jail' was addressed to the white clergy. It was the white church that sided with [police commissioner] Bull Connor over against Dr. King. The white church was negative about Dr. King and limited in their view of Jesus as a universalist; Jesus was not limited by race, by country or by culture. He was preaching a global gospel. He saw these things as transcending the nation-state."

As he says this, Jackson's tone shifts into a higher gear. His cadence becomes more pronounced. The preacher has found a groove: "The Good Samaritan who rescued the battered Jewish man was not of that man's nation, not of his race, not of his religion. The priest saw the man lying there bleeding, went to the other side of the street. The Levite saw him, went to the other side of the street. But the Samaritan—a man from another culture—stopped and helped. You see, Jesus went beyond culture and religion and race. He said, 'Look, is this guy your brother because he's your pastor? Is he your brother because he's your skin color? Who is your neighbor? Who is your brother? It's easy to love people who are in your comfort zone, but loving people outside of that zone . . . that's the kind of challenge that Jesus gives us. That's getting beyond private salvation into defining brotherhood in much broader terms."

Jackson's use of phrases like "global gospel" and "Jesus as a universalist" sets off alarms for those who hold his theology suspect. In a 1977 interview with Christianity Today, Jackson hinted at a sort of extrabiblical universalism in his understanding of salvation. "Even though we always say that you go through Jesus to get to God, Jesus did not always put on that restriction," he said back then. Thirty years later, that perspective is still intact.

When I tell Jackson that the ambiguities in his theology have sometimes troubled evangelicals, he pauses for several seconds then says, "God is older than Genesis, and he did not stop with Revelation. The Bible is a holy book but not the only book of God. God is not book-challenged. God cannot be omnipotent, omnipresent and omniscient and be limited to five thousand years of biblical history. He is much bigger than that."

LEARNING TO BE SOMEBODY

To truly understand Jesse Louis Jackson, you have to go back to Greenville, South Carolina. He was born there on October 8, 1941, in the poorest section of town, to a sixteen-year-old unwed mother. His father was the next-door neighbor, a married man in his mid-thirties who had three stepchildren.

Growing up, Jackson felt stigmatized by the ignoble circumstances of his birth. He learned as a young boy that his mother's husband—the man whose surname he had taken—was not his biological father. In later years, Jackson would tell the story in speeches of how other kids would taunt him, saying, "Your daddy ain't none of your daddy," and "You ain't nothin' but a nobody." Jackson's biological father went on to become one of the most prominent and well-to-do black men in town, but Jackson could only look in from the outside. He longed for a relationship with the man. He remembers crying a lot.

But Jackson's family instilled in him a strong sense of his somebody-ness, which helped him overcome his early insecurities. He decided to respond to the negative looks and remarks by excelling at all that he did. He became an honor-roll student, a high school football star and, most fatefully, a precocious young leader at his Baptist church.

In the 1996 biography *Jesse*, he told the late journalist Marshall Frady, "Church was like my laboratory, my first actual public stage, where I began to develop and practice my speaking powers with more and more confidence. After a while, it got to where you couldn't hardly hold me back. I'd sit there watching [other preachers], but all I was really seeing was myself up there in that pulpit."

Those who have closely followed the trajectory of Jackson's career suggest that his hyperactive compulsion to be seen, heard and accepted is driven by a deep-seated need to prove his self-worth. Rage has also propelled Jackson's determination to be acknowledged and dealt with on his own terms. That rage, it seems, is one of the consequences of growing up against the ugly backdrop of legalized racism. Jackson experienced the depressing effects of Jim Crow segregation firsthand—riding at the back of buses, using back doors to enter restaurants, not being able to check out books from the public library or play football against all-white high schools. He told Frady, "You felt the whole society was just out to erase you."

The most vexing instances of racism, however, emanated from the Christian community. Jackson recalls the irony of growing up in the shadow of Bob Jones University, the infamous fundamentalist college in Greenville, "which had the audacity to preach to us about having saved lives while they advocated a white supremacist God." And then there were the white churches where his father did janitorial work. "The strange thing," he says, "was that my father could clean up a church on Sunday afternoon but couldn't attend it on Sunday morning."

More than a decade later, while attending Chicago Theological Seminary, Jackson watched the opening salvos of Martin Luther King's march on Selma on the late news and suddenly recognized his destiny. He could not sleep that night. The next morning, he stormed into the cafeteria, jumped atop a table and began challenging his mostly white classmates. "We've been studying the cost of discipleship," he shouted, "now we have a chance to validate it with our lives. Who's gonna go with me down to Selma?"

Jackson rallied twenty of his fellow seminarians—and five professors—and launched a caravan to Alabama. Once in Selma, it took Jackson only two days to rustle a meeting with King's organization, the Southern Christian Leadership Conference (SCLC), and to persuade MLK himself to bring him on as his Chicago point man. Jackson headed up Operation Breadbasket, the economic-empowerment wing of the SCLC, which he would ultimately commandeer to form his own organization. That was March 1965. From then on, Jackson glued himself to King and quickly earned a reputation as the one member of the SCLC entourage with the right mix of charisma, brains and vision to legitimately succeed his mentor. Jackson has spent the last forty years of his life, with varying degrees of accomplishment, trying to do just that.

"Jesse Jackson represents a kind of bridge between the social-gospel voice in the African American religious community that was prominent during the civil rights movement and the contemporary focus on economic development, individual prosperity and assimilation into the American middle class," says Robert Franklin, a professor of social ethics at Emory University and former president of the historically black Interdenominational Theological Center in Atlanta.

Franklin points to Jackson's Wall Street Project—the Reverend's ambitious campaign to confront what he calls the "economic apartheid" of American capitalism—as the most recent example of his efforts to bring African Americans and other minorities into economic power. Under this new banner, Jackson has approached major corporations, demanding that they expand their opportunities for minorities or risk being boycotted. In 2001 Toyota was targeted by the campaign after running a print advertisement that some felt gave a racist portrayal of black Americans (the ad featured an extreme close-up of a black man's smiling lips and teeth and a Toyota SUV imprinted on the man's gold tooth). The company apologized and later announced an eight billion-dollar long-term commitment to increase management opportunities and dealership franchises for African Americans.

Some have labeled Jackson's efforts as shakedowns and accused Rainbow/PUSH of pocketing a portion of the money. Jackson has said that any money his organization receives, usually in the form of donations from those his efforts have benefited, is simply a thank-you gift. He in fact views the Wall Street Project as a natural continuation of Martin Luther King's work during the civil rights movement. "It's the final phase in the process," he says.

"The Wall Street Project grows naturally out of the kinds of things Jackson was doing with Operation Breadbasket and PUSH, trying to promote the involvement of black-owned businesses with corporate America," says Glenn Loury, a professor of economics at Brown University (who also has a famous testimony of becoming a born-again Christian after a fall from grace at Harvard University). Loury agrees that the project can appear opportunistic, but he doesn't necessarily think it's an inappropriate approach. "I'm realistic about the way that America works. There are back rooms where powerful people do deals. The people on Wall Street understand that."

What Loury does question is how far-reaching the campaign will be. "Real economic development for African Americans must occur from the bottom up," he says. "Most of the thirty to thirty-five million African Americans are workers. Creating a few black millionaires is not going to change the facts on the ground for most of those people. What we need—especially in the inner cities—is education, human capital and a strong economy."

Robert Franklin adds that Jackson's dependence on older civil rights strategies—boycotts, marches, protest politics—may not be well suited to the "challenges and opportunities for progress in today's society, where the skills of negotiation, merit and demonstrated excellence are important."

Still, in the end, it will not be campaigns on Wall Street that people will recall about Jesse Jackson. Ultimately, one always comes back to Jackson's role as a spiritual leader. It is at the root of his work. It is at the core of how he sees himself. And it is how most Americans think of him. That is why the revelation of his extramarital affair left most people wondering whether he could ever recover his credibility.

A SCANDALOUS SYMBOL

The tragic irony is that Jackson would father a child illegitimately after he himself entered the world under the same painful conditions. Jackson's young daughter, Ashley, was the result of his affair with Karin Stanford, a former Rainbow/PUSH staff member. The fallout led to allegations that Jackson misused Rainbow/PUSH funds to pay child support to Stanford, a claim he denies. In an NPR commentary broadcast after the news broke, Robert Franklin coined the term "unoriginal sin" to describe the sad course of events. Indeed, the story reads like a lurid episode from the Old Testament.

Jackson has been married to his wife, Jaqueline, for over forty years. They have five adult children. For his part, the Reverend has refused to discuss the matter beyond his initial statement asking his friends and supporters for "forgiveness, understanding and prayers." Still, when addressing other issues, he occasionally invokes biblical themes of forgiveness and restoration that hint at something more personal. "We must honor the ethic of the Ten Commandments," Jackson told me, "even if we fall and break them. And if we fall and break them or disobey them, it's only through mercy and grace that Humpty Dumpty is put back together again."

The love-child scandal was indeed a messy fall for Jackson. Through his sinful choices, Jackson perpetuated the same problems of fatherlessness and illegitimacy that he had so dynamically preached against in the African American community. And he had to know that it would provide terrific ammo for those wishing to blast his credibility as a spiritual leader. Yet to the consternation of many of us looking in from the outside, Jackson was almost too easily welcomed back to leadership after his shocking public admission.

When I asked his evangelical friends and supporters about the scandal and the brisk pace with which he was reinstated, most agreed that, personally, they would have preferred that Jackson spend a little more time away from the public eye. Others said they knew about the scandal long before it became public knowledge and saw that Jackson was truly remorseful. And, like Jackson himself, many of them appealed to biblical archetypes of failure and restoration—not to minimize their friend's actions but to affirm God's grace in such matters.

"Do we still read the Psalms?" asks Meeks. "David had a baby out of wedlock and he killed Bathsheba's husband. And the very people who would criticize Reverend Jackson revere David. Is David no longer a credible witness?"

This sentiment is not atypical. In general, the African American Christian community has been more forgiving of its fallen members. Though few whites will admit it aloud, this is one of the things that sustains the fissures between white and black believers—the impression that blacks are lax morally, that they too easily excuse sin or fail to take responsibility for their behavior. But such broad characterizations of blacks are based on stereotypes and false assumptions. Truth be told, I've seen some of the harshest pronouncements of church discipline dished out by black congregations. However, I've also seen a remarkable capacity for forgiveness and absolution.

After a devastating divorce from his wife, Fred Hammond, one of black gospel music's elite stars, remarked that the CCM (i.e., white) side of the Christian music industry can be very cold toward its fallen members. Indeed, once-untouchable stars like Michael English, Sandi Patty and Amy Grant have all felt the harsh judgment of the evangelical community after revelations of extramarital affairs or announcements of divorces. "They are extremely critical," Hammond told *Billboard* magazine. "I've seen that side, and it's very scary. . . . But on the gospel side, it's a culture. It's like urban and black people are a family and will understand. Some of them will have opinions, but mostly people just kind of understand and walk you through. They forgive and move on."

THE JACKSON ENIGMA

On most Fridays at 10:30 a.m., a group of about twenty-five Chicago ministers gathers at the Rainbow/PUSH headquarters to take part in a weekly meeting convened by Jesse Jackson. The pastors pray together and talk about strategies for improving their churches and communities. Jackson launched the gatherings as part of a new Rainbow/PUSH program called One Thousand Churches Connected, which provides churches with resources for teaching money management to their members.

But this meeting is also an excuse for Jackson to nurture his connection with the local church. In fact, it was at a similar meeting in 1996 that Jackson met James Meeks. The two became fast friends. Jackson invited Meeks to join the delegation of clergy who went with him to Yugoslavia in 1999 to lobby Slobodan Milosevic for the release of three American soldiers. As a result of that trip, Jackson eventually named Meeks his heir apparent at Rainbow/PUSH.

Meeks realizes that some people view his association with Jackson as odd, but he insists that theirs is a relationship of equals. "We have a good friendship. The Bible says iron sharpens iron. We get the chance to play off of each other's ideas and to scripturally compare decisions that are being made. I help him be more conservative; he helps me be more liberal."

The ministers at the Friday meetings are a varied crop—old, young, traditional, contemporary, male, female. And sprinkled in for good measure are a handful of leaders, like Meeks and Jerald January, who might be classified as evangelicals. Time after time, when I asked the pastors at one of those meetings about Jackson's importance, each insisted that Jackson still has much to offer—not just as a political figure but also as a Christian minister.

"Reverend Jackson represents the living embodiment of Dr. King's legacy," says Christopher Bullock, the former pastor of Progressive Baptist Church in Chicago and an ardent Republican. "He has an acute gift of social exegesis and analysis of the condition of America and the world. I think we do him a disservice by not viewing him as a serious critical thinker theologically."

Bullock, of course, is right. Jackson is a serious thinker, someone who needs to be taken seriously as an intellectual and political force. But, lest we forget, he is also an old-fashioned country preacher who, though not technically evangelical, has much in common with that community. In

March 2005 Jackson surprised—and emboldened—many evangelicals when he jumped into the infamous Terri Schiavo pro-life versus right-to-die fiasco in Florida and came out on the pro-life side. "This is one of the profound moral, ethical issues of our time, the saving of Terri's life," Jackson told reporters. "And today we pray for a miracle."

Years earlier Jackson told Marshall Frady, "My values come out of a conservative Christian orientation. Probably surprise a lot of people to know I think that way, but it's what I really believe, deep down in my soul." And therein lies part of the public's ongoing frustration with the man: He is forever too political to be embraced as a true minister but too religious to be accepted as a formidable politician. Yet it is the ambitious juggling of these two roles that make Jesse Jackson who he is.

Many black evangelicals in Chicago—and across the nation—believe he's still got the goods. "At the end of the day, look at what he's achieved," says Bullock. "That's the bottom line in my opinion, what he has done for the kingdom of God, what he has done for the advancement of civil rights, what he has done for the human community. He has brought hostages home. He feeds people. He does a lot of things the press will not cover."

WHY JESSE STILL MATTERS

I chose to include this chapter about Jesse Jackson because his career provocatively captures both the good and the bad aspects of racial progress in this country. Jackson's legacy will forever be highlighted by his civil and human rights accomplishments and his influential, if unsuccessful, presidential bids. But he also will be remembered for his self-serving moments of political grandstanding and his grotesquely public moral failures.

When I first proposed an article about Jackson to my editors at *Christianity Today* magazine, I took for granted its newsworthiness; this was not long after the revelation of Jackson's love-child scandal. Given those events, I was certain the article would find a place in the magazine. After all, it had been more than two decades since *CT* had done a major feature on the controversial preacher-activist. Love him or hate him, I reasoned, *CT* readers would still be curious about Jackson's ongoing relevance to many in the evangelical community.

That's what I thought. I was taken aback—though not altogether surprised—by the lukewarm reception to my proposal. Call me naive, but I underestimated the repulsion my bosses would have toward Jackson. Several working lunches later, I was given the okay to do the article. But that was only the beginning. There was no guarantee that they would approve my final article.

Once the article was written, I received a number of unannounced visits from at least two high-ranking members of *Christianity Today*'s editorial management team. Both men shared their concerns about publishing the article, that it could be a potential powder keg with our readers. Though they both agreed that I had written a balanced profile, it became apparent that, in this case, balance wasn't enough. I gathered that they wanted me to make certain the story was not too kind to Jackson and that it clearly distanced *Christianity Today* from any hint of sympathy for the man.

The room temperature during some of those meetings grew unnervingly toasty, but I sweated it out. The whole point of the article, I argued, was to give our readers an unbiased look at Jackson, of how he became the preacher-activist-politician that people either loved or hated. I had no problem showing his warts (and he had plenty), but I could not overlook that there were things to admire as well.

With some minor tweaks, the article eventually made it into the magazine. Sure, we didn't want to upset our readers any more than necessary. But I slowly came to understand that the issue was much bigger than Jesse Jackson alone. It was also about the discomfort and unease that evangelicals have grappling with the loud and impolite aspects of the race issue, the parts that might demand we actually do something.

Of course, it was also about the changing political landscape in this country. A decade or two ago, white evangelicals thought it was cool to hear Jackson's rhyming preaching and to engage his ideas, even if most of those evangelicals disagreed with his underlying politics. Back then Jackson was still viewed as a fascinating figure who proclaimed a social gospel that retained just enough moral substance to keep him relevant.

After that time, however, Jackson became persona non grata to many evangelicals. Increasingly frustrated by his reduced role on the public scene, Jackson morphed into a cartoonishly hostile and partisan figure (not unlike Pat Robertson or Rush Limbaugh on the other side of the spectrum) whose charges of racism and discrimination were as predictable as a Chicago winter.

Less a prophetic voice than a creature of ideological habit, Jackson was identified more with the Democratic machine than with the social-justice arm of the church. In a way, he was a victim of the times.

By the 1990s, the tenor of the culture wars had changed on both sides of the divide. Where once there was civil, though still fervent, disagreement, there was now distrust and partisan venom. The 2004 presidential election underscored this swelling reality. And Jackson, like the political party that had seemingly swallowed up his unique appeal, had come to look like a dissenter who had lost his soul.

Like Robert Franklin, I too suspect Jackson's devotion to old-school civil rights protest and rhetoric has outlived its usefulness in this post–civil rights era. And his eerie willingness to fall lockstep into procession with the Democratic Party's uncompromising positions on issues like abortion boggle my moral-conservative mind. (It should be noted, though, that Jackson shocked many of his left-wing fans when he limited his support of gay rights to civil unions. "In my culture," he told one audience, "marriage is a man-woman relationship.")

Yet I still respect and appreciate the old-time crusader within him. When it comes to calling attention to social ills or fingering civil wrongs, Jackson is a steadfast voice. To this day, in the public square, if he doesn't say it, it often won't get said. What ticks some people off about him is the very thing that makes him so important to others.

And that's why I think we still need Jesse Jackson—or at least the iconic meaning of Jesse Jackson. You may have to strip away some of the political posturing and unwarranted racializing, but at heart he still has something to say.

My wife, who knows my mood shifts better than anyone, sometimes accuses me of being an angry young black man. When I come home from work complaining about something that was said or done that seemed to smack of cultural prejudice or racial insensitivity, Dana will say, "Ah, the angry black man is back." And she's usually right.

The problem is, my gripes usually go unspoken—especially in an evangelical world where minority voices often get drowned out by assimilation. *My white bosses just don't get it,* I say to myself. *But if I say something again, I'll be labeled as an overreacting whiner.* Or, worse, an angry black man.

But Jesse Jackson can say something, and he usually does. He speaks for the angry black man in many of us. And though the force of his words has been diminished over the years, it still does this black evangelical's soul good to know someone's able to say the hard stuff.

9

"GOD IS NOT A DEMOCRAT OR A REPUBLICAN"

What have you done to the world, politician?
You separate brother from brother, like a magician.

Jon Gibson, "Metal Machine"

In May 2005 Calvin College, a Christian liberal arts school in Grand Rapids, Michigan, made national headlines when President George W. Bush descended on the campus to deliver the annual commencement address. Five thousand people, including nine hundred graduating students, packed the Calvin Fieldhouse to hear the president's fifteen-minute speech, in which he quipped that a mastery of grammar and verbal skills could take them far—"Just look what it did for me"—and challenged them to stay involved in churches and community-service organizations. It was not a political speech; however, some found it hard to consider a Republican president speaking at an evangelical college, against the backdrop of a controversial war, anything but political.

President Bush was warmly received—mostly. Since the announcement of his plans to address the college a month earlier, the Calvin community had been abuzz with debate about the merits and madness of Bush's visit. Election year polls of Calvin's student body showed that two-thirds of the forty-three hundred students supported Bush, and a 2001 survey of Calvin faculty revealed that 24 percent described themselves as politically liberal, 28 percent said they were conservative, and 48 percent identified themselves as political moderates. Overall, that's a pretty close reflection of American political attitudes in general. So it shouldn't have been surprising that not everyone on the campus was thrilled about Bush speaking there. Nevertheless, the media seemed to get a kick out of the idea that, even among evangelical Christians, there was disagreement over the president and his policies.

At the commencement ceremony, an estimated 20 percent of the crowd wore buttons and stickers saying, "God Is Not a Democrat or a Republican" as a silent protest, and a handful of people did not stand up to applaud when the president was introduced. "While the media have sometimes portrayed evangelicalism as unanimous in support of a particular political agenda, that's not the case [at Calvin]," said philosophy professor David Hoekema, who joined more than one hundred other Calvin faculty, students and alumni to take out a full-page advertisement in the *Grand Rapids Press*. Published on the day of the commencement, the ad featured an open letter to President Bush, which began:

> We, the undersigned, respect your office, and we join the college in welcoming you to our campus. Like you, we recognize the importance of religious commitment in American political life. We seek open and honest dialogue about the Christian faith and how it is best expressed in the political sphere. While recognizing God as sovereign over individuals and institutions alike, we understand that no single political position should be identified with God's will, and we are conscious that this applies to our own views as well as those of others. At the same time we see conflicts between our understanding of what Christians are called to do and many of the policies of your administration.

The ad went on to criticize the war in Iraq as "unjust and unjustified," and to assert that Bush's administration had "fostered intolerance and divisiveness" and had often failed to listen to those with whom it disagreed.

One of the driving forces behind the protest was Calvin history professor Randal Jelks. Jelks, one of several African American faculty members at Calvin, helped round up signatures for the newspaper ad and served as the movement's most-quoted spokesperson. "We are a serious theological and intellectual school," he told reporters, "and we try to have our students informed by thoughtful reflection about the concerns. We are not Lynchburg," he said, referring to Jerry Falwell's more conservative Liberty University in Virginia. "We are not right wing; we are not left wing. We think our faith trumps political ideology."

OUR NEW GREAT DIVIDE

Out of all the tough stuff I needed to write about in this book, I knew the subject of this chapter would be the toughest. I have learned the hard way that it's best not to talk politics among friends, especially when they're evangelical—you might get your head bitten off.

During the election season of 2004, a few members of my church small group, where my wife and I are the only African Americans, were shocked to discover I was seriously considering not voting for George W. Bush a second time (my wife, who was raised a military brat, maintained her allegiance to the Republican Party). We were studying *The Purpose-Driven Life* in small group then, and for the rest of that evening I felt like the marked man in the room.

"How could you, in good conscience, vote for a baby killer?" someone asked.

"I've been praying that God would protect us," another person said. "If Bush doesn't win, I'm scared to death of what the future could hold for my kids."

Badly outnumbered, I felt a cold sweat spreading across my body. We eventually got to the study, but I couldn't focus at all. I couldn't wait to grab the kids and get the heck out of Dodge. I wanted to be anywhere but in that room.

In many ways, political bigotry is America's new racism. Once upon a time, black and white were the classic "clashing colors" that told the story of our nation's internal strife. Racism was our country's original sin—and the black-white divide its most notorious manifestation.

Lately, however, the two primary colors have morphed from black and white to blue and red—as in "blue states" and "red states." These labels refer to the colors that TV news stations assign to various U.S. states on election night to show which party has taken them: blue for states won by Democrats, red for those won by Republicans. After the bitterly disputed 2000 presidential election, the terms were dragged into popular usage as political pundits grasped for ways to talk about the deep ideological rifts splitting our nation.

Competing political loyalties seem to be the defining mark of everything we do these days. Think about it: If you're a conservative, you watch Fox News Channel; liberals tune in to CNN. Conservatives listen to Limbaugh religiously; liberals need their daily fix of *All Things Considered*. Conservatives proclaim "Merry Christmas"; liberals mutter "Happy Holidays." Conservatives support the war unquestioningly; liberals like to flip-flop. Conservatives are patriotic; liberals should just find another country already. I'm being flippant, but you get the point. I'm sure you can think of other examples.

The problem with these broad labels, of course, is that the American people are more complicated than that. Within each American exists a wide array of opinions, allegiances and philosophies, some of them contradictory. We have never been as narrowly defined and niche-oriented as the media, marketers and special-interest groups make us out to be. But today's culture warriors have insisted that we choose sides. We must line up as either this or that—there's no room (or respect) for wishy-washy centrists. And this is especially true within the evangelical movement, where the leaders with the loudest bullhorns and greatest clout all seem to be parked in the far right wing.

In recent years, America's presidential elections have served as a mirror to our soul, lucidly reflecting our widening political gulf. But even beyond election years, the evidence of our division is disheartening. Cable news shows and talk radio are now almost exclusively driven by the rants of screaming heads from opposing camps. Civility, if ever we really had it, has been decisively displaced by in-your-face bluster.

What's really troubling is how this nastiness has found its way into the church. A few months ago on my way to work, I noticed a new billboard promoting a local conservative talk radio station, which is owned by a major Christian media company. The sign featured these words in bold block letters: "Liberals Hate Us!" It's a humorous way of saying, "We tell it like it is," I suppose. But the accompanying whispered message is, "And We Hate *Them*, Too!" The language of the culture wars and partisan politics invariably drips with enmity and prejudice, whether overt or implicit.

If I sound like I'm coming down harder on conservatives, I probably am. But it's not because I don't like them. It's because I know them better. In fact, whether I like to admit it or not, I'm generally one of them. Up until the 2004 election, there was never any doubt which party would get most of my votes. Though I have long identified myself as an Independent, the white evangelical influence runs deep in my bones. After college, I instinctively voted for Republican candidates because I figured that's what I was supposed to do as an evangelical.

Ironically, I grew up in a firmly Democratic home. My dad and mom followed the traditional African American voting pattern without fail, and I understand why. They were raised in the Deep South during an era when Republicans—the Party of Lincoln!—had gradually turned their back on the black community. During the Great Depression, with the arrival of FDR's New Deal—a heroic and desperately needed act of big government—blacks began to join the Democratic Party en masse.

Though they were loyal Democrats, my parents were never political. They were simple people with limited education who taught me, mostly by example, to respect everyone and to never carry prejudice or hate in my heart. Growing up in the segregated South, they had seen plenty of it, and they knew how it could corrupt and destroy. "Son, don't put your faith in no human being," Dad once told me. "People will always let you down, especially the ones you love. But love them anyway."

I've been without my parents for more than fifteen years now, but I often long to discuss with them the current state of our world. What would they have thought of Bill Clinton? What position would they take on the war in Iraq? How might they respond to figures like Alan Keyes or Al Sharpton? What I do know is that they would not be swept up in the current political hysteria that has settled on our country. Even back in the seventies and eighties, groups like the Moral Majority and the ACLU had no relevance to their everyday lives on the west side of Rockford, Illinois. Then, like now, the skirmishes between high-profile conservative and liberal activist groups were theater designed more for the benefit of their respective middle-class donor bases than the greater good of, say, an elderly African American couple on the poor side of town.

BAD CHRISTIANS?

In the days leading up to President Bush's visit to Calvin College, Randal Jelks and Calvin philosophy professor Ruth Groenhout appeared on Fox News's *Hannity & Colmes* to discuss their decision to protest the event. Predictably, Alan Colmes, the left-leaning co-host, gave them a warm welcome while Sean Hannity, the conservative half of the tandem, thoroughly grilled the professors and then denounced them as "bad Christians." "If you guys had your way," he said, "the torture chambers and mass graves [in Iraq] would continue. Your way would appease evil."

The most disturbing, though not surprising, part of the broadcast was Hannity's suggestion that the professors' dissenting view—i.e., non-Republican opinion—somehow indicated that they were lesser Christians. Sadly, this also has become a common line of reasoning in many evangelical churches across America, where the values of the Republican

Party have been so closely embraced by conservative Christians that it's hard to tell where one ends and the other begins. Sean Hannity, for instance, was the commencement speaker at Liberty University just a week before Bush's appearance at Calvin. In announcing Hannity's booking, Chancellor Jerry Falwell said, "Sean Hannity is America's rising young voice for social conservatism and religious liberty. There is no more articulate voice for Christian conservatives in America."

Despite mild Republican gains of black voters, the Democrats by and large are still the party of the African American community. So, inevitably, when we talk about the political divide in America, to a certain extent we're talking about the enduring racial divide as well.

Chris Williamson, who graduated from Liberty University in the late eighties, attended the 2005 graduation ceremony and heard Sean Hannity speak. "It was the traditional Republican, conservative-evangelical kind of address," he says. "But I was thinking the whole time that the African Americans who came there to support their children and grandchildren, after they'd put that tuition money up for four years and gone through ridicule from their black friends on 'why you let your kid go to that school,' then had to sit there and listen to someone bash Democrats, when the majority of those folks are Democrats. There's no sensitivity from white evangelicals on these things, mainly because they don't have to be sensitive. It's their world, and many times they don't have a clue."

In my informal survey of black evangelicals I asked the question, "What political party do you feel best addresses the issues that are important to you?" The possible answers were "Republican," "Democrat," and "Neither party satisfactorily addresses the important issues." Though 95 percent of the respondents chose the third option, on some surveys I could see where they had checked "Republican" or "Democrat" before erasing it to check the "Neither party" option. Others called or e-mailed me weeks later to change their answer to the third option. One person wanted to make it clear that, even though she checked the third box, she had voted for the Democratic presidential candidate the last two elections based on her social justice concerns. Of the remaining 5 percent who did officially check a party, 3 percent chose "Democrat" and 2 percent "Republican." Not surprisingly, many African American evangelicals feel the same way about their politics as they do about other issues in the evangelical community—torn and undecided.

BLACK-ON-BLACK POLITICS

At this point, I need to stop and say something crucial: I do not want to invalidate or devalue the viewpoints, or the very existence, of African Americans who have aligned themselves with the Republican Party. It has become popular in these polarized times for black Democrats to demonize or question the racial "loyalty" of black Republicans. Indeed, a large part of my decision to include this chapter in the book was to challenge this unfortunate trend. The political divide has not only exacerbated the separation between the races, it has exposed—and then magnified—the political rifts between African Americans themselves. There have always been black conservatives. Heck, everyone has seen the polls that show the majority of blacks coming down on the conservative side of all the big moral issues, from abortion to same-sex marriage. But to openly identify yourself as a Republican? Forget about it—unless you want to endure the wrath of the black establishment's designated haters. Even Bill Cosby, not a political conservative by any stretch, was castigated for having the audacity to suggest that the black community needs to take more responsibility for its moral and social ills. Black leaders accused him of airing his people's dirty laundry in public.

These days, when I hear black commentators on radio or TV programs such as *The Tom Joyner Morning Show* or *Tavis Smiley* (whom I really dig, by the way), at times I can sense an underlying contempt when they discuss black conservatives. Too often, black Republicans are assumed to be props of the white man, political Uncle Toms without minds of their own—or worse, self-hating traitors. The Bush administration, which has courted African American voters like no other Republican administration in recent times, has been vilified as being racist and cold toward the real concerns of the black community. The divide is even more worrisome in the church, where political allegiances have gotten in the way of Christian unity. The critics accuse some black church leaders of being seduced by the monetary promise of Bush's Faith-Based Initiative, which aims to funnel federal dollars to church-run social service programs. (Though one wonders if the critics would have had the same reaction if a Democratic president had conceived the initiative.) The sum effect of all of this scorn and derision has been an impolite, dysfunctional environment that has left some African American evangelicals feeling like pariahs in their own communities.

"You don't square these things; you just agree to disagree without being disagreeable," the Reverend Herbert Lusk of Greater Exodus Baptist Church in Philadelphia told the *New York Times*. Lusk, a black Republican, was lamenting the clashing agendas of liberal and conservative black Christians. He added soberly, "The Klan in Memphis when I was a boy denied me the right to think what I wanted. We shouldn't get to a time in our lives when our own people deny us the same right to think."

"WHY I AM NOT AN EVANGELICAL CHRISTIAN"

In 2003 Congressman Tom DeLay, the embattled Texas Republican and born-again Christian, raised eyebrows with an audacious redistricting plan designed to carve up Texas's populace by race in order to gain additional House seats for his party. The plan, which diluted black and Hispanic voting power, was later called into question as a potential violation of the Voting Rights Act. (This matter, along with other alleged scandals, led to DeLay's resignation from Congress in 2006.)

I bring this up here not to go into the specifics of this particular case, or to further bash Republicans, but to highlight the continued importance that race plays in politics. I also want to underscore the value that politicians from both parties find in exploiting—and even expanding—the separations between the American people.

It's hard not to sound cynical when addressing this, and I hope I don't. The truth is, racial and ideological divisions are politically desirable and expedient in our present political system. But the outcome will always be disastrous. Speaking to the Pharisees, Jesus himself warned, "Every kingdom divided against itself will be ruined, and every city or household divided against itself will not stand" (Matthew 12:25). Centuries later, in 1858, Jesus' words were invoked by Abraham Lincoln—a politician who would later learn firsthand the tragic consequences of a fractured nation.

I mentioned earlier how I've been burned in some evangelical circles when I made the mistake of discussing political matters. And I suspect I'll receive more severe burns once this chapter makes its way to the public. To be honest, I don't know how to talk to my Christian friends about this stuff without it turning awkward. Sometimes I get the feeling that some white evangelicals won't consider an African American believer a real Christian unless he or she subscribes to their conservative political views.

Chicago pastor Jerald January told me about a puzzling experience he had one time when he was doing a signing at a bookstore. "I was out autographing one of my books," he said, "and more than once, a [white] person walked up to me and, instead of asking whether I'm a Christian or whether I love Jesus, before they would buy the book they wanted to know whether I was conservative. And I was like, 'What? I'm a Christian, and I love the Lord!' I thought to myself, *Shouldn't that be enough?*"

What scares me most is when Christians become so zealous about their conservative politics that they bring it into their understanding of what it means to be a faithful follower of Christ. When we confuse God's kingdom for the kingdoms of this world, we eventually get things like the bombing of the Oklahoma federal building, or 9/11, or a televangelist prophesying destruction on Florida and Pennsylvania, or the confession of a close friend of mine who told me he had to pray diligently to combat his persistent feeling of hatred for Bill Clinton. In *Bird by Bird*, writer Anne Lamott recalls something her friend Tom, a priest, once told her: "You can safely assume you've created God in your own image when it turns out that God hates all the same people you do." When it comes to politics and the Christian faith, have we evangelicals somehow crafted God in our own image?

It's not that we shouldn't be politically engaged; there's certainly a place for that. The faith-based abolitionist and civil rights movements show us the value of nonviolent resistance and truth spoken to power. But the notion that America is historically a Christian nation—and the church the designated police of its values—is dubious at best, and it's disconcerting to see how far some of us take it. In our zeal, we sometimes forget Christ's command to love our neighbors—and enemies. Often in the heat of defending moral standards or the lives of unborn children, we lose sight of the individual that God has placed before us to love at that moment. Christians are called to stand apart from the venom and inhumanity of worldly politics and inject into the process compassion, grace and a spirit of reconciliation. Unfortunately, even among believers politics usually brings out our worst.

My disillusionment with evangelicals and politics was at an all-time high when God sent me a reminder about where I needed to put my focus. My church, like many evangelical congregations across the land before Election Day, had been one of those that handed out candidate scorecards to clue in its members on where the different political contestants lined up on the hot-button issues. Since these cards were produced by a conservative organization, the implication was always that the Republican candidate was the guy to go with. Though churches as nonprofit institutions are not allowed to endorse political candidates, this has been one way to get around the laws and educate churchgoers without coming out and saying, "Vote for this guy." It's a helpful tool, but I dislike seeing it in churches because of the subtle suggestion that God's stamp of approval was on a particular candidate. My church is not that different from countless other American evangelical churches in its unspoken support of conservative politics and causes.

One Sunday morning, a few months following the 2004 elections, I walked into the grade school gymnasium where my church meets to find that we were having a guest speaker. His name was Bill, and he had been one of our young senior pastor's Wheaton College classmates. He always thought he'd be pastoring a church somewhere in America himself, but instead he and his family were serving in the Middle East as missionaries. I thought we were in for the typical dry mission field report, followed by a love offering and an appeal for prayer.

But not this morning.

I knew something was amiss when Bill announced his sermon's title: "Why I Am Not an Evangelical Christian."

"It is my opinion that the greatest threat to belief in Jesus is not the religion of Islam," he began. "It is also my opinion that the greatest threat to our faith and daily following Jesus is not a liberal U.S. agenda or the onset of secularism in our culture. I believe that perhaps the greatest threat to believing and following Jesus is when we come to depend on a religious system of faith instead of daily depending on God and seeking to do his will."

I looked over at my wife, Dana, as if to say, "Uh-oh." It was clearly not going to be your typical missionary slide show.

"My wife and I moved to the Middle East three years ago, and in that time I've begun to see how much of my faith and the way that I go about making decisions is really guided by the evangelical system of Christianity—what our subculture says real Christians do and don't do—instead of being guided by my relationship with Jesus and my commitment to daily seeking to do his will. And as I've examined my own life, I've come to see how dangerous that can be to a true life of faith."

Bill talked about his background—raised in an evangelical church, Christian college and seminary graduate, youth pastor, he even taught New Testament Greek for a time. But, he said, none of that really prepared him for his life as a missionary businessman in a Middle Eastern country.

"When God called my wife and me to leave the U.S. and immerse ourselves in a new culture, a part of that calling for us was to leave organized
church, to leave contemporary worship, to leave preaching tapes and
Christian music, to leave small-group Bible studies. It even meant leaving reading and studying the Bible in English. And in the process of having all that stuff stripped away and clearing out everything that had been
built up around what it means to be a Christian in America, I found that
when it's all gone, you find that you either depend 100 percent on God
himself for everything—every aspect of life, no matter what happens—
or, like me, you begin to see how much of your faith is dependent on the
forms of Christianity or the circumstances of life instead of on God
alone."

Then, without warning, he veered even closer to home.

"Are we following a man-made system of what it means to be a Christian, or are we following Christ? And if we're following Christ, are we living out the basic truths that he called us to do? God has called us to love
our enemies and not to hate them. If you know that to be the truth, is
that reflected in how you treat people you don't agree with? Is that reflected in how you talk about people who voted for Kerry if you voted
for Bush, or people who voted for Bush if you voted for Kerry? Is that
reflected in how you talk about people who are against prayer in schools
or support homosexual rights? God has called us first and foremost to
do his will, and that begins by seeking to apply the truth we already
know every day."

He concluded: "However you may define what it is to be a Christian,
if we're not committed to seeking and doing God's will every day, we've
missed it."

When Bill began, I had been curious about how all the folks in the
gym would respond to the provocative things he was saying. Frankly, I
secretly hoped his contrarian message would convict and challenge all
the poor misguided folks in the room. But by the end of his sermon, my
attention was turned inward—and my spiritual arrogance punctured. I

was the neediest of all! How was I doing in this department? Did I really put a premium on following Jesus first? Or did I, too, get caught up in the various "forms of Christianity" that our subculture judges as most important?

I left church that morning feeling better about the whole "evangelicals and politics" thing. No, the political divide had not disappeared. We would continue to have the same vicious ranting and raving, the same painful disagreements. But as I pulled out of the parking lot, I prayed for all the other believers across the world who had heard God's Word that morning—that they, too, would leave their services with a similar determination to strip away all the trappings and simply follow Christ.

10

THE "OTHER" OTHERS

Just as God refused to answer Cain's ridiculous suppositional question—
"Am I my brother's keeper?"—
Jesus likewise did not answer the Jewish lawyer's question of
"Who is my neighbor?" Instead Jesus forced the lawyer to pick the
Samaritan—over two religious Jews!—as the person God
wanted him to imitate. How that must have stung! The lesson:
We have a responsibility to all people, not just those like us.

Randy Woodley, a Keetoowah Cherokee evangelist

In addition to teaching me how to tie my shoelaces and make my bed, my parents also impressed upon me the importance of thinking for myself. I haven't always been successful at it—but I don't always remember to make my bed either. Thinking for yourself has some disadvantages, though, especially when you're operating in an environment that expects you to say the "right" things and to conform to the party line, whatever it may be.

As a senior in high school, for reasons I cannot recall anymore, I was selected by the Daughters of the American Revolution (a century-old women's service organization that promotes patriotism) as one of its outstanding young citizens and given the chance to compete against other students in Rockford for a college scholarship. I don't remember the dollar amount of the scholarship or the exact number of students I was up against, but it was a wonderful opportunity. Each student was required to write an essay on the meaning of freedom, or something along those lines. Had I been more politically savvy, I might have come up with something calculated to really wow the sweet, gray-haired white women of our local DAR chapter. As it turns out, I was not politically savvy.

I had been troubled for months about a situation regarding a public park in Rockford. The park was originally the site of a Native American burial ground. You could still make out the locations of the Indian mounds throughout the park's hilly terrain. What bothered me was that, during the summer, this park was the site of several community festivals, including the annual Fourth of July celebration. It boggled my mind to think that as we celebrated our nation's independence, we were trampling the graves of the people to whom the nation originally belonged. I tried to communicate some of this irony in my essay, concluding with a call to remember those among us who had suffered terrible injustices, that the integrity of our freedom and liberty as Americans demanded that we look out for them too. It was not the stuff of white-bread patriotic essays. But, like I said, my parents taught me to think for myself. I can still see the women's strained expressions as the hostess read a few lines from my paper before calling me up to receive my certificate. Needless to say, I did not win the scholarship. (However, a few years later, Rockford did acknowledge the sanctity of the burial sections of the park and stopped using it as a high-traffic festival site.)

As I look back, I realize that growing up as a black kid bused to mostly white schools gave me a special sensitivity to the experiences of other minorities in America. And I eventually carried that sensitivity with me into the evangelical church, where the isolation and "otherness" of being an ethnic minority can seem even more intense.

In college I roomed with an older Mexican student named Uriel. Over the course of our three years together, Uriel and I became close friends. I know it's a cliché to say "We were like brothers," but we really were. He was the best man at my wedding, traveled to Rockford to support me at my dad's funeral, and welcomed me into his family's home in Elgin, where they introduced me to *posole* and rice milk.

Uriel loved Jesus, and he was never ashamed to shout out a praise to him in the middle of a quiet evening of homework or after getting a good grade on a paper. I went with him a few times to his vibrant Pentecostal church, which felt five times as electric as anything I'd seen in black Pentecostal settings. I remember going into Chicago to sit by his hospital bed after he underwent brain surgery to remedy the epileptic seizures that had plagued him since childhood. His face was swollen beyond recognition, but when he awoke and saw me, he flashed that same familiar smile.

There were many evenings in our dorm room that we talked about our respective journeys. He wanted to know if I had ever encountered racism. I told him about the day in Rockford when I was about fifteen. My high school buddy, Gaylin, and I were at the hospital with my mom and dad. My mom had suffered another asthma attack, and we were waiting as the emergency room doctors treated her.

Being restless teens, Gaylin and I decided to take a stroll to the hospital cafeteria to get some potato chips and pop. After leaving the cafeteria, we were confronted in the hallway by a group of hospital security guards—all white men. They grabbed our arms and abruptly shuttled us into a small room with an unmarked door. "What were you doing in the cafeteria?" one of the men demanded.

We held up our bags of chips. "Just having a snack," one of us said. "Would you like some?" We were scared to death but unable to shut off our smart-alecky teen demeanors.

"A man in the cafeteria said he overheard you two saying you planned to rob the cafeteria. Is that true?"

At that point, we didn't know whether to laugh or cry. A discussion of the latest Van Halen album had been the extent of our chatter in the cafeteria. Where someone got the idea that we planned to rob the place, I'll never know. But these stern-looking white men weren't playing around—and they had guns. Our teenage impertinence did not amuse them. As far as they were concerned, Gaylin and I were two dangerous black males. I figured we would soon be cuffed and whisked downtown. I didn't know anything then about racial profiling, and Rodney King was several years away. However, I knew we were in big trouble.

Suddenly the door swung open, and in burst my dad. "What are you doing with my boys?" he said. The rest of the event is a blur. All I know is that my dad got us out of there. I have no idea how he knew we were in the room, but in that split second, he saved us from heaven only knows. There were other incidents too, like being accused of shoplifting at a drugstore when I was ten or eleven while I was trying to read a comic book. When I think back on those episodes now, I sometimes wish I'd had a Johnnie Cochran to call afterward. As it turned out, I was powerless to do anything but plead my innocence to unconvinced accusers.

Uriel shared with me his own stories of being harassed or spoken down to by classmates, teachers and store clerks—mocked or dismissed because of his heavy accent. He also told me about the dangerous adventure of coming into the United States illegally when he was snuck into the country by "coyotes," or *polleros* (the "professional" immigrant smugglers); the joy of finally becoming a U.S. citizen; and his ultimate desire to one day return to Mexico to minister to the impoverished people in his hometown of Cuernavaca. He loved the United States and all of the opportunity here, especially the chance to get a good Christian education. But God had given him a heart for his people back home.

My friend Uriel is now married and working as a pastor and counselor in the city. We don't stay in touch as often as we used to, but I will always count it a privilege to have had my life touched by this devoted man of God. Getting to know Uriel, and my Laotian roommate, Neng, tuned me on to the immigrant experience in America and the prejudice and discrimination with which they contend.

More Invisible Than Me

In his book *Good News from the Barrio,* theologian Harold J. Recinos writes, "As a Puerto Rican, I grew up thinking of myself as a person unworthy of

American society. I attended public schools in the South Bronx where the image of 'America' was forged in white Protestant Anglo-Saxon terms and Latinos were treated in the curriculum as 'foreign others.'" He goes on to share how he and others from his community would joke about "growing up invisible in America, because if you are not black or white you are not seen." It's both fascinating and sobering for me, a member of a racial group that has been historically oppressed in the United States, to think that there are other minority groups who rank themselves below mine on the scale of American value and influence.

Recinos, a professor of church and society at the Perkins School of Theology in Dallas, writes eloquently about the twenty-first-century challenge of immigration, our culturally pluralistic society and the church's role in it all. "In America today," he says, "we are all faced with the choice between creating life together on the basis of hate for other cultures, languages, and ethnic groups, or working hard to become a free union of many." He goes on: "It is here that I think the message of the church needs to address the current national climate of increasing racial polarization by challenging people to choose between standing with those social groups who wish to shatter dreams, or walking with others who long to build society on the beauty of diversity."

Christians from Native American communities represent another race of people whose unique plights are often overlooked by the evangelical church. While sitting with fifty other people in a racial reconciliation workshop in Indianapolis (an event I will discuss later in the book), I met Randy Woodley, a Keetoowah Cherokee evangelist. Everyone in the room was mesmerized as he shared with us about the ache of being left out of the "reconciliation conversation" as a Native American believer. He came close to tears as he recounted the many times he had sat around a table with black and white evangelicals discussing racism in the church always to have America's sins against his people treated as an afterthought. "As Native people," he said, "it seems like everybody else has a slightly different agenda than we do when it come to racial issues."

Ministry leader Charles Robinson, a member of the Choctaw Nation of Oklahoma, was more explicit: "Our people are being lost to alcohol and obesity and sexual abuse, and it's all rooted in the hopelessness of poverty. So when evangelicals, who have had no real relationship with our people, suddenly show up to self-righteously crusade against the casinos on our reservations, I sometimes want to say, 'Shut your mouth about closing down the casinos until you're ready to offer other viable options. What alternatives do you have for helping these impoverished communities?'"

Over time, I have realized that my Native American, Latino and Asian brothers and sisters in the evangelical movement also have endured the frustration and loneliness of being "the first" or "only" in their Christian settings.

Perhaps a sign of growth in the racial reconciliation movement is the recognition that race relations is not just a black and white issue anymore. Though the black-white relationship still occupies a unique position in our nation's history, evangelicals must also be ready to include other ethnic minorities in their vision of a reconciled, multiracial church that reflects the ultimate reality of God's kingdom—on earth as it is in heaven.

Yes, this is a book about the black evangelical experience. But I'd be remiss if I didn't acknowledge the journeys of other minorities within the evangelical movement. They too have felt the sting of the reconciliation blues, and we must learn from their stories.

A CAUTIONARY TALE

On a breezy summer day in South Haven, Michigan, at a rustic conference center within walking distance of the beautiful Lake Michigan shore, I moderated a *Christianity Today* forum on the biblical call for multiracial churches. The forum was in response to the book *United by Faith*, which was a follow-up to *Divided by Faith*, Michael Emerson and Christian Smith's landmark tome on the evangelical race problem. Af-

ter considerable research of the Scriptures and of modern-day congregations, *United by Faith*'s team of authors, which included sociologists
Emerson, Karen Chai Kim and George Yancey, along with theologian
Curtiss Paul DeYoung, put forth the bold assertion that all Christian
churches, when possible, should be multiracial. The *CT* forum brought
together four pastors of different ethnic backgrounds to discuss the
book's findings: Noel Castellanos, founding pastor of an inner-city
church in Chicago and president of the Latino Leadership Foundation;
Bill Hybels, pastor of Willow Creek Community Church, the influential megachurch in suburban Chicago; Frank Reid, pastor of the historic Bethel African Methodist Episcopal Church in Baltimore; and
Soong-Chan Rah, the Korean-American pastor of Cambridge Community Fellowship Church, a multiethnic congregation reaching many of
the "postmodern" students from Harvard, MIT and other eminent universities in the Boston area.

I had met Soong-Chan a few years earlier at a Council for Christian
Colleges and Universities conference, and I was immediately challenged by his insights and inspired by his heart for God. I knew he
would make an excellent contribution to the *CT* forum. During the discussion, he shared a story about feeling marginalized as an Asian American in the evangelical community. The incident he described has stuck
with me ever since.

Now, you need to know that I'm the kind of guy who feels righteous
indignation over news of a woman who was treated unfairly by Neiman
Marcus after she realized she had unwittingly paid $250 for their famous
chocolate chip cookie recipe. (I later discovered the story was an urban
legend, but not before forwarding an outraged e-mail to dozens of my
friends.) I have a hard time stomaching injustice, so Soong-Chan's story
was disconcerting. Moreover, the fallout after *CT* published it added new
layers of frustration to the situation. Though I've edited out the name of
the evangelical company involved in the incident, here is Soong-Chan's
story in his own words:

It was August of 2003 and a typical summer Tuesday at our church offices in Cambridge. We were in the middle of our weekly staff meeting when we took a quick break. I took the opportunity to glance through our church's mail for that day and stumbled across a catalog for a denominational publisher of Christian education materials. In the center of the catalog was a full-page ad. At first, I thought the ad was some sort of joke or satire. I didn't want to believe it was actually what it was claiming to be: a real advertisement for a Vacation Bible School curriculum.

The ad showed a white girl dressed in a kimono with chopsticks in her hair. She held a Chinese takeout food box. The title of this VBS material was "Rickshaw Rally: Far Out, Far East." Still unwilling to believe that this could be actual VBS material, I went to the publisher's website. When I typed in the website address, a gong appeared with (for lack of a better term) "ching-chongy" music in the background— music that seemed to have been taken straight off of the soundtrack of a Charlie Chan movie. Throughout the website were images of non-Asian kids in "oriental" outfits: kimonos, karate uniforms and the like. Under the auspices of doing a VBS with a Japanese theme, the publisher caricatured and generalized all Asian cultures with various stereotypical images. Using the image of a rickshaw (a symbol of economic and social oppression used more frequently in Chinese and South Asian culture), having a theme song mocking Asian culture (the chorus of the theme song is: "Wax on, wax off, get your rickshaw ready"), and encouraging VBS teachers to dress up like geishas and samurais were examples of how the publisher was attempting to introduce diversity to their children's curriculum. But clearly, this evangelical publishing company was tapping into the only images that they have of Asians—Chinese food, *Karate Kid II,* etc. Because Asian culture was simply used as a "fun way" to teach the gospel, there was an inadvertent mocking tone to their presentation. This was particularly evident in the theme song—which mimics Asian accents and music to sing a song about Jesus.

More disturbing than the VBS material itself, says Soong-Chan, was how the publisher responded to concerns raised by many Asian American Christians. As word spread about the curriculum, the publisher was inundated with phone calls and e-mails. When Soong-Chan got through to the publishing company's assistant director of Sunday school material, he explained to her the offensive nature of the materials. She referred him to another person, but sensing that concern about the curriculum was growing, she tried to defuse the protests by saying, "You know, this curriculum is really about preaching Jesus, and I wouldn't want you to do anything that would stop Jesus from being preached." Soong-Chan picks up the story:

> The next day, I heard back from the director of the VBS curriculum. I explained for about fifteen minutes why this material was offensive to many Asian Americans and how hurtful stereotypes are to ethnic minorities. I asked him at the end of the conversation if the company would be open to reviewing and changing the curriculum given the concerns raised by the Asian American community. He said there would be no changes despite the concerns. I wanted to be certain that I had heard him clearly, so I asked him to repeat the statement. He repeated: "There will be no changes." Despite being told that this material was offensive, the company took no consideration of these concerns.
>
> The next day, those that had written an e-mail to the company received a form e-mail response. In it, the company

stated that "the Far East theme was chosen by this group because of the colorful and exciting possibilities that it held." They also explained, "While producing the material, we included folks who have served in Asian countries as missionaries and have also consulted people who are native Japanese. Some of our editorial team have actually visited Japan so that we would be as true to the culture as possible. We have not included anything in our materials other than the wonderful and fun elements of the Japanese culture that we have discovered on our own or delved into through research."

No mention was made of any Asian Americans involved in the process of the development of this curriculum (this would be confirmed by subsequent statements from the company). Instead of addressing the problem and concerns, the publisher chose to dismiss them.

Eventually, when an online petition went up, close to 1,500 signatures (with an estimated 1,000 or more signatures from Asian Americans) protested the curriculum. The publisher dismissed the petition as being unscientific. When copies of the petition were sent to the publisher and its parent denomination, no one responded. As news of the uproar spread to the media, the publisher geared up its PR machine, claiming to the Associated Press, "For every concern raised by an Asian American, we are receiving dozens of positive responses from Asian Americans. . . ." But there was never any proof of this offered.

By this time, concerns were being raised throughout the United States. A Caucasian ethics professor from the denomination in question went to great lengths to try to educate his denomination about the concerns of the Asian American community, even writing an article in a denominational newspaper. A Caucasian minister with the denomination's missions department attempted to work within the denomination to raise concerns. An Asian American pastor who is a member of the denomination's international missions board worked to have various churches in the denomination reject the VBS material. (Despite the claim by the company that they had the support and input of this particular board in creating the material, this prominent pastor was not made aware of the theme of the material until October 2003.) In addition, this pastor wrote a personal plea to the publishing company's president imploring the removal of the material. His request was rejected outright. Even as voices were raised within the denomination, the leaders continued to ignore the concerns raised by the Asian American Christian community.

After *CT* published Soong-Chan's comments about the VBS curriculum (which were considerably shorter than those above), the publishing company's president sent a letter to the editor, taking us to task for not contacting them to get their side of the story. The letter said in part: "We would have been happy to correct Rah's oversimplifications, out-of-context characterizations and factual inaccuracies." The letter cited one minor—and even then debatable—"inaccurate" statement regarding offensive lesson ideas that were posted on the VBS website and not found in the official curriculum. But the letter could not contradict the overall point of Soong-Chan's story—that the company ignored the pleas of scores of Asian American Christians, and even Caucasian leaders from its own denomination, and published a curriculum that many perceived as culturally insensitive.

The letter to *CT* continued: "The truth is that [this company's] VBS curriculum was used by tens of thousands of churches in 2004—including hundreds of Korean, Japanese, Chinese, and other ethnic churches—and resulted in more than 100,000 children, teenagers, and adults coming to faith in Jesus Christ." The company's rebuttal, that people were coming to Christ because of the VBS materials, used evangelical platitudes to obscure the issue at hand and make its critics appear numb to the idea that souls were being saved. In effect, the president's letter ignored Soong-Chan's concerns and painted him as a spiritual cad at the same time.

I understand the politics of all of this. I even understand the fact that the likely reason Soong-Chan and his cohorts were ignored was that bags of money had already been spent on the development and printing of the VBS materials. What I don't understand is how the concerns of a group of Christians desiring dialogue with the leaders of a preeminent evangelical institution could be shut down so completely.

Don't get me wrong. I think it's awesome that people came to Christ through "Rickshaw Rally," but this in no way nullifies the cultural insensitivities found in those materials. In fact, putting a premium on the salvation of each human being should mean that our commitment to their souls, to their dignity, continues even after we get them to say the "sinner's prayer." A sad tendency of evangelical faith is to elevate the act of evangelism over the humanity of the people we want to reach.

I also was troubled that *CT* didn't attempt to offer a better defense of Soong-Chan or his position. One colleague even said to me, "Based on what I heard [from the VBS publisher], I think Soong-Chan has some anger issues." Which brought to mind my own experiences with "angry black man" syndrome. I guess it's not just for black folks anymore! Apparently, anytime an ethnic minority speaks out against a race-related injustice, he risks being branded a malcontent in need of therapy.

Even as I write this, my mind flashes to thoughts of the Chief Illiniwek controversy here in my home state, in which University of Illinois leaders insist on keeping a culturally insensitive symbol as its mascot despite the outcries of Native American citizens. As with the VBS debacle, the common theme is white leaders defining the public portrayal of another culture. Wouldn't it be great if evangelicals could lead the way in countering this sort of practice?

HONORARY WHITE PEOPLE

Soong-Chan, who moved to Chicago in 2006 to join the faculty of North Park University, told me he doesn't want to be known as the belligerent defender of Asian American Christians. He hopes the VBS incident can be a cautionary tale to help evangelicals deal more seriously with cultural issues. For him, it comes down to a matter of biblical reconciliation. How can we be reconciled if we don't take the time to understand the hearts and concerns of our brothers and sisters in Christ who are different from us?

Soong-Chan asked me if I knew about the history of Asians in South Africa. Drawing a blank, I told him to fill me in.

"During the time of apartheid in that country, a special designation was created for Asian businessmen," he said. "Since Asians did not qualify as whites, nor would they want to be categorized as blacks or coloreds, a special designation was created called 'honorary white people.' There are times in the history of race relations in America where the Asian American community spent much of our time trying to become honorary white people. But only God can define who we are as a people."

He paused, then added, "Thirty years from now, if my son or daughter will have the honor of serving God in Christian ministry and they are at a conference with other believers from different parts of the country, I don't want them to have to deal with someone whose perception of Asians is based on media stereotypes that have been perpetuated by the church through a VBS curriculum. If America is to emerge as a truly multicultural nation, and if American evangelicalism is to be an important part of that growth, then voices from every race and culture must be heard—not as honorary white people, but as a reconciled community with a biblical vision and voice."

11

LET ALL CREATION SING

A great message set to simple music is a piece of portable theology.
Hardly any of us remember the sermons we have heard.
But songs, time and time again, have gone with people to the bathtub,
the coal mines, wherever they went, and made a difference.

Gloria Gaither

Some to church repair
Not for the doctrine, but the music there.

Alexander Pope

Music has a way of penetrating our lives. Sometimes when nothing else can break through, a song stirs our spirits. We all remember that Lauryn Hill song we jammed to every day the summer before senior year. The Boyz II Men song that was the final dance at the senior prom. The LeAnn Rimes ballad playing on the car radio when we kissed our future spouse for the first time. The Kenny G tune playing in the delivery room before the birth of our first child. Music is powerful stuff, like the soundtrack of our souls. A song can feature the cheesiest, most pedestrian tune in the world and still represent a precious, unforgettable memory.

Church music, in some ways, can be even more potent. Hymns we haven't heard for years can creep up on us during a worship service and remind us why we believe. A gospel choir can elevate our spirits from the pew, like laughing gas raising us from the dentist's chair. A Maranatha chorus can prompt stodgy theology professors to lift their hands. A modern praise song can turn cold-looking Goths into ardent worshipers.

In my junior year at Judson, I attended a concert on the campus of Wheaton College that featured the Soul Children of Chicago, an electrifying gospel choir of one hundred twenty African American kids ages seven to seventeen singing, clapping and dancing in the Spirit. I had never seen or heard anything like it before, a group of inner-city children whose passionate praise and worship transformed an auditorium of mostly white, staid suburbanites into a sanctuary full of Holy Ghost revelers.

The ministry of the Soul Children affected my life in two significant ways. First, I was so taken by the group that I determined to write an article about them. After graduating from Judson, I took a job crunching numbers as a marketing assistant at Christianity Today International. My dream was to be a writer, but in the meantime I was happy to be doing anything inside a publishing company, especially one as prominent as CTI. After seeing the Soul Children a second time, a year after the first concert, it occurred to me that it would be exciting to do a profile on them and their founder, Walter Whitman. I explained my vision for the article to one of the editors at *CT* magazine, and he agreed it had potential. Feeling empowered, I called the Soul Children's office and set up a date to visit the group during one of its rehearsal sessions. I remember driving down to the South Side church where they rehearsed and parking my car across the street. Broken glass and faded candy wrappers crackled under my feet as I approached the old cathedral. I remember drinking in the urban atmosphere, loving the concrete landscape.

Inside the church, I watched the kids practice. They were ordinary boys and girls, laughing and goofing around between songs. Whitman directed the group like a cross between a drill sergeant and a lion tamer, and he had the kids responding with uncanny precision to his every order. A swift handclap or vertical wave of the arm could shift the choristers into an about-face or rotate them 360 degrees. And when the children's voices were unleashed in their fullness, the effect was both beautiful and stirring:

> *This is the day that the Lord has made;*
> *This is the day to be joyful, joyful, oh yes!*

Whitman, who founded the choir as an extracurricular activity at a parochial grade school before taking it full time, told me that he intended it to be more about building character and faith than simply performing songs. And several of the kids told me that the choir had helped them learn more about God and get better grades. I wrote the profile as a fan, but by the time it was printed in *CT,* I felt like a bona fide journalist. That article, my first published piece, would ultimately lead to my position as an assistant editor at the magazine.

The second way the Soul Children changed my life was even more momentous. After years of going to white schools and attending white churches, I had become somewhat disconnected from African American culture. The Soul Children reintroduced me to gospel music and to the gritty verve of city life. From that point on, I knew I could not go back to life as usual. I sensed God was calling me not just to integrate white institutions but to reaffirm my identity as an African American Christian. This ultimately led me to attend an interracial congregation on the West Side of Chicago, where I met my future wife and discovered a real-life laboratory for working out the practical implications of racial reconciliation in the church.

All of this because I was inspired by the ministry of a youth choir. Like I said, music has a way of penetrating our lives.

STRAINED HARMONIES

Unfortunately, the power of music can be a stumbling block as well. In my current job as editor of *Today's Christian* (a more consumer-oriented sister publication of *Christianity Today*), I've received a number of articles from pastors and laypeople whose churches were torn apart by conflicts over worship—which usually boils down to disagreements over music.

To their credit, many churches today have learned to successfully blend old and new worship styles—a few organ-powered hymns here, a couple guitar-driven choruses over there. Others have stubbornly planted their stakes in one camp or the other, and everybody in town knows, for instance, that First Baptist is all dress shirts and Fanny Crosby, while Creekside Community is all Darlene Zschech and lattes in the foyer. And rarely do the twain meet.

The worship wars are bad enough in homogeneous settings, but what happens when you're trying to blend different races and cultures into one unified congregation? Indeed, when people are discussing the practical challenges of forming crosscultural churches, they usually put music and worship at the top of the list of reasons it cannot be done.

And if it is done, one of the cultures usually ends up getting slighted. In my early experience at that West Side church, for instance, the African American half of the congregation dominated over the whites and other races in attendance. Consequently, the style of the church was distinctly black, despite the rainbow of folks in attendance. I've visited other crosscultural churches where the style was decidedly white, despite the presence of significant numbers of blacks and Latinos.

During that roundtable of multicultural pastors I told you about in the last chapter, Soong-Chan Rah explained the challenge that many churches face in their attempt to attain a balanced mix of diverse cultures:

> One image that most of us have discarded by now is the "melting pot," because what it ends up becoming is a soupy mixture that has no flavor at all. A second metaphor is the "salad bowl," where you have all these different vegetables that sort of make up different flavors. But it turned out that the dressing was still creamy ranch, and it smothered everything else. . . .

Are we looking to boil everybody down into one unrecog-
nizable mass? Or are we trying to smother everything with
one culture so that everybody is the same flavor? We need to
be honest about this.

Even outside the formal church in the pop-culture realm of Christen-
dom, music has been known to segregate and divide. Nicole C. Mullen,
who happens to be black, is one of the most popular CCM artists of today. When she came to CTI's offices recently to chat up her new album
and her wonderful ministry with young girls, the other editors and I figured it would be your typical feel-good publicity visit. Instead, we were
surprised by Nicole's candor about the segregation in the Christian music industry. She said Christian radio is now programmed primarily for
white soccer moms, and that stations play her award-winning songs less
frequently.

"I grew up listening to Christian radio," she told us. "So it's ironic to
me that the same people who taught me how to write songs by allowing
me to hear the artists that influenced my life are now closing their doors
to me."

In fact, Nicole, along with CeCe Winans, is one of the only African
American artists you'll hear on mainstream Christian radio stations these
days. But, as she said, her songs get nowhere near the airplay as white
artists with fewer accolades. She's certain that it has to do with the "urban" flavor of her music.

Mullen is not alone. In a 2005 op-ed in *CCM Magazine*, singer Lisa
Kimmey, the eldest sister in the popular R&B trio Out of Eden, challenged the Christian music industry on its seemingly discriminatory
practices when it comes to nonwhite music styles. "I've seen Christian
R&B, gospel, and hip-hop get smaller, while—in the mainstream—
becoming the most popular music genres," she wrote. "We have a long
way to go. In order to operate as the family of God in music, we must be
willing to give more than one genre a platform. We must learn to appre-

ciate the many beautiful forms of music that we have in our industry."

In a ChristianityToday.com interview, Teron Carter (a.k.a. Bonafide) of the rap duo GRITS put it more bluntly: "There's blatant division within our industry. . . . In Christian music, everything's predominantly white. Black music doesn't really exist in that genre." His partner Stacey Jones (a.k.a. Coffee) added, "I don't think it's the music, the lyrics, or anything like that. . . . The black face scares them. Stacie Orrico [a white Christian singer], whom they've embraced, is doing her own version of urban music. Her beats are very urban-driven. That's why I don't think it's the music itself. They feel safer with a white face promoting that kind of music than with a black face."

You may not agree with every jot and tittle of Coffee's observation, but I think he's onto something. Many white evangelical institutions play it safe when it comes to cultural diversity—whether it applies to radio play lists or Sunday morning worship.

A friend of mine, who's black, told me about the maddening experience she's had at the church she and her husband have attended for the past year or so. It's a growing suburban church with a mostly white congregation but a desire to expand its ethnic diversity. The church's music is a mixture of modern worship songs by artists like Chris Tomlin and Matt Redman. Good stuff, but clearly more vanilla than chocolate. Once they found out my friend could sing and that she's an experienced worship leader, they recruited her for the praise team. "We'd like you to help us bring more 'soul' to our worship," the senior pastor told her, explaining that he wanted the church to be more appealing to nonwhite visitors.

But once my friend began rehearsing with the team, she felt them resisting her attempts to nudge the music in a more soulful direction. "We need to take it slow," they told her. "Our people might not be ready for that just yet."

She obliged but soon felt more like the token black person on the stage than someone who was making a unique contribution. "I love to worship God, so I didn't mind singing those particular songs," she told me. "But I was also frustrated with the leadership's rigidity. In their desire to not offend their main demographic, it seemed they weren't trusting God to broaden their worship style."

SALSA ON THE SIDE

I'm realistic. I understand that some churches simply aren't able to do the multiracial, crosscultural approach. In fact, some wouldn't know how even if they wanted to; it's just not in their DNA. But then I stop and consider the early church in Antioch (Acts 11:19-30) and how it blended Jews and a wide cultural swath of Gentiles into a reconciled body of believers. The Bible says Jesus' followers were first called "Christians" in this ancient city. Sometimes I wonder if that has some correlation to the vibrant testimony of unity that this diverse congregation displayed to the world around it. What, I wonder, was *their* worship style? Then I think about the great multitude of worshipers foreseen in Revelation 7. They are from every nation, tribe and language. As they stand before Christ declaring, "Salvation belongs to our God, who sits on the throne, and to the Lamb," I wonder if their voices are joined together in one common, heavenly tongue, or does each of their distinct languages somehow blend together in a unified chorus?

In heaven, you've got to believe the worship is going to be great. With Christ right there in front of us as both the inspiration and focus of our energies, it will be the purest offering of worship that we'll ever know. The music will be incredible too. There will be no need for accompaniment tracks, and I bet we won't even bicker over whether it's okay to use drums and electric guitars. A dream lineup for the celestial praise team might feature King David as worship leader and include folks like Stevie Wonder, Johann Sebastian Bach, George Beverly Shea, Yo-Yo Ma, Dolly Parton and maybe a special solo from Aretha—or Mahalia Jackson, if the Queen of Soul's voice is tired. There would be plenty of time to rotate people in and out.

I'm letting my imagination run wild, of course. But you get the picture. Whatever heaven's worship looks and sounds like, it's going to be an amazing collaboration between lots of disparate parts. And as we fall on our faces together before the throne, I think we'll finally understand and appreciate the true power of our diversity.

But that's heaven. Is it reasonable to expect anything resembling that kind of unity in our churches today? Most of the time, I'd say no. But then I stumble across congregations like David Anderson's.

David, whom you first met in chapter three, is senior pastor of Bridgeway Community Church in Columbia, Maryland. His church is a dynamic multicultural body, with a remarkable blend of nearly two thousand black, white, Latino and Asian believers. In many circles, David is recognized as one of the leading practitioners of racial reconciliation, and as president of the nonprofit BridgeLeader Network, he consults other churches and ministries on how to make racial diversity a reality in their organizations.

As a pastoral intern at Willow Creek Community Church in 1989, David got firsthand exposure to one of the most innovative suburban megachurch ministries of that time. He soaked it all in, but he also kept in mind his desire to lead a multicultural ministry—which, as you might imagine, wasn't one of Willow Creek's strong suits. Still, it was an instrumental part of his unique preparation to start a different kind of church.

"When we parachuted in with flares to start Bridgeway in 1992," he told me, "I had my black Baptist heritage, my Moody Bible Institute theological education and my artsy-pragmatic-seeker-sensitive Willow Creek training. I was one mixed-up dude."

But, he added, all of those diverse elements have now come to fruition, and you can see the result at Bridgeway Community Church.

How does a real-life multicultural church work? How does a typical suburban church—or an inner-city church for that matter—become a place where all races and ethnicities function as one?

"It takes some effort to transition a church from where it currently is to where you want it to go," David said. "It could take three to five years. Of course, it's a lot easier if you plant one that's already multicultural. And we did."

He believes you get what you plant. "If you plant a white seed, you're going to get a white church. If you plant a black seed, you're going to get a black church. But if you plant a multicultural seed, you're going to get a multicultural church. And that's what we did. We started with a multicultural vision, mission and values, and we're now harvesting a multicultural crop, and we thank God for that."

That's all fine and good, but in practical terms, what does it look and feel like? How do you negotiate deal-breaking issues like music and worship? David says it must start with intentionality. For instance, there should be a healthy mix of races, genders and cultural backgrounds on your ministry team. And, he insists, there needs to be a clear articulation of your vision in the church's mission statement. "If you don't put 'multicultural' in there and stick to it, you slowly become something else without even realizing it."

I told David about the situation at my old church on the West Side of Chicago (which I still love and support, by the way), and how the congregation, though multiracial, is really an African American church with a mixture of different races.

"It's easy to fall into that when one culture is subservient to another," he said. "I believe there's a difference between being 'multicultural' and 'multicolored.' What you're talking about is something that's multicolored. In other words, you can have different colors and still have a black church or a white church. You can put black people in a white church and still have a white church or white people in a black church and still have a black church because of the substance and feel of the church.

"What we try to do is to intentionally make sure what happens onstage is a variety. And what we've found music-wise is that there's a sort of middle genre that we lean on. We use the analogy of a meal to describe it. If you invite people over for dinner, for instance, you're usually going

to choose a meal that's safe, like chicken or pasta, something that everyone can eat. And that's what you need to do with your worship music—
choose something safe."

There's that word again—safe. Doesn't safe usually end up being, by
default, white?

"Ah, but that's just the beginning," David quickly added, detecting my
skepticism. "Then you pepper the meal with side dishes that are ethnic.
Because that way, you're not overwhelming your guests. For example, if
you're not Korean and you come to my house and I feed you only kimchi, it's going to blow your head off if you don't like kimchi. Only a few
people are going to enjoy it. So instead, we serve something safe, but
then we put kimchi on the side. We can put salsa and chips on the side.
We can put a lot of different ethnic dishes on the side, because no one
minds all the other side dishes being on the table; they just want to make
sure that the main dish is something they're familiar with. Once they
have that comfort level, they will be more inclined to reach out and try
something new, and they may find that they actually like it.

"So, to place it in the worship context, that's how we look at what we
do onstage," David continued, probably sensing that he was making me
hungry. "We ask, what is our main genre? What is our middle-of-the-
road meal that everyone can eat from? We find what that looks like and
feels like. Then we pepper it with side dishes—everything from rock,
country, rap, poetry, choral and classical. If we made a whole service out
of any one of those side dishes alone, some people would walk out on
us, but when we mix it up . . ."

David believes the nature of that "mix" will be different from weekend
to weekend. "'Great Is Thy Faithfulness' one way and 'Great Is Thy
Faithfulness' another way can give you two different feels," he said. "So
the question is, what feel do we want this week? The flavor and the way
we season it this week could be more spicy or less spicy, depending on
the kind of mood we want to facilitate on a particular Sunday."

When you're done talking with David Anderson, you get the gutsy feeling that this stuff could really work, that it's possible to have a living, breathing multicultural congregation in this day and age where sticky subjects like music and worship styles are dealt with head-on, and actually resolved—with some necessary compromises—to everyone's satisfaction. Of course, as David says, churches must be deliberate about it.

12

GETTING PREACHY

It is no use walking anywhere to preach unless we preach as we walk.

St. Francis of Assisi

Religion is something you do, not something you wait for.

Charles G. Finney

I've heard some amazing sermons in my time. One of the perks of being a Christian journalist is traveling around the country to attend conferences and visiting nationally known churches where some of the most dynamic preachers are doing their thing. I've heard Tony Evans, in his trademark rapid-fire style, deliver an exhaustive history of Christian theology—from the Garden of Eden to the New Jerusalem—in less than fifteen minutes. I've watched a leather-clad Charles Swindoll ride on-stage atop a roaring Harley, lead thousands of people to rededicate their lives to Christ and then ride off like Marlon Brando in *The Wild One*.

Witnessing such spectacles is thrilling; it's also a bit disheartening. Because I've heard so many great preachers work their mojo, it's sometimes a letdown when I have to go back home to hear my regular pastor. This isn't a knock against my current pastor or any of the wonderful ministers whose churches I've belonged to in the past. There's simply a difference between "event preachers" and everyday pastors. Frankly, it's easier to mesmerize and fire up an audience when you're doing drive-by sermons. It's unfair to compare those super-preachers at Promise Keepers to Average Joe Pastor back home at First Avenue Baptist. When a pastor has to prepare a message, week in and week out, in addition to budget meetings, hospital visitations and any number of daily emergencies, it's hard to get up there on Sunday morning and blow the congregation away with Max Lucado-caliber stuff each time.

I've come to believe that one of the toughest jobs on earth is that of pulpit minister in an evangelical church today. We expect him to be as profound as Spurgeon, as funny as Seinfeld and as succinct as a CNN anchor. It takes lots of study, prayer and stagecraft. And even when he has those elements down, he has to do it again and again and again, week after week after week, in front of the same old tired crowd.

Recent surveys have shown an increasing rate of burnout among clergy. Sure, we give our pastors their props after a dynamite sermon. But more often than not, pastoral ministry can be an absolutely thankless job. I thank God for the men and women who have faithfully answered God's call to lead his people in this way. I have nothing but respect and admiration for them.

(Consider everything written above a disclaimer, just in case I offend a pastor or two the rest of the way.)

Our local church pastors may not all be as dazzling as T. D. Jakes or Rick Warren, but back home at their average-size churches, they set the tone. That's why in the evangelical movement's pursuit of racial reconciliation, the role of the preacher cannot be stressed enough. For many believers, whether or not they embrace the call to racial unity in the church is often a direct result of the premium their pastors place on it.

At that pastors' forum *Christianity Today* conducted up in South Haven, Michigan, I was totally unprepared for something Bill Hybels told us. Hybels, of course, is one of the most influential evangelicals on the planet. When he launched Willow Creek Community Church in a suburban movie theater in 1975, he couldn't have anticipated the revolution he was about to jumpstart. His focus from the beginning was on reaching "unchurched Harry and Mary," those normal, middle-class suburbanites—good people who just don't see any pressing need for God. Reaching these folks meant tailoring a church service that didn't feel like a church service. It meant creating a warm, nonthreatening environment that oozed a religion-less spirit that Hybels and his early collaborators defined as "community." With professional-sounding music, dramatic skits and a casually dressed pastor whose sermons felt more like conversations than heavy pronouncements, the people came, and the church exploded. In time, Willow Creek became synonymous with the idea of the American megachurch. Church-growth experts established it as the number one case study for how to be a successful "seeker-sensitive" congregation.

Critics were quick to note that Willow Creek and its clones were a largely white phenomenon. Even David Anderson, who interned at Willow in the late eighties, observed, "They were great at reaching unchurched Harry and Mary, but what they had not locked down was how to reach unchurched Leroy and LaTonya or Juan and Juanita."

Indeed, one of the unspoken foundations of the seeker-sensitive movement was its reliance on the "homogeneous-unit principle"—a theory of church growth that focuses on a specific demographic of potential churchgoers. In this model, racial sameness was a blessing to be embraced, not a shameful thing. So it was best not to become distracted by a multicultural approach and all of its diminishing returns.

In my past interviews with Hybels and other leaders from Willow Creek, they rejected suggestions that their church model undermined racial diversity. But on that summer day in South Haven, without any prompting, Hybels stunned everyone in the room by sharing something that we all slowly recognized as . . . a confession:

> Willow Creek started in the era when the church-growth people were saying, "Don't dissipate any of your energies fighting race issues. Focus everything on evangelism." It was the homogeneous-unit principle of church growth. And I re-

member as a young pastor thinking, "That's true." I didn't know whether I wanted to chance alienating people who were seekers, whose eternity was on the line, and who might only come to church one time. I wanted to take away as many obstacles as possible, other than the cross, to help people focus on the gospel. So now, thirty years later . . . I recognize that a true biblically functioning community must include being multiethnic.

It was an amazing moment. Hybels's voice was filled with a profound mixture of passion and remorse. He went on to explain that it was the book *Divided by Faith* that finally shook him out of his complacency on racial reconciliation. Alvin Bibbs, an African American minister who is Willow Creek's executive director of multicultural church relations, had given Hybels a copy of the book to read during a vacation. It rocked his worldview.

"I was like the stereotypical person that *Divided by Faith* talked about," Hybels says. "I didn't view myself as being racist in any way. I therefore felt that there was no issue I was responsible for. If it was okay with me and my individual multiracial friendships, then it was all okay. And when I got to the section about the ongoing structural inequities, it devastated me. I thought, *How could I have not·seen this?* And that was the beginning of my journey. I felt so badly about being a pastor for twenty-five years and having been as oblivious as I was to these kinds of issues. It was embarrassing. But these days I'm trying to make up for lost time."

Making up for lost time, indeed. Hybels admits that his church has a long way to go, but they have added an African American to the board and are intentional about seeking "people of ethnicity" when filling senior staff vacancies. Hybels has worked behind the scenes to ensure that people of color are always represented on the platform. It would be unusual these days, he says, for someone to attend a Willow Creek service and not see cultural diversity intentionally represented onstage. The church also offers regular classes on cultural issues and features a Spanish-speaking service in its chapel. Most important, Hybels has publicly demonstrated his heartfelt commitment to the mission of racial reconciliation. In 2005 and again in 2006, he and other members of Willow Creek joined Salem Baptist Church's James Meeks and members from his congregation on a "Justice Journey" to civil rights landmarks across the South. The emotional, six-day trip drew the two churches together across racial lines even as they relived the history of racial division in America. On Christmas Day of 2005, Hybels was the guest preacher at Salem Baptist. And Meeks was a featured speaker at Willow's annual leadership summit in 2006.

During our roundtable, Hybels stressed the role of senior pastors in making racial reconciliation a priority in their churches. "In every congregation, someone has to have a vision for what the church should be biblically and then the practicality to ask, 'How do we move toward that?' In my opinion, a church doesn't have much of a chance of [becoming multicultural] until the senior pastor has a 'conversion experience' about this issue."

I think Bill Hybels is right. Pastors need to catch the vision for racial reconciliation before it can take root in the hearts of their congregants. But are evangelical pastors ready? Is racial reconciliation on their to-do list? There are plenty of excellent books, conferences and parachurch organizations devoted to the reconciliation message. But until our local church leaders transmit the urgency of the issue to their people, equip them with a theological foundation to understand its biblical significance, and then provide them with opportunities to live it out, the dream of a reconciled, multicultural church will remain a vague and fleeting concept—the feel-good stuff of King Day speeches and once-a-year choir exchanges.

AN INCOMPLETE THEOLOGY

Bill Hybels wasn't the only Christian leader deeply affected by *Divided by*

Faith. After the book's release in 2000, pastors, ministry leaders, students and many other laypeople devoured the book's provocative message, making it a surprise bestseller. Readers were blown away by Michael Emerson and Christian Smith's groundbreaking research and their controversial thesis: that evangelical theology and practice actually undermine racial progress and social justice in America. The authors also challenged us to shelve the language of *racism*—an increasingly imprecise term loaded with emotional baggage—to find a more accurate terminology. They suggested *racialized* as a better description of the divisions we experience today in this post–civil rights era. They argued that many white evangelicals are not so much racist as they are immersed in a "racialized society" in which race represents a huge cultural chasm between people.

On the heels of the Promise Keepers-inspired reconciliation excitement of the 1990s, *Divided by Faith* brought the church back down to earth, confronting us with the deep-seated issues that work against our good intentions. The book was the cold reality check that people who had been working in the reconciliation movement knew was needed.

One of the book's recurring themes—one I've heard repeated at nearly every conference I've attended since the book's release—is that the preaching and theology of white evangelicalism is infected by a crippling case of individualism. This also was a prevalent observation from the different black evangelicals who participated in my survey. To give you a taste of how widespread this sentiment is, here are a handful of their comments:

> "Evangelical theology tends to be so concerned with individual salvation that there's little thought about collective responsibility, collective sin or institutional concerns."

> "Evangelical theology has robbed the church of a healthy dialogue on race relations, because everything that is not primarily about evangelism—like godly social justice—is put on a shelf as secondary."

"Its emphasis on original sin gives a strong foundation for an understanding of how racial views and discrimination have come about. But it has also used a 'survival of the fittest' approach to the social position and treatment of many minorities in our society."

"In the name of evangelical theology, minorities over the years have humbly submitted to inaccurate interpretations and applications of Scripture. Too often it is not until certain issues of justice get white evangelical endorsement that they become okay."

Notice a common thread here? When so many black evangelicals possess similar reservations about the quality of our theology, there's something there to be pondered. Indeed, of all the concerns I noted from the dozens of people who took my survey, this matter about the tainting of evangelical theology—its "whiteness" and individualistic nature—is the most ubiquitous. And I suppose that shouldn't come as a shock. When you get down to the root of things, it's no longer slavery, Jim Crow or organized discrimination that we're up against in our churches, ministries and society; it's an institutionalized racialization of religion that blinds us to the systemic issues of justice and reconciliation, even as it purports to bring us together.

A few years ago Elward Ellis, senior pastor of the multiracial Crossroads Presbyterian Church in Stone Mountain, Georgia, and the former national director of black campus ministries for InterVarsity Christian Fellowship, explained the dilemma to me this way: "Historically, as we grew the nation, we had to come to terms with the economic opportunity presented by the New World and slavery. It created a moral or theological conflict, so we went to the Reverend and had him fix his preaching and doctrine so we could be both Christians and slave owners. It's at this point, where America has wrestled with how to be both profitable and ethical, that racism has taken its deepest roots. We have mixed a civil religion and pragmatism into our practice of evangelical theology."

The author and preacher John Ortberg, formerly of Willow Creek and now a teaching pastor at Menlo Park Presbyterian Church in California, once told me that the evidence of our individualistic theology is not so much in the things that we preach but the things that we *don't* preach from the pulpit: "One problem is that American evangelicals have understood the gospel to mean 'the minimal stuff I've got to do to get into heaven when I die.' And that's very individualistic," he said. "I recall hearing a prominent evangelical preacher speak on Nebuchadnezzar and the story of his recovery from insanity. When you go back through the story, you see that part of God's prophetic judgment against Nebuchadnezzar was due to his oppression of the poor. This pastor preached a whole sermon on the subject and that dimension never got mentioned; he only talked about Nebuchadnezzar's pride and arrogance—individualistic issues. And that's how it often is in our churches—certain issues get preached, other ones don't."

FIRE STARTERS

Thankfully, there are preachers who are willing to call racism and social injustice on the carpet when they see them. And some of these preachers even manage to keep their jobs.

After years of dancing around the subject, Billy Graham took a stand in 1953 when he tore down the ropes that separated the races at a Tennessee crusade and declared he would no longer preach to segregated crowds. "There is no scriptural basis for segregation," he said. "It may be there are places where such is desirable to both races, but certainly not in the church."

I marveled at the brouhaha stirred up by black televangelist Frederick Price, the charismatic minister of Crenshaw Christian Center in Los Angeles, when in the late nineties he preached a two-year series titled "Race, Religion, and Racism." Price, who is known as one of the top leaders of the

Word-Faith movement, had absolutely nothing to gain by abandoning his usual prosperity preaching to focus on racism in the church, but racist statements by another popular charismatic minister prompted him to take up the subject. And the typically brusque preacher held nothing back— even though the majority of his audience was white.

The sermon series was full of surreal moments. One Sunday morning after playing a tape from a Ku Klux Klan rally, he remarked, "I obviously don't agree with the position of the Ku Klux Klan, but I have to admire their honesty. It's too bad that the church, the so-called born-again, Spirit-filled, tongue-talking, Bible-toting, tape recorder-playing, red-orange-and-green-and-yellow-highlight-marking Christian can't be as honest as the Ku Klux Klan. They don't leave any doubt about how they feel about black folk. They don't like niggers, and they'll tell you right now: 'We don't want niggas around us, and we sure don't want to inter-marry niggas.' Hey, I can appreciate that. I mean, I don't agree with them, but at least I know where the snake is so I don't have to step on that sucker by accident and get bitten." It was as if Chris Rock had become a Pentecostal preacher.

As the series went on and on and on, many in the charismatic community grew impatient, feeling Price had sufficiently proven his point. But the feisty preacher was on a runaway train that he couldn't abandon. It made for fascinating television. Price responded to the criticism in a 1999 interview with *Emerge* magazine: "White folks always want to forget the past," he said, "but you can't forget the past because the present is always the result of the past." When the series was finally over, he turned his voluminous collection of sermons into an equally incendiary book, also titled *Race, Religion and Racism*.

Even Tony Evans, viewed by many whites as the most friendly and accessible African American preacher in evangelicalism, caused a tiny ruckus in 1992 when he authored a provocative book titled *Are Blacks Spiritually Inferior to Whites?* A small New Jersey publisher released the tome, presumably because its message was too controversial for the larger evangelical presses that usually published Evans's books.

These are extraordinary examples, of course, but they speak of the radical courage—and, some might say, recklessness—that may be required of evangelical preachers if they're serious about confronting the race issue in America.

FROM THE INSIDE OUT

Though I highlighted some of the more "in your face" statements in those survey quotes I shared earlier, there were also several hopeful comments about the state of evangelical theology. For instance, Anita Morgan wrote, "Evangelical theology has helped advances in race and justice in America because of its emphasis on a heart-change. Christians rightly believe that change must occur from the inside out, and because of this, those rare individuals who are conscientious about their relationships with people from other racial or ethic groups often work tirelessly to integrate their ideals into every area of life." *This is who I want to be*

Tony Mathews, the senior pastor at the multiracial North Garland Baptist Fellowship in Texas, said, "I honestly believe people are evolving to appreciate racial equality. I am optimistic about justice and the perception of race in America. We must not, however, overlook our responsibility to consistently teach our congregations and children about this issue and facilitate the development of a healthy, culturally competent society."

But my favorite response came from Barbara Wooding, a sixty-seven-year-old hotel mail clerk and a layperson at Emmanuel United Methodist in White Sulphur Springs, West Virginia. Regarding the state of evangelical theology, she wrote, "If we would only follow the two main commandments given by our Lord—'Love the Lord with your whole being and love your neighbor as yourself'—our theological vision would be crystal clear."

I doubt any of our great celebrity preachers could put it any better than that.

Epilogue

DO WE STILL NEED RACIAL RECONCILIATION?

There are years that ask questions and years that answer.

Zora Neale Hurston

In November 2005, I attended a racial reconciliation summit in downtown Indianapolis. It was a gathering of about fifty leaders from all over the nation. I arrived slightly late that cold, blustery morning. Walking into the fluorescent-lit meeting room at the Marriott Hotel, I wasn't sure what to expect.

The participants were seated in a circle so large that it curled into itself, like a multiracial spiral. As I nervously settled into my chair, I studied the faces of the men and women with whom I'd be spending the day. I was amazed at the number of people in attendance whom I had interviewed or written about over the last dozen years—incredibly passionate and devoted men and women. And here they were, all in the same crowded space, like a living portfolio of my work.

Leading the proceedings was Chris Rice, the codirector of the Center for Reconciliation at Duke Divinity School. Chris's book *More Than Equals: Racial Healing for the Sake of the Gospel*, which he cowrote with his late ministry partner, Spencer Perkins, was one of the most influential titles on reconciliation in the heady 1990s and is still a must-read resource for serious practitioners of community-development ministry. Sitting next to Chris was Brenda Salter McNeil, whose workshops and sermons on the pivotal role of worship in reconciliation have challenged me on more than one occasion. And there were many others: Glen Kehrein, Sam Barkat, Kathy Dudley, Rudy Carrasco, Barbara Williams-Skinner, Bart Campolo, Curtiss DeYoung, Soong-Chan Rah, Randy Woodley, Clarence Shuler. Though I didn't know him personally, it was hard not to recognize Shane Claiborne, the charmingly grungy "urban monk" who lives among the homeless in Philadelphia. Even Russell Knight, whom you may recall was one of my earliest reconciliation mentors, was in the house. I also saw many unfamiliar faces that I would soon connect to names I already knew. These leaders were black, white, Native American, Latino and Asian, and they were all movers and shakers in their vocational circles, which included churches, colleges and parachurch organizations. I had agreed to attend the meeting without giving much thought to the other folks who would be there. But as I continued to look around the room, it quickly sunk in how momentous this event was.

Slowly, however, my excitement began to dissipate into something more like sadness as I listened to the people in the circle share their stories from heavy hearts. It turned out that the work of racial reconciliation was harder than any of them had imagined. Victories and moments of progress were fleeting and usually followed by failures and setbacks. Each of them had no doubt they were called to their ministries, but the journeys had been long and taxing. At times, the summit felt like a wake.

I looked at Chris Rice, his full head of hair grizzled from years of hardcore ministry—most notably with the interracial Voice of Calvary Church and faith-based community in Jackson, Mississippi. In 1998 his best friend and colaborer Spencer Perkins, the son of reconciliation pioneer John Perkins, died of heart failure at age forty-three. It was as if he had given his whole heart to the ministry and had no more to give. Spencer and Chris had become one of the reconciliation movement's most prominent black-white duos. So after Spencer's untimely death, it was hard to imagine Chris without his yokefellow. Now one of the senior

statesmen of the movement, Chris was bravely carrying the mantle he
and Spencer once shared.

"Much blood, sweat and tears have been given to this call to reconciliation over the years," he told the group. "It's only God who has sustained us. We want to make this a time to learn from one another's experiences and to perhaps identify new ways to advance the ministry of
reconciliation."

"We are wounded healers who have been at this for a long time,"
added Glen Kehrein, who runs Circle Urban Ministries on Chicago's
West Side. "We are tired of 'reconciliation lite.' We need something genuine."

As the morning wore on, more raw feelings surfaced. "Over the years,
we've analyzed this race thing to death," said Russ Knight, whose hair
was now considerably grayer than when he had spoken at Judson College fourteen years earlier. "We've researched, written books and done a
lot of talking and agreeing. And now here we are in another meeting.
How far have we really gotten?"

"Very little of this kind of stuff hits the ground," said Leroy Barber,
president of Mission Year, a growing community-service ministry. "Very
little of this stuff makes it into the neighborhoods. The systems ultimately must change. The monster of racism is not at all bothered by our
meetings and discussions."

Soon, people became more intense in questioning the conventions
and trappings of the reconciliation movement—even the movement's
vocabulary was tossed up for debate.

"I struggle with the term *reconciliation*," said Clarence Shuler. "I mean,
we were never *conciled*. So why, then, are we pursuing *re*-conciliation? It's
like getting married without dating. We never really knew each other in
the first place."

Russ Knight proposed that, instead of "racial reconciliation," we
change our terminology to something like "racial righteousness"—a
phrase he'd been using since 2000. "We need something that captures

the idea of justice, because that has often been the missing link."

By this time, it was becoming clear that we were spinning our wheels, reaching for a better truth but not able to move the conversation forward. At that moment, a question occurred to me: *Do we still need racial reconciliation?*

THE RECONCILIATION REVUE

That question spun in my head as I began to flash back through my experiences in covering the racial reconciliation movement over the previous decade. A flood of memories filled my brain as I reviewed the ups and downs that brought us to where we were that November day.

In the 1990s, Promise Keepers used its massive clout to challenge Christian men and their pastors to confront racism and build crosscultural friendships. Repentance for personal and corporate sins of racism was the focus, and that message spread to other organizations. In 1994, black and white Pentecostals drafted a Racial Reconciliation Manifesto among their churches in a historic meeting now known as "the Memphis Miracle." The following year the Southern Baptist Convention, whose proslavery stance led it to split from its Northern members in 1845, issued an official apology for its segregationist past and denounced racism as a "deplorable sin." Meanwhile, the National Association of Evangelicals and the National Black Evangelical Association held joint meetings to encourage racial cooperation, and high-profile Christian ministries hired African American leaders like Clarence Shuler in bold efforts to diversify their organizations. Taken as a whole, these events suggested rumblings of a major awakening among evangelicals.

Unfortunately, when PK's popularity began to wane in the late nineties, so, it seems, did the urgency of the reconciliation trend. (In fact, some even attribute PK's gradual decline to an overemphasis on racial issues.) Without PK stirring things up, white evangelicals seemed to lose interest in the topic of race relations. And those men and women who

had always been committed to reconciliation figured the fad was over—
back to business as usual.

Today we find ourselves at an interesting crossroads. There has been
undeniable progress. A whole new generation of leaders committed to
justice and racial diversity is taking its place in churches, ministries and
academic institutions. In our need to examine what's broken (which is
what we often do at conferences and meetings), it's easy to overlook the
strides that have been made. There are now scores of multiracial
churches and organizations across the country whose young leaders
have grown up in diverse communities with crosscultural friendships,
and they have brought that sensibility to their ministries. As I said in the
beginning, things have improved. Our experiences bear it out.

However, our experiences also tell us that things are not all good. In
our everyday existence, just when we've managed to get it off our minds,
we sometimes trip over the remaining rubble of our racialized world.
The church's dysfunctional past rears its head to remind us that, on a systemic level, old injustices linger.

An impulsive reaction for Christians immersed in the work of social
justice and reconciliation is to become flustered, angry or bitter even as
they trudge along in their ministries. We answer the call, but the song
we sing is blue.

I could detect traces of this at the Indianapolis meeting.

I was reminded of the many times I had felt that frustration in my own
journey. How for a period a few years earlier I had strongly considered
quitting my job at *Christianity Today* and finding a gig that did not dis-
appoint me so regularly. I recalled the anger and mistrust I had harbored
against certain coworkers. I didn't like myself very much back then. I
frankly was tired of being mad every day. But then God intervened to
shake me out of my selfish pity.

One weekend afternoon soon after that time, I took my kids, DeMara
and Daniel, on one of our regular trips to the park. Daniel, who was
about three then, has always been an outgoing kid. He loves to introduce

himself to people at the supermarket. This particular day in the park, he decided to befriend two slightly older white boys who were chasing each other around the brightly colored playground equipment. When Daniel attempted to join in, one of the boys shouted, "No, we don't want to play with you!" I could hear the disgust in the young boy's voice.

Forgetting the fact that four-year-olds are often just nasty by nature, the first thought to pop into my mind was that this little boy was a pocket-sized racist. My hypersensitive reaction was the result, I guess, of living too long in a racialized world. I looked around to see if the boy's mother had heard her child's remark. She was busy talking to another mom. My first instinct was to quietly get my son away from those other boys. "Daniel, come over here and play with DeMara," I said.

Daniel was having none of that. "I'm going to play with my friends here," he told me. And he did. Though the little boys coldly ignored him at first, Daniel smiled and kept pushing his way in, until eventually the little white boys were playing with him too.

As I reflected on this incident, it occurred to me that my three-year-old was a better man than I. He was not yet familiar with the concept of prejudice or hate. The social construct of race meant nothing to him. He simply wanted to play tag with these two new friends he had met in the park. To him, every child he saw at the park was his friend.

I realized that I needed more of this childlike grace.

I know youthful innocence will only go so far, that life's ugliness will creep its way in soon enough. But I also know that one of the things that we often lack in our attempts at racial unity and reconciliation is a demeanor of grace. We talk about it a lot, and sometimes we even show it. But when the reality of injustice, ignorance and cultural division bears down on us, we forget what it means to die to ourselves and live out the truth of Christ's love. It's often easier to leave the playground in a huff.

I don't want to live in that place all the time. And I knew none of the leaders in that hotel meeting room wanted to dwell there either.

CLOSING WORDS

By the afternoon, I wasn't sure where this reconciliation summit was going. Would we all leave more disillusioned than when we came? Or did God have something else in store?

The answer came toward the end of the day when John Perkins suddenly walked into the room. If I were to ask for a show of hands on how many people there had gone into ministry because of Dr. Perkins, virtually everyone in the room would have reached for the sky. Alvin Bibbs of Willow Creek once dubbed him "the godfather of racial reconciliation."

In 1970, Dr. Perkins was beaten to within an inch of his life by racist cops in a Mississippi jail. The preacher and social activist had been leading protest marches and boycotts against discrimination and unjust laws. "Like many other black leaders during that period, I was willing to die to change America for our children," he later said. That violent episode in the jail became one of his defining moments.

What set Dr. Perkins apart from many other civil rights activists of that post-Martin Luther King era was his evangelical faith—his determination to live out the truth of the gospel of Jesus Christ. Instead of allowing his pain and despair to turn to hate, Dr. Perkins decided to love those who persecuted him, to answer their injustice with grace. During the 1960s he and his wife, Vera Mae, had launched Voice of Calvary—a network of community development ministries aimed at lifting black Mississippians out of their spiritual and economic poverty. A tireless force, he hosted a weekly radio broadcast, did youth outreach, ran a Bible mission and opened a daycare center.

Over time, Dr. Perkins began to articulate a sophisticated theology that grew out of his understanding of biblical Christianity and social justice. He called it the "three Rs"—relocation, redistribution and reconciliation. "These comprised the trinity of disciplines that became the core of his expanded ministry," writes religion scholar Charles Marsh. According to Marsh:

The focus on Evangelical faith is a little off-putting. As it the access to a cool club.

Relocation meant "<u>incarnational</u> evangelism" . . . the lived
expression of the great Pauline theme that Jesus Christ did
not consider equality with God something to be grasped but
took on "the very nature of a servant. . . ."

Redistribution meant sharing talents and resources with
the poor, but . . . also working for observable changes in public policy. . . .

Reconciliation meant embodying the message that "ye are
all one in Christ Jesus" and that Christ has "destroyed the bar-
rier, the dividing wall of hostility" in lived social experience.

In 1989 Dr. Perkins founded the Christian Community Development
Association (CCDA), an organization that encompasses eight thousand
individual members and some five hundred ministries around the nation. At its core, the CCDA is the national expression of Dr. Perkins's
vision—the "three Rs" incarnate.

Today, one cannot overestimate the extraordinary contribution of this
man whom many call a modern-day evangelical prophet. So when he
entered the room in Indianapolis that afternoon, everyone's eyes bright-
ened. The surge of respect for him was almost palpable.

Sensing an opportunity to lift the spirits of the people in the room,
Chris Rice asked Dr. Perkins to address the meeting. "So many of us are
weary and our vision is dim," Chris said. "What is your sense of God's
message for us today?"

Dr. Perkins stood in the middle of the circle, with all eyes fixed upon
him. At seventy-five he seemed a little slower than usual but still full of
personality. His face, with its strong brown features, was accented by the
lines of time. What would he tell us? What wisdom could he, the patri-
arch of the movement, impart to us on staying the course and fighting
the good fight? Gathering his thoughts, he looked at us with a gentle but
fierce gaze. And then . . . he began to sob.

"On the night of Spencer's wake," he said in a shaky voice, "I asked

God why he had to take my son." Tears rolled down his cheeks. "I said,
'I'm mad at you, God. I can't bear this pain.' But God quickly sobered me
up, and he brought to my mind Jim Elliot's quote: 'He is no fool who
gives what he cannot keep to gain what he cannot lose.'"

He paused several seconds for a deep breath. "I love Spencer, but God
loves him more . . ."

Those of us nearby reached out to hug him or touch his shoulder. He
produced a handkerchief from his pocket to wipe his face, even as many
of our eyes moistened. Then he slowly looked around the circle, making
contact with each of us.

"What is God telling us?" Dr. Perkins continued. "I feel he's telling us
Philippians 1:6—'He who has begun this good work in you will carry it
on to completion until the day of Christ Jesus.' It is God who gave us this
ministry, and he will be the one to fulfill it. We just need to continue to
give our hearts and souls to loving others and living the gospel in an in-
carnational way, and then trust God to bring the change."

It was not a magic answer by any means. But it was the right one. And
I think everyone was encouraged. We all understood.

Do we still need racial reconciliation?

Sometimes I am tempted to throw my hands up and be done with it,
like my friend who e-mailed me saying she was sick and tired of racial
reconciliation. But then I think about the dedication of the men and
women at that meeting in Indy. I think about the selfless example of a
man like John Perkins. I think about the college student who put her
neck on the line to bring healing to her campus. I think about the compelling testimony of the many multiracial churches that are springing up
around our nation. And I think about Jesus' prayer for his followers,
"that all of them may be one, Father, just as you are in me and I am in
you. May they also be in us so that the world may believe that you sent
me" (John 17:21).

Nah, I'm not ready to leave the playground just yet.

ACKNOWLEDGMENTS

I knew this was going to be hard. I had always imagined my acknowledgements page being this elegantly worded record of all the people who helped me bring this book to life. But as I write this, it's becoming painfully clear that I'll never be able to thank all the folks who in some way contributed to the creation of this thing. So, if you don't see your name here but think it should be, please forgive this fallible but eternally grateful brother.

Thanks to the many friends and colleagues (old and new) who offered helpful suggestions, honest opinions or needed encouragement: Debra Akins, Vince Bacote, Michael Emerson, Gregg Glotzbach, Jocelyn Green, Mike Haas, Howard Jones, Jennifer Jukanovich, Ginger Kolbaba, Carmen Leal, Mickey Maudlin, Pete Menjares, Nate Mouttet, Dwight Perry, Brian Peterson, Carol Pipes and Brenda Salter McNeil.

Thank you to all the men and women who graciously responded to my survey. I cannot list all of you here, but I'm grateful for your time commitment and candid responses. Several individuals spent time with me on the phone or corresponded with me at great length via e-mail. Many of you I cannot name in print (per your wishes), but you know who you are. Among those whom I can name, David Anderson, Justine Conley, Rodney Cooper, Bob Fomer, Chanel Graham, William Pannell,

Soong-Chan Rah, Verley Sangster, Clarence Shuler, Chris Williamson and Randy Woodley were particularly generous with their time.

Several of my CTI colleagues were helpful in different ways and at different times (in some instances long before this book began to take shape): Harold Myra, Harold Smith, David Neff, Mark Galli, Phil Marcelo, Cynthia Thomas and Chris Lutes.

A hearty helping of thanks is reserved for LaTonya Taylor, my little sister in Christ, whose feedback on the manuscript and development of this book's discussion guide were invaluable assists.

To all my pastors, past and present, whose teaching and example have had a profound effect on my life and thinking: Eugene Garner (deceased), Charles Butler, Arthur Jackson, Ronn Smith, David Steinhart, Raleigh Washington and Ed Johnson (who's a pretty swell father-in-law to boot).

A special shout-out goes to the wonderful men and women in my small group. Thanks much for allowing me to share a bit of our journey together in the service of bringing an honest, real-life flavor to this book.

My heartfelt appreciation goes to Janet Kobobel Grant, who has been both a fine agent and a wise teacher on publishing matters.

A very special thanks to Cindy Bunch, Bob Fryling and the amazing team at IVP. Thanks for believing in this project from the beginning. Your heart for ministry has been a great inspiration.

But the biggest serving of thanks belongs to you, Dana, for your patient love and support. Your grace and quiet strength continually amaze me. And to you, DeMara and Daniel, for allowing Daddy to miss all those bedtime stories and goodnight kisses, yet loving me the same when I came back. I am also thankful to God for the lives of my late parents, Ed and Florence Gilbreath.

As I look at this amazing list of my peers, colleagues, friends and family, I'm reminded how incredibly blessed I am to be living this life. And so I thank you, Lord, for all your gifts. May this book be used for your purposes.

DISCUSSION GUIDE

PROLOGUE: SINGING THE RECONCILIATION BLUES

1. On page 9, a young woman says she doesn't believe true racial reconciliation will take place in the church during her lifetime. Why do you think someone would make such a statement?

2. What do you think she meant by "true" racial reconciliation?

3. Do you believe "true," large-scale racial reconciliation is possible? Discuss experiences that have contributed to your beliefs or feelings about racial reconciliation.

4. This prologue describes how evangelicals "have been throwing our best stuff at [racism] for the last forty years." How have you experienced this or witnessed it in your own life? In what ways did participating in important events or movements encourage you or change your life for the better? Did some of these events discourage you or make you feel resistant to change? If so, share how.

5. How do you feel about the question, "If we've made such progress in race relations, why do many [African American evangelicals] sound so glum about the subject?" What answers come to your mind?

6. What do you think about the statement that white evangelicals don't realize how much their "whiteness" affects their faith?

7. Do you believe that "despite our frequent missteps, the church is the one institution that's best equipped to overcome the racial divide?" Why or why not?

CHAPTER 1: LIVING IN TWO WORLDS

1. In this chapter, buses and the river that divided the east and west sides of Rockford, Illinois, symbolize how issues of race and class can shape life. If you were to choose similar symbols to describe your life, what would they be?

2. Tell a story of a person who, like the white Sunday school teacher Mr. Kaiser, defied what you thought you knew about a person from a different racial or ethnic group.

3. This chapter mentions the privileges of being the only African American in the house. What do you think that means? Have you ever been in a situation where you benefited from standing out due to your race, gender or class? What was it like?

4. Have you ever had a realization that you were "a black Christian in a white Christian's world," or something similar? If so, how did it come about? If not, how does this statement make you feel? How do you respond to terms like "black Christian" and "white Christian's world?"

5. Have you ever felt like a reluctant "race cop"? Has someone around you acted like a "race cop"?

6. Think about the stories of Clarence Schuler and Chanel Graham. Have you ever felt called to a situation that seemed less than ideal, frustrating or difficult? What made you comfortable or uncomfortable about it?

CHAPTER 2: "EVANGELICAL" . . . THERE'S JUST SOMETHING ABOUT THAT NAME

1. Have you ever been prejudged, treated with suspicion or misunderstood because of your faith? If so, how does that help you understand how others experience prejudice?

2. How do your preconceived notions affect the way you interact with

other Christians? Do you have a "denominational alarm" that alerts you to uncomfortable differences of opinion and practice within the Christian faith?

3. Have you ever tried to "convert" someone from a different Christian denomination? Have you been on the receiving end of such efforts?

4. Do you identify yourself as an evangelical Christian? What does the term *evangelical* mean to you?

5. What do you think the word *evangelical* means to people outside the evangelical subculture? Why do you think some people respond negatively to the term?

6. Why do you think several of the black evangelicals quoted in this chapter choose not to identify themselves as evangelical?

7. Talk about some of the paradoxes that are part of Christian life. Do you agree with the idea that race adds a complication? Why or why not? Talk about how you came to this belief.

CHAPTER 3: "WHY DO ALL THE BLACK STUDENTS SIT TOGETHER?"

1. This chapter states that self-discovery is one of the most significant things we gain from college education. Why do you think the author calls that self-discovery "dangerous"?

2. If you attended college, did you discover significant things about yourself? If so, what were they? Did your experience include any significant self-discovery regarding race or class?

3. Did you have an experience that gave you a sense of your calling during college?

4. If you attended (or attend) a Christian college, share some of your observations regarding how students of color perceive themselves or are

perceived on campus. Do your observations come from close friendships, from being one of those students or from a more removed perspective?

5. What do you think it means for a chapel speaker to seem "safe enough"? Have you ever gauged whether a person's ideas make him or her "safe"? If so, how have you measured that?

6. The chapel speaker tells the audience, "To be born white in America makes it almost impossible to escape being a racist." What do you think of this statement?

7. This chapter compares Russell Knight's sermon to the "safe" sermons usually preached on the Judson campus. Is your experience mostly with safe sermons, or do you often feel challenged by what you hear in church or chapel? Why do you think that is?

8. Do you remember the first time you heard the phrase "racial reconciliation"? How did you feel, and how did you respond?

9. When people of color bring up issues of race or class, are you ever tempted to see them as "rabble-rousers"? Does this perception differ among people of different races in the discussion group?

CHAPTER 4: A PROPHET OUT OF HARLEM: THE LEGACY OF TOM SKINNER

1. This chapter describes the influential Tom Skinner book *Black and Free*. Has a particular book, film, person or experience affected your life in a profound way? If so, talk about what that was and how it affected you. How has it affected the choices you've made and the way you live your life today?

2. The chapter refers to Skinner as unconcerned about winning popularity contests and portrays him as someone who is fearless about sharing his passions. Do you have a belief that is greater than your fears?

3. Skinner talks about not relating to the depictions of Christ he often saw. How do you respond to this idea?

4. Why do you think Skinner seemed too radical for blacks and whites alike? What makes a person "radical" when it comes to race relations and religion?

5. Why do you think Skinner's ministry struck a chord with college students?

6. In your mind, does Tom Skinner's message still matter today? Why or why not?

CHAPTER 5: THE FIRST SHALL BE LAST: ON BEING THE "FIRST BLACK"

1. Have you ever been the "first" in a situation? If so, how did you prepare yourself? Do you know anyone who has been such a "first"?

2. Do distinctions like "first African American" still seem significant to you, or not?

3. Why do you think "firsts" sometimes have to prepare themselves to "turn the other cheek" or show passive resistance to violence or unfair treatment?

4. Do you know any "first blacks" (or "firsts" of other ethnicities) in leadership in the evangelical subculture? If you know them personally, what have you observed about how they seem to experience the evangelical world?

5. In Rodney Cooper's narrative, he finds that older white faculty members seem most resistant to efforts to diversify seminary faculty. Assuming his observation is valid, why do you think that might be? What other reasons might there be for this attitude?

6. This chapter states that everyone benefits from diversity. Do you be-

lieve this is true? Why or why not? Do you believe everyone benefits *equally* from diversity?

7. What role do you think money and funding issues play when it comes to dealing with issues of race and class in evangelical institutions?

8. In your opinion, how do generational differences affect the ways racial reconciliation and related issues are handled in the church?

9. Page 81 says, "As Christians, it's possible for us to do wonderfully holy things crossculturally without ever experiencing a fundamental change in our thinking about crosscultural matters." Have you observed this in your own life? How about in the institutions you belong to? What can you do to promote change in the relationships or institutions you are part of?

10. What is your response to Ray Bakke's interpretation of Acts 10?

CHAPTER 6: WHEN BLACKS QUIT EVANGELICAL INSTITUTIONS

1. Have you ever felt the pressure to represent a community's perspective, perhaps more often than you wanted to? If so, how did you balance your loyalty to that community with your own needs?

2. Talk about an experience you've had where you sensed others perceived you as unworthy or not quite good enough because you were different. How did you sense this, and how did you respond?

3. This chapter touches on themes of masks and invisibility in African American literature and art. Talk about some of the books, films or works of art in which you've observed these themes. How did they affect you?

4. Page 89 asks, "Why do so many successful black evangelicals still

feel compelled to wear their masks? Or worse, why are some giving up on the idea of racial unity in the church altogether?" What conclusions have you reached so far?

5. Anita Morgan describes two experiences: One with a well-meaning white woman who strong-armed her into a friendship, and a second with a well-meaning white woman who believed she was an expert on African American culture. Have you ever been in a similar situation? How did it unfold? What kind of resolution did it reach?

6. Anita defines racial reconciliation as "creating a climate where people deal honestly with racial and cultural issues. It should put an emphasis on action, so that leaders make changes based on feedback learned through dialogue (both formal and informal)." How do you define racial reconciliation?

7. Do you believe it's possible for black evangelicals to say they are not bitter yet also resolve never to work closely with white evangelicals again, or vice versa? Why or why not?

8. How does the existence of strong, successful Christian organizations that are also monoracial challenge your assumptions or complicate your thinking about racial reconciliation?

CHAPTER 7: WAKING UP TO THE DREAM: EVANGELICALS AND MARTIN LUTHER KING JR.

1. What does Martin Luther King represent for you? If you were alive at the time of his death, how did it affect you? If he lived and died before you were born, how has his story affected your life and the way you view issues of race?

2. What were you taught to think about King? How has that view expanded or changed? Has King meant different things to you at different times in your life? Talk about this.

3. On page 102, Dolphus Weary notes that "King's heart was to look at the broader picture. The small picture is to be angry. The broader, more prophetic picture is to devote yourself to changing the system and changing minds." What does that "more prophetic picture" look like in your life?

4. This chapter asserts that as a young man, King "had to learn how to be King." How are you still learning to be the person God has called you to be? How might that apply to racial reconciliation?

5. How do you think the white community's response to the civil rights movement of the 1950s and 1960s has affected race relations today?

6. In your opinion, how does the "dream language" prevent evangelicals from grappling with some of the deeper issues that King dealt with?

7. For what causes or beliefs have you placed yourself on the line? What has that looked like in your life?

CHAPTER 8: IS JESSE JACKSON AN EVANGELICAL?

1. In your mind, what does Jesse Jackson represent? How do your friends and colleagues of different races or political affiliations respond to him?

2. This chapter states that some Christians are uncomfortable with Jackson's unorthodox beliefs. For you, how important is it to ally yourself with people who share your degree of conservatism or liberalism?

3. What can white evangelicals learn from the way many black evangelicals view Jackson? In what ways might Jackson's story be instructive for black evangelicals?

4. How do you respond to the biographical details of Jackson's life? In what ways is your approach to racial issues affected by the story of your life?

5. Page 122 quotes Robert Franklin, who points out that Jackson often employs tactics associated with the civil rights movement of the 1950s and 1960s. What kinds of strategies do you believe are effective today? How can these new strategies be taught effectively?

6. How did Jackson's affair affect the way that you view him?

7. Several pastors quoted in this chapter believe that Jackson is still an important figure, both politically and religiously. What are your thoughts?

CHAPTER 9: "GOD IS NOT A DEMOCRAT OR A REPUBLICAN"

1. Calvin College professor Randal Jelks told reporters that "our faith trumps political ideology." How do you respond to this statement?

2. Do you feel comfortable talking with fellow evangelicals about your political ideologies? Do most of the people you encounter share your views? What are the challenges of relating to those with whom you disagree?

3. Do you agree with the statement that "political bigotry is the new racism"? What shapes your beliefs?

4. How does holding differing political ideologies prevent black and white Christians from working together?

5. How can Christians with different political views walk together? What key steps can unify these groups?

6. What have you observed about the way conservative or Republican African Americans are received by blacks and whites?

7. Do you know politically engaged people who hold strong conservative or liberal beliefs yet also avoid vilifying fellow believers with different views? What spiritual or temperamental qualities do they exhibit?

CHAPTER 10: THE "OTHER" OTHERS

1. In your opinion, why has the issue of racial reconciliation among evangelicals focused largely on issues between African Americans and whites? What are the positive and negative results of this focus?

2. How can the discussion of racial reconciliation be broadened beyond black and white? How can black and white Christians avoid treating the concerns of other groups as an afterthought?

3. How can listening to the stories of Latino, Native American and Asian Christians affect the ways white and black Christians interact with these groups or with one another?

5. Were you aware of the controversy regarding the "Rickshaw Rally" Vacation Bible School curriculum? How did you respond? In your opinion, how could the publisher have responded in a way that promoted reconciliation?

6. One person suggests that Soong-Chan Rah's outrage surrounding stereotypes of Asian cultures is based on "anger issues" rather than valid concerns. Have you ever observed Christians from a majority group playing the "rage card" against outspoken individuals from a minority community? Why do you think this happens?

7. In your opinion, is it ever acceptable for one racial or ethnic group to decide how another should be depicted or represented? How should Christians respond to this practice?

CHAPTER 11: LET ALL CREATION SING

1. How has music been part of your journey as a Christian? Has it played a role in your journey as a reconciler? Tell how, and share the songs and experiences that have been significant for you.

2. Has your church or another Christian group you're part of been af-

fected by the "worship wars"? What were the issues involved, and how did it play out?

3. In your experience, how can music unify? How can it divide?

4. What are the challenges of creating a church with a multicultural worship style? Where have you seen this done poorly or well? What are the characteristics of churches that have succeeded in this area?

5. In your opinion, what are some effective ways to become musically diverse without alienating certain groups? How can musicians and pastors prepare their congregations for these changes?

6. How does David Anderson's meal analogy of multicultural worship encourage or discourage you? How realistic would it be to implement this model at your church?

CHAPTER 12: GETTING PREACHY

1. Why is it so important for Christian pastors to "set the tone" for their local churches when it comes to racial reconciliation?

2. Which elements of evangelical theology and practice encourage racial reconciliation? Which elements are incompatible with racial reconciliation?

3. What concrete steps can you take to bring change to your church or Christian organization?

4. Bill Hybels asserts that pastors must have a "conversion experience" on issues of race before they can lead their congregations on it. Share your "conversion experience" regarding racial reconciliation.

5. How do you feel about the idea of replacing the language of "racism" with terms like "racialized"? In your opinion, what are the positives and negatives related to such a shift?

EPILOGUE: DO WE STILL NEED RACIAL RECONCILIATION?

1. What does a move from "reconciliation lite" to genuine reconciliation look like in your life? If you've already experienced such a shift, tell how. What events or people were pivotal in your journey?

2. Leroy Barber suggests that serious grappling with deeper issues of racial reconciliation rarely affects people's day-to-day lives. Do you agree? If so, how can this be changed?

3. What do you think about replacing the phrase "racial reconciliation" with "racial righteousness?" What new expressions, if any, would you suggest?

4. How has your own journey intersected with the landmark racial reconciliation events chronicled in this chapter?

5. The author recalls a memory involving his three-year-old son that challenged him to persevere as a racial reconciler. What stories or experiences renew you when you are tired of dealing with racial reconciliation?

6. How does this book leave you feeling about racial reconciliation—hopeful, discouraged, indifferent? How can we pray more intelligently about this issue? What will be *your* next step?

NOTES

PROLOGUE: SINGING THE RECONCILIATION BLUES

Page 10   I worked with the evangelist Howard O. Jones: The resulting book was *Gospel Trailblazer: An African-American Preacher's Historic Journey Across Racial Lines* (Chicago: Moody Press, 2003).

Page 11   "Institutional racism": Stokely Carmichael and Charles V. Hamilton, *Black Power: The Politics of Liberation* (New York: Random House, 1967).

Page 11   "Those established laws, customs, and practices": James Jones, quoted in Alan J. Levine, "Redefining Racism," *American Outlook*, Spring 2002 <www.americanout look.com>.

Page 12   Many will remember: Russ W. Baker, "Truth, Lies, and Videotape," *Columbia Journalism Review*, July-August 1993 <archives.cjr.org/year/93/4/primetive.asp>.

Page 13   In the summer of 1999: "Midwest shooting spree ends with apparent suicide of suspect," CNN.com, July 5, 1999.

Page 13   A 2004 Gallup-AARP survey: Adam Goodheart, "A Change of Heart," *AARP: The Magazine*, May-June 2004 <www.aarpmagazine.org>.

Page 13   And four years earlier: Quoted in John H. McWhorter, "Double Consciousness in Black America," *Cato Policy Report*, March-April 2003, p. 14.

Page 16   He coined the phrase: John McWhorter, *Losing the Race: Self-Sabotage in Black America* (New York: Free Press, 2000), pp. 1-3.

Page 18   They are people like Dwight Perry: Dwight Perry, *Breaking Down Barriers: A Black Evangelical Explains the Black Church* (Grand Rapids: Baker, 1998), p. 113.

Page 18   They are people like Brenda Salter McNeil: Brenda Salter McNeil, "The Issue Is Power," *World Vision Today*, 1999 <www.worldvision.org>.

Page 19   Ellis Cose observes: Ellis Cose, *The Rage of a Privileged Class: Why Are Middle-class Blacks Angry? Why Should America Care?* (New York: HarperCollins, 1993), p. 4.

Page 20   In 2002 the Latino population: Tyche Hendricks, "Asian Americans, Latinos setting pace in population growth," *San Francisco Chronicle*, June 15, 2004, p. B-2.

Page 20   Already, in states like California, Texas and Hawaii: Alicia A. Caldwell, "Nonwhites now majority in Texas," *The Boston Globe*, August 11, 2005 <www .boston.com>.

Page 20   The blues "are like having the flu": Julius Lester, *The Blues Singers: Ten Who Rocked the World* (New York: Jump at the Sun/Hyperion, 2001), p. 4.

CHAPTER 1: LIVING IN TWO WORLDS

Page 24   In Rockford, the dividing line: For a great article on Rockford's racial woes, see Elizabeth Austin's "A River Knifes Through It," *Chicago Tribune Magazine*, September 1, 1998, pp. 10-19.

Page 30   My friend Clarence Shuler: In addition to a full schedule as a conference speaker, Clarence is gifted author on issues like marriage and race. Read *Winning the Race to Unity* (Chicago: Moody Press, 1998) for an excellent perspective on race relations in the church.

CHAPTER 2: "EVANGELICAL" . . . THERE'S JUST SOMETHING ABOUT THAT NAME

Page 33   My main assignment was: The resulting article, "We Repent," appeared in *New Man*, November-December 1997, pp. 28-33.

Page 37   In the New Testament: Larry Eskridge, "Defining Evangelicalism," Institute for the Study of American Evangelicals website, 1995 <www.wheaton.edu/isae/defining_evangelicalism.html>.

Page 37   Historically, the term: According to Larry Eskridge, associate director of the Institute for the Study of American Evangelicals, during the sixteenth-century Reformation, Martin Luther adapted the term, dubbing his breakaway movement the *evangelische kirke*, or "evangelical church"—a name still generally applied to the Lutheran Church in Germany.

Page 37   Author Philip Yancey: Philip Yancey, "My Gallery of Saints," *Christianity Today*, February 3, 1997, p. 136.

Page 40   Your spirituality may be personal: This is an idea that I've heard expressed on various occasions by *Sojourners* founder Jim Wallis.

Page 40   "Our business is to present": C. S. Lewis, "Christian Apologetics," *The Joyful Christian* (New York: Collier/Macmillan, 1977), p. 184.

Page 41   Recent studies by sociologists: Larry Eskridge, "Defining Evangelicalism," Institute for the Study of American Evangelicals website, 1995 <www.wheaton.edu/isae/defining_evangelicalism.html>.

CHAPTER 3: "WHY DO ALL THE BLACK STUDENTS SIT TOGETHER?"

Page 44   Adoniram Judson, a pioneering American missionary: Philip Yancey, *Rumors of Another World: What on Earth Are We Missing?* (Grand Rapids: Zondervan, 2003), pp. 213-14. Yancey's book was a helpful resource for some of the background information on Judson.

Page 45   We were still a few years away: Beverly Daniel Tatum's groundbreaking *"Why Are All the Black Kids Sitting Together in the Cafeteria?"* (New York: HarperCollins, 1997) is a fascinating study of racial-identity development and self-segregation.

Page 47   "Who will speak for justice": My old recordings of Judson College chapel services came in handy for reviewing parts of Russell Knight's sermon. His message was delivered February 25, 1991.

Page 53   Race and higher education: For information here, I am indebted to discussions with Vincent Bacote and portions of his article, "When Will There Be Room in the Inn? Minorities and Evangelical Leadership Development," *Urban Mission*, December 1, 1994, pp. 25-33.

Page 54   For instance, at Columbia Bible College: E-mail correspondence with Columbia's former president Robertson McQuilkin and current vice president Bob Kallgren were helpful in confirming this episode. It's interesting to note that, despite the resignations, the school was willingly moving toward integration a full year before the Civil Rights Act of 1964.

CHAPTER 4: A PROPHET OUT OF HARLEM: THE LEGACY OF TOM SKINNER

Page 56   When I said that self-discovery: Portions of this chapter were adapted from Edward Gilbreath, "A Prophet Out of Harlem," *Christianity Today,* September 16, 1996, pp. 36-43.

Page 57   Thomas Skinner was born: Most autobiographical information is taken from Tom Skinner, *Black and Free* (Grand Rapids: Zondervan, 1968).

Page 58   "It would have involved five gangs": Tom Skinner, *If Christ Is the Answer, What Are the Questions?* (Grand Rapids: Zondervan, 1974), pp. 22-23.

Page 64   In countless speeches and books: Tom Skinner, *How Black Is the Gospel?* (Philadelphia: J. B. Lippincott, 1970), pp. 92-104; *Words of Revolution* (Grand Rapids: Zondervan, 1970), pp. 44-45.

Page 70   "Tom poured hundreds of hours": Patrick Morley, quoted in Joanie Perkins Potter, "Tom Skinner: The Man, the Prophet, the Legacy," *Urban Family,* Fall 1994, pp. 6-11.

Page 71   However, out of that movement: Indeed, it's easy to hear Skinner's influence in Tony Evans's fiery but intellectual preaching style. Several people told me this in interviews, but it really became clear after I listened to old tapes of Skinner's sermons.

Page 71   In 1968, at age thirty-nine: Though out of print, *My Friend, The Enemy* (Waco, Tex.: Word, 1968) can still be found at used bookstores or through private sellers online. The *Christianity Today* review, "Evangelicals' Racial Paralysis" by Dirk W. Jellema, appeared in the August 30, 1968, issue, p. 29.

CHAPTER 5: THE FIRST SHALL BE LAST: ON BEING THE "FIRST BLACK"

Page 73   When Brooklyn Dodgers manager: David Falkner's *Great Time Coming: The Life of Jackie Robinson from Baseball to Birmingham* (New York: Simon & Schuster, 1995) was a helpful general resource, as was an interview with Scott Simon about his book *Jackie Robinson and the Integration of Baseball* (Wiley, 2002) at the website Jerry Jazz Musician <www.jerryjazzmusician.com/mainHTML.cfm?page=simon.html>.

Page 76   "It's great that we have advanced": Clarence Page, "Why Condi's Star Is Rising," *Chicago Tribune,* January 4, 2006 <www.chicagotribune.com>.

Page 77   A recent Stanford University study: "The Effects of Racial Diversity on Complex Thinking in College Students" originally appeared in the August 2004 issue of *Psychological Science.* For information, visit The Racial Diversity Experiment homepage <www.stanford.edu/group/diversity>.

Page 79   Many books and articles have noted: See, for example, George Barna's *Revolution: Finding Vibrant Faith Beyond the Walls of the Sanctuary* (BarnaBooks/Tyndale,

2005) and Andy Crouch's excellent "The Emergent Mystique" in the November 2004 issue of *Christianity Today,* pp. 36-41.

Page 80   "By the year 2010": Crawford Loritts, "Interviews with Crawford Wheeler Loritts," Wheaton College's Billy Graham Center archives, Tape Collection 419, June 24, 1989.

Page 82   "Peter reminds me of myself": Ray Bakke, *A Theology as Big as the City* (Downers Grove, Ill.: InterVarsity Press, 1997), pp. 144-45.

CHAPTER 6: WHEN BLACKS QUIT EVANGELICAL INSTITUTIONS

Pages 84-85 "There's a social responsibility": Michael Wilbon, quoted by Justin Brown, "Should Woods carry the black man's burden?" *The Christian Science Monitor,* August 16, 2002 <www.csmonitor.com>.

Page 85   "I know that I have a certain responsibility": Jackie Robinson, in an interview with Scott Simon at the website Jerry Jazz Musician <www.jerryjazzmusician.com /mainHTML.cfm?page=simon.html>.

Page 87   Paul Laurence Dunbar, an African American poet: Lida Keck Wiggins, *The Life and Works of Paul Laurence Dunbar* (Nashville: Winston-Derek Publishers, 1992).

Page 88   "Please him? . . . Why, the dumbest": Ralph Ellison, *Invisible Man* (New York: Vintage, 1972), p. 137.

Page 97   Perhaps one of the most famous: Edward Gilbreath, "An Agent of Healing and Hope," *Wheaton,* Autumn 1999, pp. 14-15.

CHAPTER 7: WAKING UP TO THE DREAM: EVANGELICALS AND MARTIN LUTHER KING JR.

Page 100   As one of the only two blacks: Portions of this chapter were adapted from Edward Gilbreath, "Catching Up with a Dream," *Christianity Today,* March 2, 1998, pp. 20-29.

Page 104   "The movement made Martin": Civil rights activist Ella Baker, quoted in Kevin Boyle's "To the Mountaintop," *Chicago Tribune,* Jan. 8, 2006 <www.chicago tribune.com>.

Page 104   "Through nonviolent resistance": Martin Luther King Jr., *Testament of Hope: The Essential Writings and Speeches of Martin Luther King, Jr.,* ed. James M. Washington (San Francisco: HarperSanFrancisco, 1986), p. 496.

Page 105   "In the midst of a mighty struggle": Ibid., p. 299.

Page 106   "The Black Power slogan": King, *Testament of Hope,* p. 575.

Page 107   "Whites, it must frankly be said": Ibid., p. 561.

Page 108   "Some extreme Negro leaders": Billy Graham, quoted in William Martin, *Prophet with Honor: The Billy Graham Story* (New York: William Morrow, 1991), p. 295.

Page 108   "The essence of the Epistles of Paul": Ibid., p. 345.

Page 109   We've missed the heart of the man: Read Taylor Branch's phenomenal trilogy of books—*Parting the Waters* (1988, Simon & Schuster), *Pillar of Fire* (1998, Simon

& Schuster) and *At Canaan's Edge* (2006, Simon & Schuster)—for the most complete treatment of King history.

Page 110   "Every night when I get down on my knees": Charles Johnson, *Dreamer* (New York: Scribner, 1998), p. 139. I am deeply indebted to Glenn Loury and his May 25, 1998, commencement address at Eastern Nazarene College for turning me on to that incredible passage from Charles Johnson's *Dreamer*. Read Loury's inspiring speech at <www.bu.edu/irsd/articles/nazarene.htm>.

CHAPTER 8: IS JESSE JACKSON AN EVANGELICAL?

Page 112   In the early 1960s: Portions of this chapter were adapted from Edward Gilbreath, "Still Somebody," *Christianity Today*, February 4, 2002, pp. 64-70.

Page 117   "We in the black community": Eugene Rivers, quoted in "Some Black Leaders May Part Ways with Jesse Jackson," CNN.com, Jan. 23, 2001.

Page 118   "Even though we always say": Jesse Jackson, quoted by Glenn Arnold, "You Can Pray If You Want To," *Christianity Today*, August 12, 1977.

Page 119   To truly understand Jesse Louis Jackson: I particularly relied on Marshall Frady's excellent *Jesse: A Biography* (New York: Random House, 1996).

Page 124   "They are extremely critical": Fred Hammond, quoted in Deborah Evans Price, "In the Spirit: Hammond Feels the Love As Album Shoots to No. 1," *Billboard*, July 3, 2004 <www.billboard.biz>.

Page 126   "This is one of the profound": Jesse Jackson, quoted in "Terri Schiavo's Mom Pleads: 'Give My Child Back,'" CNN.com, March 30, 2005.

Page 128   "In my culture": Jesse Jackson, quoted in Michael J. Meade, "Jesse Jackson: Gay Rights Not Civil Rights," MarriageWatch.org, February 17, 2004.

CHAPTER 9: "GOD IS NOT A DEMOCRAT OR A REPUBLICAN"

Page 130   Epigraph: The song "Metal Machine" is featured on Jon Gibson's 1986 album *On the Run*. Visit his website at <www.jongibson.com>.

Page 130   In May 2005: Details on President Bush's Calvin visit came from Collin Hansen, "Bush Visit to Calvin College Exposes Divisions," ChristianityToday.com, May 20, 2005, and Julia Duin, "College Ad to Protest Bush visit," *The Washington Times*, May 17, 2005 <www.washingtontimes.com>.

Page 135   In the days leading up: A partial transcript for Jelks and Groenhout's May 13, 2005, appearance on Hannity & Colmes can be found on FoxNews.com <www.foxnews.com/story/0,2933,156931,00.html>.

Page 136   In announcing Hannity's booking: Jerry Falwell, quoted in "Sean Hannity to Speak at LU Graduation," Liberty.edu, May 5, 2005.

Page 138   "You don't square these things": Herbert Lusk, quoted in Neela Banerjee, "Black Churches Struggle Over Their Role in Politics," *The New York Times*, March 6, 2005 <www.nytimes.com>.

Page 138   In 2003 Congressman Tom DeLay: See Dan Eggen, "Justice Staff Saw Texas Districting As Illegal," *The Washington Post*, December 2, 2005 <www.washingtonpost.com>.

Page 140   "You can safely assume": Anne Lamott, *Bird by Bird: Some Instructions on Writing and Life* (New York: Anchor/Doubleday, 1995), p. 22.

CHAPTER 10: THE "OTHER" OTHERS

Page 147   "As a Puerto Rican": Harold J. Recinos, *Good News from the Barrio: Prophetic Witness for the Church* (Louisville, Ky.: Westminster John Knox, 2006), pp. 5-7.

Page 149   On a breezy summer day: That *Christianity Today* forum, "Harder Than Anyone Can Imagine," appeared in *Christianity Today*, April 2005, pp. 36-43.

CHAPTER 11: LET ALL CREATION SING

Page 159   That article, my first published piece: Edward Gilbreath, "The Soul Man," *Christianity Today*, April 26, 1993, pp. 14-15.

Page 160   "One image that most of us": From "Harder Than Anyone Can Imagine," *Christianity Today*, April 2005, p. 39.

Page 161   "I've seen Christian R&B": Lisa Kimmey, "The Goal Is Soul," *CCM Magazine*, September 2005, p. 64.

Page 162   "There's blatant division": Andree Farias, "A House Divided," ChristianMusic Today.com, July 12, 2004 <www.christianitytoday.com/music/interviews/2004/grits-0704.html>.

Page 164   David, whom you first met in chapter three, is senior pastor: For more information about David Anderson's ministry, visit BridgeLeader Network at <www.bridgeleader.com>.

CHAPTER 12: GETTING PREACHY

Page 170   "Willow Creek started in the era": Bill Hybels in "Harder Than Anyone Can Imagine," *Christianity Today*, April 2005, p. 38.

Page 172   "In every congregation": Ibid., p. 40.

Page 172   Bill Hybels wasn't the only Christian leader: If you haven't read it, do grab a copy of Michael O. Emerson and Christian Smith, *Divided by Faith: Evangelical Religion and the Problem of Race in America* (New York: Oxford University Press, 2000).

Page 174   "Historically, as we grew the nation": Elward Ellis in "We Can Overcome," *Christianity Today*, October 2, 2000, p. 43.

Page 175   "One problem is that American": John Ortberg in "We Can Overcome," pp. 43, 45-46.

Page 175   Billy Graham took a stand: See William Martin, *Prophet with Honor: The Billy Graham Story* (New York: William Morrow, 1991), pp. 170-71.

Page 175   Black televangelist Frederick Price: Great background information for this section came from Rhonda B. Graham, "Holy War," *Emerge,* December-January 1999, pp. 44-51.

Page 176   Even Tony Evans: *Are Blacks Spiritually Inferior to Whites? The Dispelling of an American Myth* (Wenonah, N.J.: Renaissance Productions, 1992). In the book, Evans "appraises the strengths and weaknesses of the Black and white church in America . . . [and] assesses the strategic role of Blacks back to the earliest days of biblical history." Three years later, Evans released a reworked version of the book through Thomas Nelson, and this version carried a less-provocative title: *Let's Get to Know Each Other: What White Christians Should Know About Black Christians*.

EPILOGUE: DO WE STILL NEED RACIAL RECONCILIATION?

Page 178   Brenda Salter McNeil, whose workshops and sermons: Brenda, along with co-author Rick Richardson, lays out some important concepts and principles in *The Heart of Racial Justice: How Soul Change Leads to Social Change* (Downers Grove, Ill.: InterVarsity Press, 2004).

Page 179   I looked at Chris Rice: Chris shares the amazing story of his and Spencer's friendship in his poignant memoir *Grace Matters: A True Story of Race, Friendship, and Faith in the Heart of the South* (San Francisco: Jossey-Bass, 2002).

Page 180   "We are wounded healers": Glen Kehrein is coauthor, with Raleigh Washington, of the influential book *Breaking Down Walls: A Model for Reconciliation in an Age of Racial Strife* (Chicago: Moody Press, 1993). For a good chunk of the nineties, I attended services at Rock of Our Salvation Free Church in Chicago, where Glen is an elder and where Raleigh was senior pastor.

Page 181   Black and white Pentecostals: To read the Racial Reconciliation Manifesto, go to <www.pccna.org/manifesto.html>.

Page 181   The following year the Southern Baptist Convention: Read the SBC's Resolution on Racial Reconciliation at <www.sbc.net/resolutions/amResolution.asp?ID=899>.

Page 184   "Like many other black leaders": John Perkins, "Who Speaks for the Black Community." Originally from a 1995 issue of the now-defunct *Urban Family*, this article is posted on ChristianityToday.com at <www.christianitytoday.com/holidays/bhmonth/features/jpspeaks.html>.

Page 185   Relocation meant: Charles Marsh, *The Beloved Community: How Faith Shapes Social Justice, from the Civil Rights Movement to Today* (New York: Basic, 2005). This brilliant book is perhaps the first major historical treatment to place John Perkins's ministry in its proper context as a continuation of the civil rights movement. Pages 174-77 were particularly helpful in my research.

Page 185   In 1989 Dr. Perkins founded: The Christian Community Development Association, a network of churches, parachurch ministries and individual reconcilers, is an excellent resource for the church as a laboratory for how to do community ministry, a place of encouragement and fellowship for "holistic" ministry leaders and workers, and a living example of racial reconciliation in action. Find out more at <www.ccda.org>.